C000053466

Inward Conquest

In the nineteenth and early twentieth centuries, modern states began to provide many of the public services we now take for granted. *Inward Conquest* presents the first comprehensive analysis of the political origins of modern public services during this period. Ansell and Lindvall show how struggles among political parties and religious groups shaped the structure of diverse yet crucially important public services, including policing, schooling, and public health. Liberals, Catholics, conservatives, socialists, and fascists all fought bitterly over both the provision and political control of public services, with profound consequences for contemporary political developments. Integrating data on the historical development of public order, education, and public health with novel measures on the ideological orientation of governments, the authors provide a wealth of new evidence on a missing link in the history of the modern state.

Ben W. Ansell is Professor of Comparative Democratic Institutions, Department of Politics and International Relations, University of Oxford, Nuffield College. He works on the political economy of education, inequality, and wealth. Coauthored with David Samuels, his book *Inequality and Democratization: An Elite-Competition Approach* won the 2014 Woodrow Wilson Award for best book in political science. He is a Fellow of the British Academy and coeditor of *Comparative Political Studies*.

Johannes Lindvall is Professor of Political Science, Lund University. He works on comparative politics, especially political institutions, public policy, and political economy. He is the author of *Mass Unemployment and the State* (2010) and *Reform Capacity* (2017), and his work has been published in journals such as *World Politics*, the *Journal of Politics*, and the *American Political Science Review*.

Cambridge Studies in Comparative Politics

General Editors
Kathleen Thelen, *Massachusetts Institute of Technology*

Associate Editors
Catherine Boone, *London School of Economics*
Thad Dunning, *University of California, Berkeley*
Anna Grzymala-Busse, *Stanford University*
Torben Iversen, *Harvard University*
Stathis Kalyvas, *University of Oxford*
Margaret Levi, *Stanford University*
Melanie Manion, *Duke University*
Helen Milner, *Princeton University*
Frances Rosenbluth, *Yale University*
Susan Stokes, *Yale University*
Tariq Thachil, *University of Pennsylvania*
Erik Wibbels, *Duke University*

Series Founder
Peter Lange, *Duke University*

Other Books in the Series

(Continued after the Index)

Inward Conquest

The Political Origins of Modern Public Services

BEN W. ANSELL
University of Oxford

JOHANNES LINDVALL
Lund University

CAMBRIDGE
UNIVERSITY PRESS

CAMBRIDGE
UNIVERSITY PRESS

University Printing House, Cambridge CB2 8BS, United Kingdom

One Liberty Plaza, 20th Floor, New York, NY 10006, USA

477 Williamstown Road, Port Melbourne, VIC 3207, Australia

314–321, 3rd Floor, Plot 3, Splendor Forum, Jasola District Centre,
New Delhi – 110025, India

79 Anson Road, #06–04/06, Singapore 079906

Cambridge University Press is part of the University of Cambridge.

It furthers the University's mission by disseminating knowledge in the pursuit of
education, learning, and research at the highest international levels of excellence.

www.cambridge.org
Information on this title: www.cambridge.org/9781107197398
DOI: 10.1017/9781108178440

First published 2021

A catalogue record for this publication is available from the British Library.

ISBN 978-1-107-19739-8 Hardback
ISBN 978-1-316-64776-9 Paperback

Contents

Figures

Tables

Acknowledgments

We thank Serkant Adiguzel, Rafael Ahlskog, Michael Albertus, Niklas Altermark, Jens Bartelson, Kyle Beardsley, Daniel Béland, Pablo Beramendi, Philippe Bezès, Rikhil Bhavnani, André Blais, Ketevan Bolkvadze, Marius Busemeyer, Carl Dahlström, David Dow, Holger Döring, Erika Dyck, Sabine Engel, Jane Gingrich, Martin Hall, Peter Hall, Ida Hjermitslev, Silja Häusermann, Sara Kalm, Herbert Kitschelt, Patrick Le Lidec, Danny Loss, Philip Manow, Cathie Jo Martin, Mathew McCubbins, Henry Milner, Rita Nikolai, Emerson Niou, Soomin Oh, Sigrun Olafsdottir, Nathaniel Olin, Tom Pepinsky, Katren Rogers, Paul André Rosental, Bo Rothstein, David Rueda, Björn Rönnerstrand, Livia Schubiger, Kenneth Shepsle, Hillel Soifer, Jeremy Spater, Daniel Stegmüller, James Snyder, Kathleen Thelen, Wenkai He, Kees van Keesbergen, Erik Wibbels, and Joseph Wong for excellent comments and advice, as well as Jan Teorell and the rest of the STANCE team at Lund University. We are also grateful to Robert Dreesen, Sara Doskow, and three anonymous reviewers for Cambridge University Press.

David Adler, Valerie Belu, Nicolas Rodriguez Hedenbratt, Alvina Erman, Selina Furgler, Carl Gahnberg, Jacob Nyrup, Moa Olin, Nicolás Palacios, Elle Pfeiffer, Annika Stjernquist, Henry Thomson, and Anna Wilson provided excellent research assistance.

Many historians and social scientists have kindly responded to our questions about the organization of public services in different countries around the world. In particular, we thank Hilda Amsing, Arne Apelseth, David Bayley, Hervé Bazin, Jean-Marc Berlière, Alistair Black, Gerda Bonderup, Geertje Boschma, Deborah Brunton,

Warwick Brunton, Franco Buonaguro, Margaret Burgess, Donald S. Burke, Helen Varney Burst, Yves Cartuyvels, David Churchill, Gary B. Cohen, Vicky Conway, Michèle Dagenais, Fabrizio Dalpasso, Antoinette Daly, John David, Vincent Denis, Marc Depaepe, Isabelle Devos, Martin Dyrbye, Hjørdis Birgitte Ellefsen, Eric J. Engstrom, Markus Feigl, Cyrille Fijnaut, Daniel Fink, Anders Frenander, Björn Furuhagen, Donald Fyson, Helmut Gebhardt, Jolien Gijbels, Jan Goldstein, Gutmaro Gomez Bravo, Anne Goulding, Patrizia Guarnieri, John D. Grabenstein, Christoph Gradmann, Brian Griffin, Kristin Hammer, Elsbeth Heaman, Philippe Hebeisen, John Hickok, Richard Hill, Tuija Hietaniemi, Peter Hoare, Sonia Horn, Stephen Hughes, Frank Huysmans, Ulf Högberg, Jessica Jacobs, François Jacquet-Francillon, Ralph Jessen, Carl Gustav Johanssen, David D. Jones, Greta Jones, Brendan Kelly, Ove Korsgaard, Jennifer Kosmin, Einar Kringlen, Marjorie Lamberti, Jesper Eckhardt Larsen, Helene Laurent, Elmar Lechner, Axel Liégeois, Manuel Linares Abad, Maria Luddy, Anne Løkke, Benoît Majerus, Núria Mallorquí Ruscalleda, Hilary Marland, Gregory Marquis, Christa Matthys, Peter McCandless, Marietta Meier, Philippa Mein Smith, Wilbur Miller, Ole Georg Moseng, Anne Marie Moulin, Miguel C. Muñoz Feliu, Ingomar Mutz, Ilkka Mäkinen, Jette Møllerhøj, Greg Newbold, Roddy Nilsson, André Normandeau, Ian O'Donnell, Enrique Perdiguero-Gil, Anna M. Peterson, Arno Pilgram, María-Isabel Porras-Gallo, John Pratt, Helen Proctor, Roger Qvarsell, Jukka Rantala, Alice Reid, Andrée Rivard, Philip Rieder, Cecilia Riving, Christina Romlid, Willibrord Rutten, Christopher Rutty, Hermann Rösch, Nathalie Sage Pranchère, Peter Scharff Smith, Jürgen Schlumbohm, Gabi Schneider, Alfred Springer, Hubert Steinke, Akihito Suzuki, Yuki Terazawa, Gaëtan Thomas, Michael Tonry, Signild Vallgårda, Wilbert van Panhuis, Dominique Varry, Olga Villasante, Hans von Rütte, Paul Weindling, Richard Wetzell, Wayne Wiegand, Gareth Williams, Michael Willrich, David Wilson, Nick Wilson, Eberhard Woolf, Satoko Yanagisawa, Paola Zocchi, and Lisa Öberg. It goes without saying that the responsibility for any remaining errors – and there are bound to be a few – falls on us.

We are also grateful to the helpful staff of the Bibliothèque et Archives nationales du Québec and the Provincial Archives of Saskatchewan in Saskatoon and Regina and to Robert Chevrier at the Montreal Police Museum.

Parts of this book have been presented at the University of Bremen, the University of Copenhagen, Cornell University, Harvard University, the University of Konstanz, the London School of Economics, Lund

I

Two Cities

The great towns are making themselves over, and providing themselves with all the appointments of a new civilization, because their permanent existence is now accepted as a fact. Energetic and intelligent action has already been taken here and there to render city life more tolerable for the bulk of city people, and such action must be copied everywhere.

Theodore Roosevelt, 'The City in Modern Life' (1895)

Consider a modern city. Almost any city will do, really, as long as it is more than 200 years old and wasn't heavily bombed in the Second World War. Let us pick Sweden's second-largest city, Gothenburg (Figure 1.1). We are looking for something amid its streets, parks, and office blocks: we are looking for the traces of a revolution in government.

Our first stop is a redbrick building just west of the city's center. Above the entrance, we find a statue of a man and a dog. The man wears a police uniform, so we know the building is a police station. As in many other cities in Western Europe and North America, the old city watch was replaced by a modern police force in the middle of the nineteenth century (the first commissioner, Lars Norin, was appointed in 1849). The police department first had offices in City Hall, and then, from 1893, in a nearby building that it shared with the bureau of detectives, founded in 1856 (Palmgren 1923, 226–230, 240). That building is now a museum of the history of medicine; the building with the statue, once the city's largest police station, was constructed just before the First World War; it remained a police station until 2006.

In the nineteenth century, it was increasingly common for those who were convicted of crimes to be sent to prison. Unlike the police,

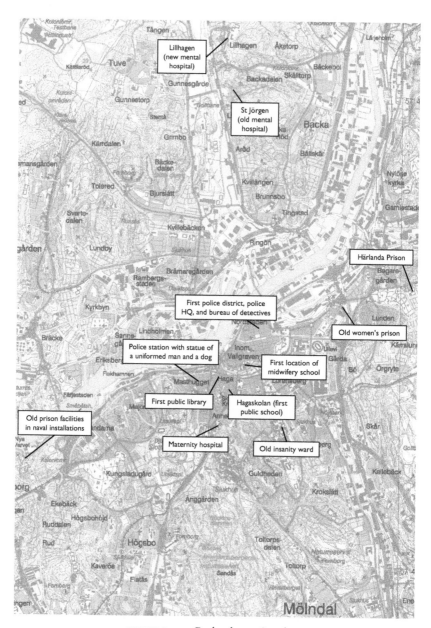

FIGURE 1.1 Gothenburg, Sweden.

Source: The map was drawn using a tool provided by Lantmäteriet (the Swedish mapping, cadastral, and land registration authority) and made available under the open-data license Creative Commons 0

which remained municipal until the 1960s (Furuhagen 2009, Chapter 7), Sweden's prisons have long been operated by the national government. Gothenburg's largest prison, Härlanda, opened in 1907 (Lundberg 1997, 9–21). It replaced an old prison that was erected in 1854–1857 (located near the old police headquarters, it was demolished in the 1970s) and a temporary prison in abandoned naval installations downriver. Female prisoners were held in an eighteenth-century workhouse until 1908. The last prisoner left Härlanda in 1997, but the buildings are intact; there are some sports facilities in there now, and a public library.

There have been schools in Gothenburg ever since the city's founding in the seventeenth century, but modern public schools date back to 1842, when Sweden's estates parliament established a national education system (Ohlander 1923, 812–813). The wood building that housed Gothenburg's first public school, Hagaskolan, is, remarkably, still a public school. Another dozen nineteenth-century school buildings remain. Their often grand edifices are the most visible traces of the nineteenth century's revolution in government. One notes right away that many of them are located near churches. Well into the twentieth century, Sweden's schools were administered by the Lutheran state church.

As in many other cities around the world – but, interestingly, unlike in other *Swedish* cities – the first public library in Gothenburg was the result of philanthropy. In 1861, James Dickson, a wealthy industrialist of Scottish extraction, founded a public library that would later be named after him. It was first located in an apartment building in a working-class neighborhood and then, from 1898, in a new library building around the corner. That building, which continued to house Gothenburg's main public library until the municipal city library opened in the 1960s, is now a senior citizens' center. By the 1920s, the charitable foundation that operated the Dickson Library relied greatly on funds from the city government (Wåhlin and Romdahl 1923, 901; Atlestam, Bergmark, and Halász 1997 describe the library's incorporation in the municipal government after the Second World War). The result was a mix of public and private authority of which we will see many other examples in this book.

In the nineteenth and the first half of the twentieth centuries, a growing share of Sweden's population was committed to mental institutions. New facilities for the old Gothenburg asylum, now largely demolished, opened north of the river in 1872 (Brockman 1994, 27, 32). From the late eighteenth century to the 1950s, most lunatic asylums, as they were known in English at the time, were administered by Sweden's national government. In the larger cities, however, there was a more complicated division of labor between national and city authorities, and by 1925, the responsibility for many of Gothenburg's mentally ill was taken over by the city itself. They were treated in several different locations until, in 1932, a modern mental hospital, Lillhagen, opened just north of the old asylum (Punell 1995, 180).

Before the introduction of modern methods of vaccination in Sweden in 1802, just a few years after Edward Jenner's discovery of the smallpox vaccine, so-called variolation was the main method used to prevent the spread of history's deadliest disease, smallpox. Already in 1757, Gothenburg's Masonic lodge established an orphanage where variolations were performed (Lundh 1957, 14–19). Variolations were also carried out in the city hospital. By the early nineteenth century, when Jennerian vaccination was made compulsory for all children, vaccinations were performed at large public meetings around the city (Gezelius 1923, 345).

We end our tour of Gothenburg with the beginning of life. Starting in the middle of the eighteenth century, Swedish parishes were required to employ a midwife and pay for her training. The first school of midwifery was in the capital, Stockholm; the one in Gothenburg opened in 1856. The new school was first housed in a big city hospital that was constructed in 1849–1855 (the hospital buildings are now used by the university), but it moved to different premises in the early 1870s, and then again, at the turn of the century, to a new maternity hospital south of the city center (Gezelius 1923, 364). That building, too, is now used by the university.

From cradle to classroom to grave, through order, disorder, and madness, the nineteenth century saw the construction of grand new institutions that turned what had been managed by the family or the local community into modern public services. The map of Gothenburg today is still harnessed to these imposing buildings, the architectural residue of the nineteenth-century state's first forays into controlling, teaching, and healing its citizens.

Now, let's consider a very different city: Montreal, which is the second-largest city in Canada, was once the largest city in colonial Lower Canada and is now the largest city in the province of Quebec (Figure 1.2). Just like Gothenburg, Montreal bears many traces of the nineteenth century's revolution in government, but its public services emerged in a very different political, social, and religious environment.

The middle of the nineteenth century was a period of great political and social unrest in Lower Canada. For a few years after the rebellion

FIGURE 1.2 Montreal, Canada.

Source: Contains information licensed under the Open Government Licence – Canada

of 1837–1838 – known as the *rébellion des patriotes* among French-speaking Québécois – the police force in Montreal answered to provincial authorities, not to the city government (Atherton 1914, 419). Authority over policing was transferred to the town corporation a few years later, in 1843, which was also the year in which the Montreal police department was formed (Fyson 2012, 105, 113; Greer 1992, 28). Its first headquarters were located in the Bonsecours Market building, which still stands in Old Montreal.

The main prison in Montreal in the nineteenth century, first called the Montreal Gaol and later known as the Pied-du-Courant Prison, opened in 1836 (Borthwick 1886). More than a thousand rebels were held here in the wake of the 1837–1838 rebellion. The buildings, which are still intact, are currently being renovated for the use of a provincial government agency and a public broadcasting corporation. The old city prison was replaced by the new Bordeaux Prison in 1912 (Bossé and Bouchard 2013, 58–61). Located on the northwestern shore of Montreal Island, the Bordeaux Prison is still in use and remains the largest provincial prison in Quebec. In Sweden, a unitary state, prisons have long been operated by a national prison service; in federal Canada, by contrast, offenders sentenced to fewer than two years are typically held in provincial prisons, not federal ones.

For decades, even centuries, schooling in Montreal has been a source of conflict between Protestants and Catholics and between English speakers and French speakers (Milner 1986). From the 1840s to the 1990s, the city's school authorities were divided along religious lines, with one school board for Protestant schools and one for Catholic schools.[1] This again sets Montreal apart from Gothenburg, where the established Lutheran church controlled almost all schools until the school system was secularized, without much conflict, in the early twentieth century. The first school that was administered by Montreal's Protestant Board of School Commissioners, on Ann Street, has been demolished, but one of the oldest Protestant school buildings, the British and Canadian School on the corner of rue de La Gauchetière and rue Coté, remains (MacLeod and Poutanen 2004, 116). Located in Montreal's Chinatown,

---

[1] On the 'confessionalization' of the school system that began in the middle of the nineteenth century, see Dufour (1997, 46–50). Jewish children in Montreal attended the schools of the Protestant School Board, and at one point, 40 percent of all children in the Protestant Schools were in fact Jewish. On the education of Jewish children in Montréal, see Corcos (1997).

the building now houses a noodle factory. Across the street, the Christian Brothers, a Catholic association with enormous influence in Quebec's education system in the nineteenth and twentieth centuries, once had its headquarters (Symphorien-Louis 1921, 18–19). The oldest Christian Brothers school building that remains at least partly intact – the École de Sainte-Brigide on the corner of rue Sainte-Rose and rue de Champlain – has been converted into housing.[2]

Public libraries came later to Canada than to its neighbor, the United States, where northern cities, such as Boston, established some of the first public libraries in the world. By the outbreak of the First World War, only two libraries in Montreal were open to the public: the small Civic Library and the larger Fraser Institute, which had opened in 1885 (Atherton 1914, 350–351). Neither of these old library buildings remains, but the building of the French-language, church-run Saint-Sulpice Library, which opened in 1915, does remain, as does the building of the French-speaking Municipal Library that opened, after long delays, in 1917 (Dagenais 2006, Chapter 3).[3] The Saint-Sulpice library originated in the nineteenth century, when the Sulpician order in Montreal made books available in a chapel and created a parish reading room. It moved its collection to the Saint-Suplice Library building in 1915, to make it more accessible. The circulation department closed in 1926, and the library itself closed in 1931 (Hubert 2013, 508–514).

In Lower Canada, and, later, in the province of Quebec, charitable organizations and religious orders have long cared for the mentally ill, with funding from the government. Through this so-called farming-out system, the government first granted an effective monopoly over mental health care to a private hospital at Beauport, Quebec City; later on, it entered into a contract with a Catholic sisterhood (Moran 2001, Chapter 1; see also Hurd et al. 1916, Chapter XIII, Section V). The largest insane asylum in Montreal – the Longue Pointe Asylum, now known as Saint-Jean de Dieu Hospital – was constructed in the 1870s for the benefit of a religious order (Appleton 1967); it remains a psychiatric hospital today. Montreal was also the location of Quebec's first, temporary, lunatic asylum, which was housed on the third floor of the Pied-du-Courant Prison between 1839 and 1845 (Cellard and Nadon 1986).

---

[2] On the history of the Christian Brothers, see also Voisine (1987).
[3] In English-speaking Westmount, an enclave within the city of Montreal, two public libraries were established already in the nineteenth century: the Atwater Library, which was associated with the Mechanics' Institutes, and the Public Library.

In Gothenburg, as we have seen, vaccination was compulsory for all children from 1816, and there was no significant antivaccination movement. In Montreal, matters were different, for antivaccinationism was strong, especially in the French-speaking community. When the City Board of Health introduced compulsory smallpox vaccinations during the great epidemic of 1885, riots broke out all over Montreal (Bliss 1991). On September 28 of that year, a large crowd attacked both the East End branch of the Health Office and the homes of several public health officers, before heading for City Hall, where the Board of Health was convening. The next day, troops were called out, and the riots ended.

In nineteenth-century Sweden, midwifery was a strong and recognized profession; in most parts of Canada, by contrast, midwifery had been banned by the early twentieth century. In Quebec, the midwives held out the longest – until the First World War – and provincial legislation from 1879 licensed midwives to practice if they received training at a maternity hospital that was affiliated with a university (Relyea 1992, 161). The Montreal Maternity Hospital, at McGill, was one such institution. Its first buildings have been demolished, but the building to which it moved in 1905, later known as the Sainte Jeanne d'Arc Hospital (Kenneally 1983), still stands; it is now used by a treatment center for young drug users.

We could have taken a similar tour through many different cities: the physical traces of the nineteenth century's revolution in government, when public authorities began to provide most of the public services we now take for granted, are everywhere. As our tours through Gothenburg and Montreal have also shown, however, public services have been organized differently in different countries and at different points in time. Some services have been administered by national governments, others by provinces, still others by local authorities. Some services have been provided by secular public authorities, others by churches, others by voluntary associations. Public services expanded everywhere, but *how* they were provided and *by whom* has varied substantially across countries and over time. In this book, we explain why.

2

Public Services

From the village school of Chesney Wold, intact as it is this minute,
to the whole framework of society; from the whole framework of
society, to the aforesaid framework receiving tremendous cracks
in consequence of people (iron-masters, lead-mistresses, and what
not) not minding their catechism, and getting out of the station
unto which they are called – necessarily and for ever, according to
Sir Leicester's rapid logic, the first station in which they happen to
find themselves; and from that, to their educating other people out
of THEIR stations, and so obliterating the landmarks, and opening
the floodgates, and all the rest of it.

Charles Dickens, *Bleak House* (1852–1853)

In the nineteenth and early twentieth centuries, an era of industrialization, nation building, and democratization, modern states transformed themselves from protectors into providers. The seventeenth- and
eighteenth-century early modern state raised armies of soldiers to protect its subjects, while insisting on its right to tax their land and their
resources; the industrial-era state, by contrast, raised armies of professionals to provide new public services to its citizens, and to secure their
loyalty and obedience. For the first time in the history of government,
states put in place broad-based public programs that reached deep into
the lives of communities, families, and individuals.

This revolution in government is not well understood. We know
a great deal about state building in the early modern period, when
monarchs and governments established new, powerful bureaucracies and
increased their capacity to rule and raise revenue. We also know a
great deal about the twentieth century's many political conflicts over
distribution and redistribution. But the development of modern public

services in the nineteenth century is something of a missing link in the history of government. This omission is surprising, for the transformation of the state from protector to provider changed the nature of politics, probably forever.

This book studies the origins of seven public services: policing and prisons, which promoted public order; schools and libraries, which promoted knowledge; and mental institutions, vaccinations, and midwifery, which promoted mental and public health. We analyze the development of these seven services in nineteen states in Western Europe, North America, and the Asia-Pacific region between the turn of the nineteenth century and the outbreak of the Second World War: Australia, Austria, Belgium, Canada, Denmark, Finland, France, Germany, Ireland, Italy, Japan, the Netherlands, New Zealand, Norway, Spain, Sweden, Switzerland, the United Kingdom, and the United States.

Our first goal is to account for the sheer expansion of public services in the nineteenth and early twentieth centuries. Relying on several types of evidence – including data on legislation, government employment, and the proportion of the population that was incarcerated, attended school, or were committed to mental institutions – we show when, where, and how modern public services emerged and spread between the years 1800 and 1939. There are many excellent historical studies of individual public services – typically within particular countries during particular periods – but there is no other broad, synthetic overview that compares many policies, countries, and periods.[1] We find that by the interwar period, all the countries in our study provided each of the public services we cover, at least in some form, with the intriguing exception of midwifery. We also show, for each policy area, which countries were pioneers, and which countries followed.

Our second goal is to analyze political conflicts over emerging public services. When public authorities began to promote order, knowledge, and mental and public health, they started to engage more systematically – and insidiously – in social control. The nineteenth century's new machinery of public order reduced crime and violence, but also allowed the state to define social deviance and defeat challenges to its authority. Public education had important social and economic benefits, but was also used to foster either nationalism or regionalism and either secularism or clericalism. Public health programs increased the welfare of the population, but also permitted the state to put human resources to better

---

[1] Some country-specific, synthetic historical studies, such as Fraser's *The Evolution of the British Welfare State* (1973), cover most of the policy areas that we discuss in this book.

Of course, public services often existed in some rudimentary form before the nineteenth century. There were public officials who were responsible for apprehending and punishing criminals; at least some children went to school; and local authorities had some responsibility for the aged, the infirm, and the mentally ill. But there are several crucial differences between the services that were once provided by parishes and other local institutions and the modern public services that emerged in the nineteenth century.[4]

Most importantly, the involvement of early modern central governments in things like the maintenance of order, the education of children, and care for the mentally ill was remote and perfunctory. Such services were typically provided locally, if at all, and national legislation, if it existed, had the form of broad enabling acts such as the Elizabethan Poor Laws in England. It would be wrong to say that early modern governments were mere legal-military machines, for they also promoted public welfare by addressing social problems that local governments were too small to handle, including famines, plagues, and large-scale public works (He 2018). But these efforts were societal and collective and did not reach individuals. With a few notable exceptions – such as the early development of national midwifery training in Sweden (see Chapter 9) and the creation of individual, centrally administered early modern hospitals in a few national capitals – central governments did not provide services to individuals in a systematic manner before the nineteenth century.

Moreover, public services were not clearly differentiated from each other in the early modern period. Today, we think of policing, prisons, schooling, librarianship, psychiatry, vaccinations, and midwifery as distinct policies and institutions. That was not necessarily how they were perceived, if they existed, in the eighteenth-century world. Under the old English Poor Laws, for example, parishes had a general responsibility for the parentless, the disabled, the mentally ill, the old, and the sick. But in the nineteenth century, these groups were increasingly treated as distinct, and states developed specific policies and institutions for each of them. For example, whereas England's old Poor Laws and Vagrancy Laws included lunatics in a long, undifferentiated list of persons for

---

4 English historians in the 1950s and 1960s referred to the nineteenth century as a period of 'revolution in government,' comparing it to the Tudor period's political revolution; for different perspectives on this question, see MacDonagh (1958), Parris (1960), and Hume (1967).

whom parishes were responsible and over whom parishes had authority (see Chapter 7), the 1834 Poor Law Amendments, the 'New Poor Law,' provided that 'nothing in this Act contained shall authorize the Detention in any Workhouse of any dangerous Lunatic, insane Person, or Idiot, for any longer Period than Fourteen Days' (§ 45). By the first half of the nineteenth century, separate provisions were being made for 'lunatics' and 'the insane' through legislation such as the County Asylums Act 1808 and the Lunacy Act 1845 (separate provisions were made for 'idiots' through the Idiots Act 1886).

As a consequence of this differentiation of policies and institutions, new types of professionals emerged in the nineteenth century and developed into increasingly prominent political constituencies of their own: policemen, prison guards, teachers, librarians, psychiatrists, doctors, and midwives. These groups played an increasingly important role in modern societies, also politically, and they formed their own organizations, associations, and unions, to defend their interests and to press for policy reforms. Even today, these professional groups constitute the majority of government civilian employees in the advanced democratic states.

Last, but not least, many of the services we study in this book were long seen as prerogatives of the church. In the nineteenth century, those old prerogatives clashed with the ambitions of the emergent bureaucratic state and modernizing political elites in national capitals. This led to one of the nineteenth century's defining political conflicts: the struggle between the 'centralizing, standardizing, and mobilizing *Nation-State*' and the 'historically established corporate privileges of the *Church*' (Lipset and Rokkan 1967, 14–15, emphasis in original). As Lipset and Rokkan point out, this conflict was most intense in the area of education, which is why education features so prominently in this book.

When we cross from the eighteenth century into the nineteenth, we consequently enter a recognizably modern world where national governments sought to establish new forms of public services, under specific national legislation, in domains where earlier, rudimentary services had been local, undifferentiated, and often religious. In their place, states often tried to introduce services that were more centralized, differentiated, and secular.

There are many important policies and services that are not covered in this book. We exclude cash transfers and, more generally, policies that pertain to the transfer of resources among people and groups. In other words, we do not only exclude resource-extracting policies such as taxation but also resource-granting policies such as poor relief, unemployment insurance, family benefits, and pensions.[5] We also exclude policies that developed physical infrastructure that was intended to have beneficial but indirect effects on people. This means excluding many of the great projects of the Victorian era, such as sanitation systems, transportation networks, and postal and telegraph infrastructures. While such policies changed the physical environment in ways that facilitated people's transformation into more orderly, more educated, and healthier citizens, these were indirect outcomes of public policies, not direct ones.[6] Moreover, we exclude purely regulatory policies that determined what private agents were and were not allowed to do. This means excluding the nineteenth century's many laws on child labor, food adulteration, and working hours. Finally, and perhaps most controversially, we exclude institutions and policies whose role was to 'sustain' rather than to 'shape' people. That means excluding orphanages and sanatoria as well as most hospitals. One might argue that hospitals ought to be included given their modern functions of diagnosis and healing. However, the surgical revolution in hospitals only occurred toward the end of our period – following developments in surgical techniques and antibacterial technology – and the medical care that existed before that time was largely ambulatory or palliative.[7]

---

5 We also limit our analysis to services that were provided for nonmilitary reasons. Although conscription, military training, and, indeed, warfare all 'transform' people, sometimes fatally so, they are outside the scope of this study. The line between military and nonmilitary services is sometimes faint, however. For example, many domestic police forces have military origins and were created to violently compel citizens with the state's authority in a manner that was not necessarily dissimilar to military compulsion in wartime. Moreover, education, prisons, vaccinations, and other policies analyzed in this book were often implemented with the intention of improving the stock of fighting men that were available to the nation-state. We include all these policies, but exclude purely military ones.

6 On sewage, sanitation, and public health in Victorian cities, see Hennock (1973) and, for a comparison with Germany, Hennock (2000); on public programs for urban refuse, see Melosi (1981).

7 As documented by Rosen (1963), among many others, the hospital, as we understand it now – an institution dedicated to surgery and the treatment of disease, dominated by the medical professions – is a fairly recent phenomenon. There have been hospitals at least since the middle ages, probably longer, if by 'hospital' we mean an institution that cared for the sick, but early modern institutions were not functionally differentiated in the way that modern hospitals are: etymologically, the word hospital, which has medieval origins, comes from the Latin word *hospitale*, for 'guest house,' and medieval hospitals cared not only for the sick but also for travelers, for the young, for the old, and for the infirm. The first specialized hospitals emerged in the early nineteenth century (Gloyne 1944, 16), but as Rosenberg (1995 [1987], 5) notes, 'Aside from a handful of surgical procedures, there was little in the way of medical capability in 1800 that could not be made easily available outside the hospital's walls.'

Of the institutions we do cover, the one closest to 'sustaining' institutions is the insane asylum, but great efforts were made in the nineteenth century, inspired by the ideas of men like the French physician Philippe Pinel, to cure the insane instead of merely confining them. We do exclude workhouses, poorhouses and almshouses. In all three cases, the role of the physical institution was largely to store people who had in common their health status or their poverty. Unlike in a prison, the goal was not to alter people – neither negatively, through punishment, nor positively, through redemptive rehabilitation.

How do our choices over what to include compare with existing work on the origins of public services? That terrain is not entirely barren. Ernest Barker's *The Development of Public Services in Western Europe* (1943) is an early contribution by a political scientist to the comparative literature on the history of public services. His stated aims are to examine 'systems of administration in the modern type of state,' the 'treatment of person and property, by the methods used for raising armies and imposing taxes,' and 'the promotion of physical and mental welfare by means of State public services and State provision for education.' The chapter on social 'services' is concerned first with poor relief, then factory legislation, then social insurance; then there is the chapter on education. There is very little on other types of public services, even if Barker had a broad concept of public services that also included conscription, taxation, and cash benefits.

More recently, and closer – in terms of coverage – to what we do in this book, De Swaan's *In the Care of the State* (1988) provides a sweeping overview of health care, education and welfare since the medieval era, discussing local and religious provision as well as industrial capitalism and the ambitions of nation-states. De Swaan tells a more explicitly political story about the preferences and behavior of various political parties and actors. Still, his book lacks a systematic conceptualization of how services differ, and it offers little analysis of how political preferences over the organization of services might be abstracted from particular historical cases. Moreover, De Swaan's choice of services only partly overlaps with ours: he includes sanitation, poor relief, and pensions, and mixes transfers and infrastructure; he does not concentrate on human services, as we do here.

In addition to these broader studies – which, like our book, cover several services at once – there are many excellent studies, with great historical sweep and depth, of individual public services. Kimberly Morgan's work on early-childhood education is particularly close in spirit to our project, since it investigates the long-run consequences of state–church conflicts in the nineteenth century for the organization and scope of child care and education (Morgan 2002, 2006).

But these are the exceptions. In general, political science has left an important period of recent history underexamined and whole swathes of public policy underexplored. In particular, we lack clear theories about how and why the governance of public services differs among countries and over time. We now turn to developing our own framework to understand these choices about governance.

2.2 HOW MUCH, AND BY WHOM

We are not the first to examine the origin and spread of public services, but most existing work is concerned with describing and explaining their increasing extent, and the increasing cost of providing them (consider, for example, Lindert's influential 2004 analysis of schooling). What we add is a detailed, comparative analysis of political conflicts over how public services were organized. Political battles in the nineteenth and early twentieth centuries were often fought over the question 'By whom?' (who should provide and control services), not the question 'How much?' (should services be provided more widely).

Indeed, in the long history of political conflicts over what we now call the welfare state, the question 'By whom?' has often been more important then the question 'How much?' Esping-Andersen (1990, 19) famously noted, for instance, that public spending on social insurance programs is 'epiphenomenal to the theoretical substance of welfare states,' and before him, Briggs (1961, 17) included public services in a similar argument:

There is controversy ... not only about the range of services and who shall enjoy them but about the means of providing them. The choice of means influences all "welfare state" history. "Welfare states" can and do employ a remarkable variety of instruments, such as social insurance, direct provision in cash or in kind, subsidy, partnership with other agencies, including private business agencies, and action through local authorities.

In the early nineteenth century, most public services were provided locally, if at all, and they were often provided by churches, religious orders, or philanthropic associations, not by secular, public authorities. When nineteenth-century governments introduced new legislation

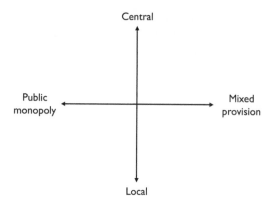

FIGURE 2.1 Governing public services.

on services such as policing, schooling, and public health, they therefore challenged two forms of authority: on the one hand, the authority of local elites and assemblies, and on the other hand, the authority of religious institutions and private associations. We wish to understand the consequences of this dual challenge to established institutions.

To examine similarities and differences over time, among countries, and among policy areas, it is necessary to develop concepts that can be applied to different political systems, historical periods, and public services. Our basic analytical construct is two-dimensional (see Figure 2.1). The vertical dimension represents the distribution of power and competencies among different levels of government, with local and central as the endpoints. The horizontal dimension represents the distribution of power and competencies between public, secular authorities and other institutions and organizations – which might be churches, religious orders, lay foundations, philanthropic associations, or other private organizations, including for-profit corporations.[8] In this dimension, the endpoints are public and mixed, where public means that all publicly funded services are provided by public, secular institutions (we can call this type of arrangement a 'public monopoly') and mixed means that publicly funded services are provided by some combination of public, private, secular, and religious institutions and organizations. It would in theory have

---

[8] The concept of 'public' and its separation from the 'private' sphere was emergent and contested during the period we study – in part as a consequence of legal developments separating monarchical sovereignty from the public domain in the early modern period – and indeed varied dramatically among countries (for a discussion, see Horwitz 1982).

been possible to have 'private' as the endpoint, but it was very rare for the services we consider to be provided entirely by private institutions.

In the northeast quadrant (central and mixed), we find services that were controlled by national governments but involved a mix of providers – some public, some private; some religious, some secular. This type of arrangement has been rare (approximately 5 percent of all services we study in this book), and the proportion has changed little over time. When governments sought to centralize public services, they often did so precisely to wrest control from private and religious organizations, which explains why most centralized systems were dominated by public authorities.

In the northwest quadrant (central and public), we find services that were provided by national governments, but with all public funding going to public, secular providers. In 1839, 11 percent of the services in our study were governed in this manner; in 1939, 100 years later, 36 percent were. In other words, having a centralized system with a public monopoly on service provision became much more common over time.

In the southwest quadrant (local and public), we find services that were provided locally, with all public funding going to public, secular providers. Over the 140-year period we study, this has been the most common type of arrangement, but by the middle of the 1930s, centralized, public systems had become slightly more common: in 1839, 55 percent of all services were local and secular; in 1939, 34 percent were.

In the southeast quadrant, finally (local and mixed), we find services that were provided locally by a mix of public and private and religious and secular providers. In 1839, 28 percent of the services in our study were provided in this way; in 1939, 23 percent were.

The two dimensions in Figure 2.1 are a simplification of a complex reality, and the empirical chapters will have more to say about the varied arrangements that have existed in different countries, at different points in time, for different types of services. In particular, the label 'mixed' covers many different types of arrangements, since there are many types of institutions and organizations that have provided public services alongside secular and public authorities.

Centralization – the vertical dimension in Figure 2.1 – is the degree of control that national-level political authorities had over public services. Were public services directed from national capitals, by central bureaucracies controlled by national executives and legislatures, or were they controlled by local decision makers, whether those were voluntary organizations, municipal authorities, or parishes? Or were services perhaps controlled by regional authorities that were responsive to regional legislatures or officials? For generations, scholars have emphasized the importance of political tensions between core and periphery in determining state capacity, defining party–political conflicts, and shaping political identities in the modern world (Beramendi 2012; Caramani 2004; Rokkan 1973; Ziblatt 2008). Public services have long influenced – and been influenced by – these struggles.

There are numerous ways to conceptualize and measure the level of centralization. One approach is to concentrate on legislation and regulation. Another approach is to concentrate on funding and on financial flows from the center to the periphery (or vice versa). We choose a public administration approach: we concentrate on the employment of policemen, teachers, midwives, and other individuals who carried out public policies. We thus ask where the ultimate responsibility lay for the selection of individuals who actually provided services – that is, who had the responsibility for 'hiring and firing.' We distinguish among three levels of government – local, regional, or national – although in parts of our analysis, we combine the first two categories into one.

In his book *The Tools of Government*, Hood (1983, 4–7) distinguishes among four basic government 'resources': 'nodality,' 'treasure,' 'authority,' and 'organization.' Our approach is to concentrate on 'organization,' which is 'the possession of a stock of people with whatever skills they may have (soldiers, workers, bureaucrats), land, buildings, materials and equipment, somehow arranged' (Hood 1983, 6). This seems to us the most direct measure of the authority of different levels of government, institutions, and organizations. In the domain of schooling, to take one example, concentrating on 'nodality' would have meant emphasizing the influence of the government over the curriculum and over the diffusion of pedagogical ideas and techniques, concentrating on 'treasure' would have meant emphasizing the sources of education financing, and concentrating on 'authority' would have meant emphasizing the adoption and implementation of school laws and other authoritative political directives (Westberg et al. 2019). These things are all important, but it is no coincidence that many of the great education reforms involved the teachers themselves – who they worked for, who promoted them, and who set their salaries and determined their other employment conditions.

By concentrating on who employed those who provided public services, we follow other studies of the transformation of the state in the nineteenth and early twentieth centuries, notably Hillel Soifer's study of state-making in Latin America. 'Where local bureaucrats were deployed from centre to periphery,' Soifer writes (2015, 5–6), 'the implementation of state-initiated policies was more successful than in countries where the appointment of public offices was delegated to local elites.' He notes that the mechanism is straightforward: 'while centrally deployed bureaucrats' salaries and status depended on their loyalty toward the central government, locally elected office holders were more susceptible to the influence of regional elites.'

It is not always straightforward to infer from the formal separation of a country's political structure into different levels of government how powers over specific services were allocated. Consider France, for example. In the nineteenth century, like now, France was divided into several departments, each of which was run by a prefect. The role of the prefects changed over time and varied among policy domains (Machin 1977). In periods when regional governments had some autonomy, the prefect had a dual role: on the one hand, he was the agent of the central government 'in regard to those matters of general administration which are thought to concern the whole country'; on the other hand, the prefect was an agent of the department 'for local affairs' (Lowell 1896, 36–37). In the former capacity, the prefect thus implemented the national government's policy; in the second capacity, he was more autonomous, and carried out 'the resolutions of the General Council' (Lowell 1896, 38), which was the representative body at the regional level. It is therefore necessary to consult the historical literature on individual policies to determine how centralized each particular policy was.

It is also difficult to distinguish, at times, between *de jure* and *de facto* centralization. In Germany, the formal organization of mental health care did not change much when the National Socialist Party took power in the 1930s: legally, the mental institutions were still regulated at the level of the *Länder*, the state governments. But the National Socialist government's two most well-known programs in the domain of mental health and 'racial hygiene' – the program of forced sterilization that began in the middle of the 1930s and the program of outright killing that started a few years later – were both run directly from Berlin. The first program, which was legally sanctioned, was run from the Interior Ministry (Evans 2005, 507). The second program, carried out in secret, was run from a special office at Tiergartenstraße 4 in Berlin (hence the program's name, T4). In Chapter 7, we treat mental institutions in Germany as centralized in this period, but it is important to keep in mind that many decisions about admissions and treatment were still made by *Land* authorities.[9]

In the horizontal dimension in Figure 2.1, we find many different sorts of arrangements, spanning the range from a public monopoly to a fully mixed economy of public, religious, and private provision. There were many services that were under full control, funding, and provision by central, regional, or local governments. In those cases, the employees who provided services were state bureaucrats or local officials, with allegiance to public authorities only and performing services in institutions built, owned, and kept by the state or by local governments. Outside of these cases of public monopoly, however, there have been many hybrid systems of provision, often retaining strong connections to networks of preindustrial service provision. In such systems, the state might have a say in regulation and funding, but little direct control.

One type of mixed service provision is where public services are provided by the church: public and religious institutions are fused in the sense that the clergy, or other religious authorities, effectively control how a service is delivered (by, for example, hiring and firing those who provide it). We refer to this form of governance as *fusion*. A public service may well be secular, which is the opposite of fusion, even if religious individuals, groups, or parties have a great deal of influence over legislation, which is the sort of influence that Gryzmala-Busse investigates in her recent book *Nations under God* from 2015. The question we ask in this book is rather if the officials who controlled or carried out a public service did so *ex officio* as members of the clergy or in holy orders. As we show in Chapters 4 and 6, many of those who were active in the prison-reform and public library movements in the nineteenth century were deeply religious men and women, but that does not preclude the possibility that the prisons and the public libraries were themselves secular in an administrative sense – indeed, in most cases, they were.

---

[9] An added difficulty in the case of Nazi Germany is that administrative centralization often involved the superimposition of party organizations on underlying bureaucratic structures. In a recent assessment of the health care sector in Nazi Germany as a whole, Busse et al. (2017, p. 886) write, 'The organisation of the health care sector, and the balance of power among the main actors were also changed during the Nazi regime. The sickness funds (1934), community health departments (1935), as well as professional associations, medical chambers, and charitable institutions dealing with public welfare or health education (1933–1935) were each centralised and placed under the authority of a director nominated by the Nazi Party. Members of the self-governing institutions within the system of joint self-government were chosen by the Nazi Party rather than elected.'

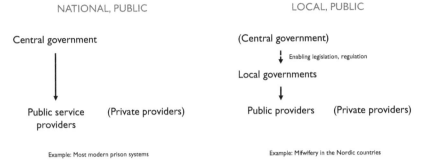

FIGURE 2.2 Governance I: Public monopolies.

A mixed economy of public services also emerges when significant public funding is channelled to private service providers through an arrangement that we call *subsidization*. In the nineteenth century, private providers were usually religious organizations, but they need not be; several different 'owners' of public services, whether religious or nonreligious, were typically eligible to receive public funding, creating a contractual, potentially arms-length relationship between the state, local governments, and public services. We say 'significant' public funding since we wish to concentrate on cases where private service providers were an important part of the whole system and where the funding stream was sufficient to cover a large part of the running costs. In the United States, direct transfers to religious institutions from the public purse have largely been banned, but there has at times been implicit subsidization through tax breaks, or by permitting the funding of ancillary services, including books or transportation, for religious schools (see Hackett 2020). Although there are important line-drawing problems, as Supreme Court jurisprudence in the United States demonstrates, we think of these sorts of arrangements as qualitatively different from the direct support of private, potentially religious services we emphasize here.

Figures 2.2 and 2.3 illustrate the main combinations of central, local, public, church-controlled, and subsidized private service provision. Figure 2.2 describes systems with a public monopoly: private services – if they exist at all – receive no or negligible public funding. The main distinction here is between services that are provided directly by the national government (the left-hand panel) and services that are provided by local authorities with national governments stopping at enabling legislation, regulations, and perhaps grants-in-aid (the right-hand panel).

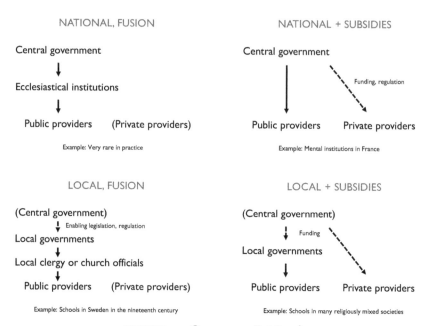

FIGURE 2.3 Governance II: Mixed.

Figure 2.3, by contrast, describes systems in which there is no public monopoly, either because there is a fusion of church and state since the government cedes authority over some public services to ecclesiastical institutions or members of the clergy or because the government enters into a contractual relationship with private associations (religious or secular), which receive government subsidies to provide public services.

2.3 COMMON TRENDS

When did modern public services emerge? When did they centralize? Was there common a trend toward public monopolies? And what explains these overall patterns? We start our analysis in the year 1800, just after the appointment of Napoleon Bonaparte as First Consul of France, and we end in the year 1939, when the Second World War began. The world was obviously a very different place in 1939 than it was in 1800. When we analyze the policies that were adopted in different countries and at different points in time, we must therefore take into account the great economic, social and political changes that occurred over this period of almost a century and a half.

In this section, we examine the broader structural forces that were at play in this era. This book examines nineteen countries: Australia, Austria, Belgium, Canada, Denmark, Finland, France, Germany, Ireland, Italy, Japan, the Netherlands, New Zealand, Norway, Spain, Sweden, Switzerland, the United Kingdom, and the United States. These countries were selected because they represented the wealthiest nation-states by the end of our period, just before the outbreak of the second world war This of course means that they experienced dramatic economic growth over the period we examine, along with the restructuring of their national identities, cultures, and politics.

Until recently, the study of public services in this period has been the domain of sociologists and economic and social historians, not political scientists. This literature has largely emphasized the importance of structural forces in shaping the extent and governance of public services. A particularly useful way to think about structural change is to follow Lipset and Rokkan (1967) and Rokkan (1973), who identified two key 'revolutions' that shaped the nineteenth century: the 'Industrial Revolution' and the 'National Revolution.'

In the beginning of the nineteenth century, the First Industrial Revolution had just begun; by 1939, industrialization had profoundly changed the economic structure of all the countries in our study. Around 1870, in the very middle of the period we analyze, industrialization took off outside the early industrializers. Industrialization matters in at least three important ways for the story we tell. First of all, as Lipset and Rokkan (1967) and Rokkan (1973) discussed, industrialization changed the class structure, which created new types of political conflicts, including conflicts over services, between landowners and the emerging commercial and industrial classes and between capital and labor. Second, industrialization changed the state itself. As Samuel Finer notes in his *History of Government* (1997, Book III, 1610–1618), the development of the modern state in the nineteenth century was only possible because of technological changes associated with the Industrial Revolution, and as Mann (1984) observed, the increase in the state's 'infrastructural power' in the nineteenth and twentieth centuries was a consequence of new industrial-era technologies that allowed the state to penetrate civil society – including new means of transportation and communication and new administrative practices. Third, industrialization brought about new machinery, equipment, and techniques, and thus generated economies of scale that made it possible and desirable for governments to create big institutions in lieu of small, local establishments.

Industrialization also contributed to another great social transformation: urbanization. The migration from the countryside to the cities was an economic and social transformation with important consequences for the provision of public services and for political conflicts. Urbanization creates new social risks, since the concentration of people in urban agglomerations creates new threats to health and social order. It thus increases the demand for public services. But it also increases the supply, since the concentration of people in cities generates economies of scale in service provision and makes training new types of professionals – such as policemen, teachers, and doctors – more cost-effective. As a consequence of the demand for and supply of public services in the cities, innovations in public services often began there and spread elsewhere. Urbanization also influenced political conflicts since it created an urban-rural cleavage. Industrialization and urbanization are related, since those who moved to the cities often worked in factories. But their effects are quite different. Put simply, industrialization changed people's relationship with time whereas urbanization changed people's relationship with space: industrialization made it more difficult for families to raise the young and take care of the sick and the old; urbanization, meanwhile, made it more difficult for local communities to perform those tasks.

The nineteenth century was not only an era of economic and social change, but also an era of ideological changes. As Lipset and Rokkan (1967) and Rokkan (1973) argued, chief among these were the growth of a national identity – nationalism – and the decline of old religious identities – secularization.

Nationalism required great efforts to make the nation-state's authority universal across its subjects, and to inculcate subjects who were often spread over vast territories with the language, ideology, and often also the religious norms of the center (Anderson 1983; Gellner 1983). Eugen Weber (1976) famously referred to this social process as one of turning 'peasants into Frenchmen.' The nationalist mission typically required the deliberate expansion of public services that could shape the minds and behavior of citizens.

The period between 1800 and 1939 was also characterized by both religious conflict and secularization. In the book, we are studying one element of secularization: the creation of public services outside the church. But it was a much broader process. Scholars of secularization such as McLeod (1997) emphasize the dual challenge to majority churches from other Christian sects on the one hand and secular, even anticlerical, groups on the other hand. Culturally, socially, and politically, the once unquestioned authority of the church in matters of family and community life was being challenged.

Political systems were also changing, not least through state formation itself. The structures of modern states as territorial entities changed greatly between 1800 and 1939. In the beginning of the period we are studying, countries such as Australia, Canada, Germany, and Italy did not even exist. The middle to late nineteenth century was a period of intense conflict over the structure of states, as several new federal states were formed and the northern and southern states in the United States went to war with each other. The centralization or decentralization of public services was one important source of these broader conflicts over state structure – and, at times, an outcome of those conflicts.

These structural forces have clear implications for our two dimensions of public services – the vertical dimension that accounts for the relative centralization of policies and the horizontal dimension that accounts for the importance of public versus private or religious provision. Industrialization and urbanization weakened old peripheral localities, both politically and economically, as populations and production became centered in the cities. They also permitted economies of scale in the development of public services, while increasing demand among citizens. These forces the suggest greater centralization and a larger role for exclusively public provision – a shift to the northwest in Figure 2.1. The National Revolution, combined with secularization, similarly suggests a greater role for the core and capital over peripheries and a weakening of traditional religious providers (or indeed any private entities whose allegiance to the state might not be fully trusted). Thus, again, structural forces suggest a northwest movement in Figure 2.1. In general, one would thus expect the historical trends we have discussed here to have resulted in uniformly centralized and secular public services.

Indeed, there are such general tendencies in the data we have compiled, but those average tendencies hide a great deal of variation among countries and policy areas. Figure 2.4 describes the average level of centralization among the countries in our study. In order to analyze the overall trend, we have taken the means of our 'centralization' variable across all the seven policy areas we study (0 is local, 1 is regional, 2 is national), and then we have taken the mean for all countries that existed in each year. This means that the figure displays the average level of centralization across all policies and all countries. The overall level of centralization increased from just over 0.3 in the early nineteenth century to approximately 1.1 in the year 1939. By and large, then, centralization

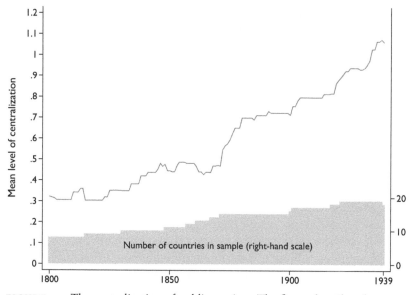

FIGURE 2.4 The centralization of public services. The figure describes the mean
level of centralization (where 0 is the minimum and 2 is the maximum) of
policing, prison services, primary education, public libraries, mental institutions,
vaccination services, and midwifery.
Sources: Calculated on the basis of the categorization of different public services in
Chapters 3–9

rose markedly over time. But even at the end of the period, there was
a great deal of variation among countries and policy areas – indeed, by
the 1920s and early 1930s, the mean level of centralization was only
half-way between the extremes of complete local control and complete
national control.

Figure 2.5 describes the proportion of services that were both secular
and provided by public authorities – a 'public monopoly.' There was an
upward trend between 1800 and 1939, but it is far less pronounced than
the upward trend in centralization. The proportion of public services in
which a public monopoly existed only increased from a little over 0.5 in
1800 to just under 0.7 in 1939, with much of the increase occurring early
on, in the first half of the nineteenth century, when tasks such as mental
health care were removed from old parish-based systems of poor relief
and placed in the hands of new, secular institutions.

The apparent stability is misleading, however. Figure 2.6 splits the
trends in the two main forms of non-public-monopoly provision: the
fusion of church and state and the subsidization of privately provided

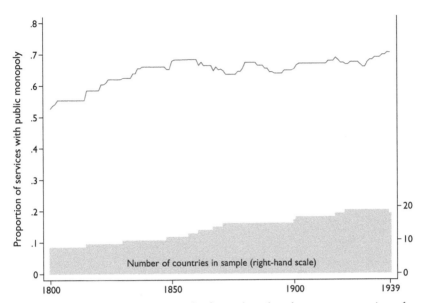

FIGURE 2.5 Public monopolies. The figure describes the mean proportion of public services that were provided exclusively by secular and public authorities (including policing, prison services, primary education, public libraries, mental institutions, vaccinations, and midwifery).
Sources: Calculated on the basis of the categorization of different public services in Chapters 3–9

services. The proportion of services that were characterized by a fusion of church and state declined dramatically during the whole period we study. By contrast, the proportion of services where nonpublic providers retained direct control but received public monies – subsidization – increased substantially, especially in the second half of the nineteenth century. In the aggregate, we thus see a shift from fusion to subsidization. Interestingly, however, there was rarely a direct substitution effect: countries that secularized their public services, ending the fusion of church and state, did not typically introduce subsidization; instead, they were more likely to introduce public monopolies (a trend that is especially noteworthy in the Nordic countries). Subsidization emerged, instead, as an independent model.

All these averages hide a great deal of policy variation and political conflict. In each of the empirical chapters, we explore in depth the particular configurations of control that emerged over time, the contingencies of provision in different policy areas and national environments, and the changing nature of political debates over public services. Moreover in

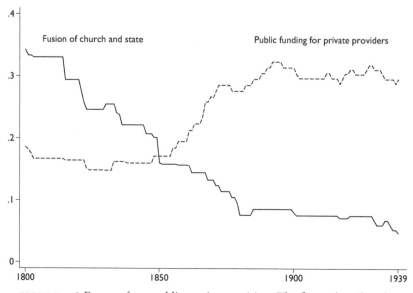

FIGURE 2.6 Forms of nonpublic service provision. The figure describes the proportion of services in which there was a fusion of church and state (among policing, prison services, primary education, public libraries, mental institutions, vaccinations, and midwifery) and the proportion of services that were carried out, at least in part, by private organizations with public funding.
Sources: Calculated on the basis of the categorization of different public services in Chapters 3–9

Chapter 10 we analyse the determinants of reform across different policy types. Nonetheless, Figures 2.4, 2.5, and 2.6 do demonstrate that there were overall trends toward centralized governance, the end of state–church fusion, and a new mixed economy of subsidization. These trends can be explained in part by the broad historical changes that we have discussed here: industry, cities, and nationalism contributed to centralization and the decline of religious authority, combined with the rise of democracy, contributed to secularization, but also to demands for subsidization from religious and other minorities. Yet, these grand historical shifts are not the whole story. They were by no means universal, suggesting that structural forces provide an incomplete explanation for the development of public services. Our own explanation of public service governance emphasizes the agency of political parties, while recognizing how that agency is constrained by political institutions and the power of the church. Before we turn to our *political* argument, however, it is worth discussing at greater length existing structural arguments and their limitations given the variation we see in the data.

We are not the first authors to draw attention to the combined importance of the Industrial and National Revolutions for state-building and the emergence of public services. Michael Mann's magnum opus *The Sources of Social Power* (1993) surveys state building since time immemorial, with its second volume, on the period between 1760 and 1914, focusing on the period that interests us here. Mann subtitled this volume *The Rise of Classes and Nation States*, which is indicative of his core explanatory factors: for Mann, state-building is a function of the development of new industrial-era classes (a capitalist class and a working class) and the creation of nation-states.

The nineteenth century's new public services were, for Mann, a functional response to the demands of a modern economy on the one hand and the military and diplomatic aims of nation-states on the other. A representative quote about education makes this functionalism quite clear:

The expansion of state education was partly a function of the job requirements of capitalism and modern states ... But it also reflected dominant class desires for social control and subordinate class desires for "ideological citizenship" – revealing the class and national crystallizations of the state. (Mann 1993, 572)

Mann tells a similar story at the more coercive end of the public-service spectrum. The origins of policing, in his analysis, are also functional:

Regimes now had a broader "policing" problem. Capitalism and urbanization had weakened local-regional segmental controls over the lower classes ... [and] more universal forms of social control were required, especially in the burgeoning towns. (Mann 1993, 500)

Classic accounts of the development of policing, schooling, and medical provision – particularly those written before the 1960s – tended to have in mind an implicit 'modernization' story of growing social complexity, which produced, more or less automatically, a professionalized, centralized, and secular system of social provision. For policing, for instance, early work by Reith (1943, 1956) took a 'Whiggish' view of British political development: urbanization and industrialization led to a rising middle class and active urban groups who desired safer streets and more effectively secured property rights; Robert Peel then responded to these demands with the creation of a professionalized London Metropolitan Force, which served as an exemplar to other British cities and to reformers abroad.

A similarly linear progressive story has often been told in the history of education, dating back at least to Durkheim and most pronounced in the sociological functionalism of the 1950s, as in Floud and Halsey (1958) and (Parsons 1959). In this view, schooling emerged as a way to supply the more diverse array of skills and competencies required by an industrial society, and as a way to bind together an otherwise anonymous, increasingly urban community. A more contemporary rendering of this approach can be seen in the 'world society' school, which examines the spread of modern social services, particularly education, through a process of isomorphism, as developing countries adopt the policies of early industrializers (Meyer, Ramirez, and Soysal 1992; Meyer and Thomas 1984).

Although these sorts of arguments have long been dismissed as teleological and overly functionalist, they do get the broad trends right: all of the public services we examine in this book did grow in their size, complexity, and professionalism over the long nineteenth century, and while some have eventually declined, notably mental institutions, that downturn typically happened in the postwar era. Moreover, this growth must almost certainly have been related to the growing wealth and complexity of what would become known as the developed world; we consistently find the most established and resource-consuming social institutions in countries that were relatively wealthy.

But these modernization approaches were always less useful when explaining differences *among* the developed countries, and they were least useful in explaining 'By whom?' questions, as opposed to 'How much?' questions. Modernization theories have little to say about why the church remained powerful in many domains, from education through health, for so long. Moreover, they do not explain why many countries retained decentralized social institutions, whereas others centralized decision-making in their national capitals. The heirs to this tradition – such as Lindert (2004) – see rising income and democratic transitions as underpinning growing spending, but they too lack purchase when it comes to explaining how social institutions were governed.

We see similar blind spots in the more 'critical' traditions of thinking about social institutions, whether they be Marxist, and therefore materialist, or inspired by the work of intellectual historians such as Michel Foucault. In the Marxist tradition, social institutions are structures of state control over the proletariat – hence the expansion of prisons, according to Melossi and Pavarini (1981) and, before them, Rusche and Kirchheimer (1939), reflects a need to coerce labor into acquiescence and apathy by harshly punishing any transgressions of property rights, or indeed pro-labor political activism. Schooling, meanwhile, has been viewed as a way to train labor into obedience to the demands of capitalist production (Bowles and Gintis 1976; Sharp 1980).[10] The critical tradition, following Foucault, has also presumed that social institutions operate on behalf of the powerful, structuring both material conditions and common interpretations of social reality. The prison, of course, was the paradigmatic form of social control for Foucault, but schools, medical interventions, conceptions of 'order' and of 'sanity' could all be placed within this framework.

We do not wish to argue that these class-based or critical approaches are without merit. Governments did not introduce public services for entirely charitable reasons, and schools, policing, and vaccinations could all be invasive and coercive. But again, such approaches are better able to account for the expansion of social institutions than for how they were governed. Clashes between periphery and center and between church and layman can be squeezed into such theories, but the clothing is typically ill-fitting. Marxist theories are at their most helpful in noting that social democratic parties, when in power, are likely to bring social provision under their control; indeed that is an argument we also make. They are less effective at explaining why liberal parties also typically sought the same ends in the late nineteenth or early twentieth centuries, or indeed why authoritarian leaders sometimes produced secularized and centralized policies that were similar to those of social democrats.

A more challenging account for us is the large institutionalist literature on the origins and path-dependent development of various social institutions, particularly in education (Thelen 2004) and health (Immergut 1992). These studies focus not on convergent processes of modernization or class structure shifts, but on the divergent legacies of policies themselves. Choices made by industrial or political actors about the design of public policy become embedded in country-specific forms. They shape their own support bases, complementary institutions, and economic logics; hence, the design of modern public services reflects choices made long ago, not contemporary needs or the contemporary balance of political power.

---

[10] Even class-based accounts of welfare state development that are not explicitly Marxist, such as Esping-Andersen (1985, 1990) and Stephens (1979), tend to view the growth of spending on social institutions as reflecting the relative balance of class power between labor and capital, as promulgated by their representative political agents and organized interests.

As we shall see, we find a good deal of within-country stasis in the design of social institutions – indeed, some countries retain decentralized or mixed public–private institutions for certain public services during the entire century and a half we study. Given the dramatic shifts in industrial structure and the composition of the population over time, these findings speak to the powerful role of path dependence. And yet, we do see policy change and great political battles over reform. Concentrating to much on stability may lead one to neglect the possibilities and actualities of change.

Finally, a recent literature in political economy (for example, Onorato, Scheve, and Stasavage 2014) has returned to Tilly's (1986) and Levi's (1988) insight that episodes of military rivalry and conflict are crucial for state-building. A related literature argues that social institutions such as education and libraries are products of nationalism and empire (Anderson 1983; Gellner 1983; Weber 1976). Again, we think these are serious arguments that help to explain both divergence – for example, the different pressures on distant settler colonies than among the European Great Powers of the nineteenth century – and change – the shock of military defeat drove French education reformers after the Franco-Prussian war and English health reformers after the Boer War. As we focus on the 'inward conquest' of the domestic territories and citizens of modern states, we need to take into account the threats – and opportunities – they faced in their 'outward conquests.' These arguments are helpful in explaining the relative desire of political reformers – particularly those with universalizing ideologies – to reshape the nation-state from the center. But again, they are perhaps less useful in explaining many of the important domestic conflicts of the time – for example, those between minority and majority religious groups, or between liberals and socialists. We turn to these questions in the next section.

2.4 THE POLITICS OF PUBLIC SERVICES

Why were public services governed differently? Why did some countries follow, or even lead, the trend toward increasing centralization and public monopoly, while others retained more local and parochial systems of governance? What explains the timing of the great public service reforms? To be more specific, what were the preferences of different political parties, factions, and interest groups, and when were they able – or, indeed, unable – to get what they wanted? In this section, we spell out our own political and institutional argument about the governance public services. We show that different political factions and parties and religious groups and authorities had different preferences over both the vertical dimension of governance (centralization versus local) and its horizontal dimension (public monopoly versus mixed provision), but we also argue that political institutions and state capacity shaped the policies that governments eventually adopted.

Our argument begins with a historical and sociological analysis of the principal social and political fault lines in the nineteenth and early twentieth centuries, based largely on the pioneering work of Stein Rokkan. But it is not enough to ask what different groups and parties wanted. We must also consider whether they were able to achieve their goals, which means taking institutional constraints seriously. We therefore complement our argument about the role of social cleavages with an analysis of the growth of democracy, the development of administrative capacities, and the inherent differences among public order, knowledge, and mental and public health, which mattered greatly for the priorities of political parties and factions.

Conservatives, Liberals, Socialists, and Fascists

Social scientists have long sought to understand the social cleavages that structure modern societies. Generally speaking, there are two types of cleavages: those that are defined by the organization of the economy, such as social class, and those that are defined by social and cultural factors such as religion and language. For Lipset and Rokkan (1967) and Rokkan (1973), four main cleavages structured political developments in Europe after the early modern period: the class divide, the urban–rural divide, the state–church divide, and the core–periphery divide. Those cleavages were the result of the nineteenth century's two great 'revolutions' – the Industrial Revolution, which led to new conflicts between landowners and industrialists and capital owners and workers, and the National Revolution, which led to new conflicts over place and religion.

In order to make our analysis tractable, we concentrate on two main dimensions, one based on wealth and one based on attitudes to traditional, often religious, authority. The wealth dimension separates well-to-do landowners, industrialists and professionals from the peasantry and the emerging working class. The cultural dimension separates the main beneficiaries of the *ancien régime* – local notables, adherents of the majority religion, and dominant regional and linguistic groups – from those who were outside the cultural and religious mainstream: adherents of minority religions, secularists, and inhabitants of the periphery. These social cleavages defined the groups that emerging political parties appealed to. They also structured preferences over the provision and organization of public services.

The most long-standing political parties in the nineteenth century were the conservatives and the liberals. Conservative parties typically defended the monarchy and traditional class-based and religious hierarchies. Their core constituency was wealthy land-owning citizens with traditional cultural identities. In countries without representative government – or with a limited franchise – conservative groups normally controlled the state. When the franchise expanded, conservative parties sometimes tried to widen their electoral support by appealing to socially conservative middle- and working-class voters. Alternatively, new types of parties emerged that resembled conservatives ideologically but had a broader class base, notably the Catholic parties that were formed in Western Europe in the second half of the nineteenth century (Kalyvas 1996).

Liberal parties represented well-to-do groups whose material interests or cultural identities differed from those represented by conservatives. They were typically supported by an alliance of industrial and commercial elites, professionals such as doctors and lawyers, and religious nonconformists and anticlericals. At the outset, many liberals, like conservatives, were skeptical of large public expenditures for public services and the welfare of the poor. Indeed, they were skeptical of extending the franchise to the poor in the first place (Fawcett 2015; Kahan 2003). Once the franchise was expanded, however, liberals began to favor higher levels of public spending, to draw in support from middle- and even low-income groups.

Socialist parties only emerged toward the end of the nineteenth century, once a large working class had emerged in the cities. Their core constituency was workers who were anticlerical, nonconformist, or simply separated from the mainline church and its parishes. The electoral strategy of socialist parties, as they expanded, often involved appealing to the rural poor in competition with more conservative and religious parties (Bartolini 2000, Chapters 5 and 8). During the twentieth century, they also began to win over middle-class or even upper-middle-class radicals.

The final party family that we consider here is fascist parties, which only emerged after the First World War. Fascism as an ideology was emphatically conformist, and it was typically economically conservative, but it was also a mass movement that relied on support from lower-middle-class socially conservative voters, especially in rural areas and small towns (Mann 2004). As we discuss below, fascists therefore favored broad-based provision of public services, but they also sought to use those services for political ends, promoting a nationalist political agenda as well as nativist and eugenic policies.

Not all political activity is channeled through political parties, however, so our inventory of the main political forces of the nineteenth- and early twentieth-century world cannot stop here. Churches, for instance, were important social institutions and political agents in their own right, and in countries with several religious denominations existing side by side – that is, all countries in our study except the Lutheran countries in Northern Europe and the Catholic countries south of the Alps – there were not one but several churches that shaped public services. At times, churches sought political influence through established political parties; at other times, religious groups were the backbone of social movements that later turned into new parties.

The professionals who were employed in the services we are studying – such as policemen, teachers, doctors, and nurses – were also important interest groups in the late nineteenth and early twentieth centuries. Professional groups often favored more centralized governance models since they were better organized in the center than in the periphery; in her study of French mental institutions, Jan Goldstein (1987) notes, for instance, that learned societies and professional organizations for psychiatrists – and their precursors – had better access to national-level political decision-making in the capital than to regional and local authorities in towns and provinces. Similarly, as we will show in Chapter 5, most associations for teachers were organized nationally, even in countries where the schools themselves were governed locally.

What Parties Wanted

Because of their different class bases, conservative, liberal, socialist, and fascist parties had distinct ideas about the scope of public services and how services should be provided.

Conservative parties typically wished to contain the expansion of public services and leave them in the hands of traditional social, religious, and political authorities. Consequently, they often delegated public services to the clergy or to local notables and assemblies (Sir Leicester

Dedlock's views in the opening quote from Dickens's *Bleak House* are representative of nineteenth-century conservative opinion). Conservatives were often unwilling to raise the revenues needed to expand the scope of public services, since those revenues came out of the pockets of their constituents. As the franchise expanded, however, conservative parties often became more favorable to public services, or were superseded by parties that were. Consequently, although they were rarely in the forefront of the expansion of public services, they often accepted reforms adopted by others. When Benjamin Disraeli's conservatives returned to power in England after the defeat of Gladstone's first government in the 1874 elections, for example, they did not unravel the landmark Education Act that the liberals had passed in 1870.

Both in cultural and economic terms, nineteenth-century liberals challenged existing social hierarchies. When it came to public services, liberals therefore sought to wrest control from the majority church and from local notables and landed elites. However, liberal parties also represented groups with high and rising incomes – the new middle classes – who were sensitive to tax increases and the costs of extending services to the masses. Early liberals were thus conflicted: they wished to change the governance and organization of public services, but nevertheless wanted to limit their scope. Over time, however, liberals sought to broaden their electoral appeal, and in the beginning of the twentieth century, they often allied with socialists in promoting the expansion of public services. This reorientation of liberal opinion in more democratic regimes was reinforced during the final third of the nineteenth century.

With the urban working class as their core constituency, socialists were interested both in expanding provision and in ensuring that services were not provided by traditional authorities that represented long-standing social hierarchies. This meant divesting the church and local notables of control, as liberals also wanted, and rationalizing, regulating and centralizing service provision. In this sense, the socialists were the clearest contrast to conservative parties – especially toward the end of the nineteenth century, when liberal parties became more favorable to higher levels of public spending.

Fascists, finally, sought to bind society into an organic whole, based around the defense of the nation and traditional culture. In that sense, the fascist political project was emphatically one of defending social hierarchies. But unlike conservatism, fascism was also a mass movement based on the organization of the population into civic and paramilitary organizations that were defined by the party itself. Those ambitions could not

services emerged, political power became more complex and differenti-ated. The struggle for political power was no longer just a struggle for the control of coercive organizations, whose power is essentially negative; it was also a struggle for the control of organizations whose power is posi-tive, in that they provide things for people rather than taking things from them or preventing them from doing what they would otherwise do.[11]

Consequently, nineteenth-century nation-states did not only do *more* things than early modern states; they also did *different* things. Parties, political leaders, and interest groups now fought over a political appa-ratus that was more complex than the revenue-generating and coercive apparatus of early modern central states: they fought over the power to control people's bodies and behavior, change people's minds, and manage entire populations.

Political and religious leaders cared more about some of these powers than others. The relationship between the organizations that provided services and the individuals and groups to whom they were provided therefore mattered for the political choices governments made. For exam-ple, religious authorities cared most about the ideological power that education offered – as opposed to coercive power, which the church had largely abandoned in the early modern era, or the powers over the body that came with modern medicine and public health. For fascists, what mattered most, by contrast, was coercive power through internal order. Liberals, conservatives, and socialists too viewed different pub-lic services through distinct lenses, depending on whether those services promised to increase coercive power, ideological power or biopower over the citizenry.

---

[11] The idea that power in modern societies is complex, multifaceted, and positive is the main theme of the work of Michel Foucault, who himself studied many of the insti-tutions we analyze or discuss in this book – from insane asylums and hospitals to prisons and public health. According to Foucault, 'sovereign' power – which demands and expects obedience to the king or some other ruler – coexisted, from the seventeenth and eighteenth centuries onward, with at least two other forms of power: 'disciplinary' power and 'biopower' (Foucault 2004b). Disciplinary power, the main theme of Fou-cault's *Discipline and Punish* (1975), is exercised over individuals, shaping their lives, beliefs, and sense of self, whereas biopower, one of the themes of Foucault's *History of Sexuality* (1976; see also 2004a), is exercised over the population, which modern states treat as a resource to be managed for political ends. One way of thinking about the pub-lic services we study in this book is that they represent different combinations of modern forms of power: the police is principally a manifestation of sovereign power; prisons, mental institutions, and schools are principally manifestations of disciplinary power; and midwifery and vaccinations are principally manifestations of biopower. The estab-lishment of libraries can be seen as an attempt to control the production of knowledge – which was itself an important theme of Foucault's work.

Two Paths to Centralization

To understand the development and organization of public services, one must thus understand not only what political leaders wanted, but also how political institutions evolved, how the state's administrative capacity developed, and what the main differences were among public order, knowledge, and mental and public health. The interactions among these four explanatory factors are complicated, and in the policy-specific empirical chapters, we will provide many different examples of how they combined. But it is possible to outline a few general claims at this stage.

We begin with the idea that there were *two paths to centralization*. In the beginning of the nineteenth century, rudimentary public services were typically provided locally, if at all. National political leaders that sought to centralize public services therefore needed both the will and the capacity to wrest power over services from local authorities and create new central bureaucracies. There were two types of governments that did: on the one hand, governments in autocratic and authoritarian states, such as absolute monarchies in the beginning of the period we study or fascist regimes toward the end, which were often conservative; on the other hand, governments in democracies with powerful liberal or – later – socialist parties.

Although these two types of governments were in many other ways each other's opposites, they were both centralizers. Centralization was motivated in part by a desire to increase the provision of public services, since centralization creates economies of scale in training, deployment, and payment and in the construction and financing of large establishments. But other political motivations also mattered. More authoritarian governments typically centralized services since they wished to use them for their own political ends, including coercion and propaganda. Fascists in particular had totalizing ideologies that led to a preference for centralization. Whereas conservatives in democratizing or democratic countries often sought to preserve the status quo by leaving public services in the hands of local authorities, fascists sought to recreate a more homogeneous social, political, and sometimes also racial national community through party- and government-led mobilization.

Liberals and socialists in democracies, on the other hand, sought to centralize public services because they wanted to provide them more uniformly among social classes and other groups. Local authority often meant traditional authority, imbued in local notables, the 'squirearchy,' and the parishes of the mainline church; hence, liberals and socialists had strong reasons to pursue uniform public policies, which required a national lead and a large role for the government in directly controlling and running institutions throughout the territory, avoiding the perceived arbitrariness and venality of local elites and the obscurantism of the church. Liberals had more mixed motives than socialists. Distrust of vested local, traditional authority recommended the breaking of conservative dominance through centralization, but liberals were also concerned about limiting costs since they represented relatively wealthy groups. Once countries democratized and liberals began to expand their support base, however, they often began to favor more generous service provision, which meant that centralized solutions became more appealing to them.

The governments that were least likely to centralize were conservative parties in democracies, who typically preferred a more limited extent of provision and the defense of traditional authority and control. Only in nondemocratic regimes where the hold of conservative forces at the central level of government was so secure that leaving public services to local authorities did not offer conservatives any political advantages but rather impeded the government's efforts to use public services, such as policing, to defend the regime from challenges to its authority, was centralization an option for conservatives as well.

Our argument about two paths to centralization is strongly related to Gerring et al.'s argument about so-called agenda-centered reasons for imposing direct rule (2011). 'An agenda-centered hypothesis,' Gerring et al. note (2011, 379), 'supposes that the more transformative *A*'s agenda, the more likely it is that *A* will impose a system of direct rule. Only by grasping the levers of power will *A* be able to engineer a thorough transformation of *B*'s economy, society, or government.' We will show that this mechanism applies equally to liberals and socialists in democracies, twentieth-century fascists, late nineteenth-century authoritarian modernizers such as Japan, and, in some policy domains, nineteenth-century monarchies.

The argument about two paths to centralization helps to explain the variation in centralization among countries and over time. We also have a secondary argument about centralization, which concerns the variation among public services, as opposed to among political regimes. Two key mechanisms explain why some public services have been more centralized than others: on the one hand, how coercive the services were; on the other hand, whether it was possible to achieve economies of scale through the construction of large establishments.

Inherently coercive public services – notably services that are imposed on individuals involuntarily for the good of society, such as prisons, policing, and asylums – are more likely to be centralized since they involve the state's monopoly on violence. The monopolization of the state's coercive powers had begun already during the early modern period and continued in the nineteenth and early twentieth centuries. As ideas about civic rights and constitutional protections spread, parliaments sought to restrict and regulate the state's coercive powers by putting in place new legal provisions, such as the rules about involuntary confinement in mental institutions in nineteenth-century 'lunacy laws' (see Chapter 7). This only reinforced centralization, for the new legal protections were typically implemented by national bureaucracies, not local decision makers.

Meanwhile, economies of scale mattered since centralization was more straightforward if the introduction of modern public services involved the creation of large institutions that catered to many different localities at once. In these cases, the state did not displace older service networks, but created a new layer that was distinct from what came before, and in doing so, it made public services more efficient since large establishments, such as insane asylums and mass prisons, could house large populations, sometimes thousands of individuals. In countries with geographically dispersed populations, these economies of scale were difficult to achieve, with the exception of prisons, since governments had few qualms about housing convicts far away from their homes, which explains why prisons were the most centralized of all the institutions that emerged in the nineteenth century.

When we test these ideas about centralization, one institutional factor that must be taken into account is that some countries in our study had a federal structure, whereas some did not. In the United States, federalism was already enshrined in the constitution when our story begins. Other countries developed their modern federal structures during the nineteenth century – notably Australia, Canada, Germany, and Switzerland (on the German case, see especially Ziblatt 2008). Federalism placed a major hurdle in the way of centralizing reformers, since sub-national units often retained the right to govern public services regardless of the preferences of central authorities. In federal states, we therefore expect conflicts over centralization to play out differently, with progressive reformers in democracies seeking to centralize services to the highest level possible (often state governments rather than the central government), and authoritarian reformers seeking to abolish federalism itself in order to achieve their political goals.

Church, State, and the Mixed Economy of Public Services

We now turn to the second, horizontal dimension in our analysis: the relationship between public, religious, and private provision of services. The main protagonists in our story about the mix of public and private services are majority churches and their conservative political supporters, religious minorities, and secular, at times anticlerical, modernizing elites.

When it came to centralization, we started with the observation that before the nineteenth century, public services were provided locally, if at all. We start our discussion of the mix of public and private provision with the observation that before the nineteenth century, public services were often provided by churches, religious orders, lay foundations, and other private organization. This meant that governments faced an important choice between cooperating with existing service providers and replacing them. To create a public monopoly in the presence of existing nonstate provision, the state must strip control from nonstate actors – through secularization in the case where the church had control and through nationalization where non-religious actors did. The other options were to absorb the organizations that provided services – typically the established church – through a fusion of church and state, or to enter into a contractual relationship with organizations that were prepared to provide public services with public subsidies, often religious organizations.

When it comes to the mix of public, religious, and private authority, the differences among public order, knowledge, and mental and public health are starker than they were in our analysis of centralization (where we expected the 'two paths' to centralization to be relevant across policy domains). The reason is that the involvement of ecclesiastical institutions and religious organizations depended both on the relative *capacity* of churches and private organizations to provide services and on their *desire* to do so. Both factors varied systematically among policy areas.

Public order is easiest to understand. Policing and prisons were so closely associated with the sovereign power of the state that the precursors of modern police and prisons were secularized already in the early modern period (with the exception of the *Stati della Chiesa* – the Papal States – which were only dissolved in 1870). In other words, whether religious and private organizations desired to provide services or not, they did not have the capacity to do so.

When it comes to mental and public health, by contrast, early nineteenth-century governments often did rely on ecclesiastical institutions, religious organizations, and private associations. But this was largely because those institutions and organizations often had the capacity to provide services, not because religious leaders had a strong desire to influence mental health and public health policy. In each of the chapters on mental and public health, we find that when the fusion of church and state ended, and public health authorities were removed from the church, the separation was usually amicable.

Schooling was very different, which explains the remarkable fierceness of the late nineteenth- and early twentieth-century School Wars, the *guerres scolaires*. Ecclesiastical institutions and religious organizations typically had both the capacity and the desire to offer schooling. This meant that the choices governments made depended much more directly on nineteenth- and early twentieth-century conflicts between church and state.

Concerning the fusion of church and state – or, rather, ending that fusion through secularization – the main pattern that we wish to highlight is a simple partisan one: the secularization of public services was associated with the ambitions of liberal and socialist governments. If the church had established some administrative capacity for the provision of public services, conservative governments typically had an interest in mobilizing and utilizing this capacity rather than creating new, secular bureaucracies. This directly parallels the preferences of most political conservatives for maintaining local capacity, if such capacity already existed. Replacing the infrastructure of the church *in toto* was capital-intensive and required the training of new secular armies of professionals.

By contrast, the parties that had the strongest incentives to end the fusion of church and state were the liberals and the socialists, since they represented nonconformist and anticlerical groups and since their political agendas required a clearer break with the manner in which churches provided services.

State–church conflicts were typically most divisive in countries where the Catholic church was hegemonic, since the rise of modernizing liberal political elites led to a direct confrontation between the Catholic hierarchy and worldly rulers. In religiously mixed societies, the fusion of church and state was rare – although subsidization was more common – and the Catholic church was not an equally serious threat to political rulers, even in the Ultramontane heyday of Pius IX. In Protestant countries, there was typically a more gradual path to secularization: services were secularized in a piecemeal fashion as liberals and socialists sought to end the post-Reformation fusion of church and state, which lingered even as societies evolved and modernized.

The main preexisting factor that we need to take into consideration when we test these ideas about the fusion of church and state is that some countries had an established state church. In countries where the church was integrated in the state bureaucracy before the nineteenth century, early nineteenth-century service provision outside the domain of public order was typically based on the fusion of church and state. The reason, quite simply, is that the church had the capacity: the parish was typically the only public authority at the local level. A the same time the level of conflict between church and state was fairly low (Morgan 2002). Liberal and socialist parties had an interest in removing public services from church control, where possible, in these countries too, but the confrontation was less direct than in Catholic states.

Countries in which religious denominations existed alongside one another – which we refer to as religiously 'mixed' – were likely to have secular institutions, but they were nevertheless least likely to introduce public monopolies, since governments in religiously mixed countries had particularly strong reasons to support nonpublic service providers. This brings us to the final question that we will consider in this section: what factors explain the subsidization of religious and private organizations who provided public services.

Again, the argument we make depends on the differences among public services. In policy domains where religious conflicts were divisive, especially education, the main function of subsidization was to alleviate religious conflicts among denominations. Religious heterogeneity means that there can be conflicts not only between the state and the mainline church, but also among religious groups. Lijphart (1979) distinguishes, therefore, between what he calls 'Religious Cleavage I' and 'Religious Cleavage II,' one being the conflict between church and state and the other being the conflict among churches.

The subsidization of private service providers was often an appealing political option in heterogeneous societies. In the presence of religious heterogeneity, different sects are likely to have strong preferences for providing their own services to their own adherents. In particular, followers of minority religions typically object to having their children raised by officials representing the majority religion. Where several religious groups had the capacity to provide services, especially education, we expect subsidization to be an important solution to group conflict. By allowing each religious group to run its own institutions, with the backing of public money, the government could keep both majority and minority religious groups happy.

But subsidization was not only a solution to the the problem of religious conflict – it was also a solution to the problem of administrative capacity. Put simply, state bureaucracies often could not keep up with the rising demand for new public services in the nineteenth century, and governments therefore paid religious and private organizations to provide public services instead of relying fully on public institutions. Religion mattered here too, for countries with Lutheran state churches could typically rely on the established church until they were ready and able to shift the responsibility for public services to secular institutions, but the effect of religion was more indirect than it was in the domain of schooling. The main implication of these arguments about subsidization for our empirical analyses are that subsidization is likely to be most common in religiously mixed societies and least common in Protestant societies, with Catholic societies in between.

2.5 OUR APPROACH

To explore these ideas and arguments, our book follows nineteen countries from 1800 – or their year of independence – to 1939: Australia, Austria, Belgium, Canada, Denmark, Finland, France, Germany, Ireland, Italy, Japan, the Netherlands, New Zealand, Norway, Spain, Sweden, Switzerland, the United Kingdom, and the United States of America.

The main reason for selecting these particular cases is that many other important works about social policy and political change in the nineteenth and early twentieth centuries cover the same countries, which allows us to compare our findings with theirs. There is, for example. almost complete overlap with the case selection of Esping-Andersen (1990), Cusack, Iversen, and Soskice (2007), and Martin and Swank (2012). Moreover, our study covers most of the richest and most economically advanced countries in the world during the period we examine.

Admittedly, as data from Maddison (2011) show, Japan was significantly poorer than the other countries we study in the nineteenth century, but by the end of the period Japan had become a key global political player and had grown quickly enough to catch up with other advanced states.[12]

The reason for the choice of time period is that the seven public services we cover in the book emerged as distinct policy domains in the nineteenth century, and by the 1930s, all states in our study provided each of the services – with the intriguing exception of midwifery, which was banned in Canada in the early twentieth century and lost ground to care provided by competing medical professions in other parts of the world.

To study the development of public services, we have compiled several types of data. Our main data set contains summary information about how policing, prisons, schools, public libraries, mental institutions, vaccinations, and midwifery were governed: centralization of those services (local, regional, and national), the fusion of church and state (yes or no), and the provision of public funding for private service providers (yes or no).

The coding of centralization is meant to pick up the modal level of centralization in a given policy area in a given country-year. In other words, if a service was provided at several different levels of government, we sought to determine at what level the service was typically provided. For instance, several types of police have coexisted in France in the nineteenth and twentieth centuries (Berlière and Lévy 2011). We have therefore tried to establish during which periods local and national police forces were predominant. As we noted in more detail in Section 2.2, we code centralization by establishing which level of government had responsibility for hiring and firing service providers.

When we characterize the fusion of church and state and the subsidization of private providers, we ask whether there was at least some significant church involvement in the administration of public services or some significant subsidization of private service providers. When it

[12] Three rich South American countries are not included in our analysis: Argentina, Chile, and Uruguay. We exclude those countries since the state-building process was very different in South America than in Western Europe, North America, Australia and New Zealand, and Japan (the Meiji reformers famously used the European state as a benchmark when constructing a new Japanese state in the late nineteenth century) (Centeno 2002; Soifer 2015). We are thus not confident that we could do justice to the interregional comparisons the inclusion of Latin American cases would require. We do examine these countries' experience in education in Ansell and Lindvall (2013).

comes to fusion and subsidization, we are thus mainly concerned with existence, not with prevalence. For instance, although the state-based system of mental health care in Upper Canada (later Ontario) was different from the 'farming-out' system of mental health care in Lower Canada (Quebec), in that only Quebec funded private mental institutions (Moran 2001), we categorize Canada as a country where subsidized institutions have existed.

Our main sources are country-specific and policy-specific historical studies of the public services we are interested in. From these many sources, with the help of research assistants, we have extracted information about centralization, fusion, and subsidization. We have also been able to find some information about how public services were governed in other sources, notably in country-specific statistical yearbooks and in cross-country comparative studies of policy domains where there is a comparative tradition (notably policing). We have also cross-checked our decisions about how to categorize services in individual countries with country experts.

For most historians who work on public services, the governance mechanisms that we are interested in – legal frameworks and bureaucratic structures – are of secondary concern. For example, many scholars of mental institutions and prisons, following in the footsteps of Michel Foucault (1961, 1975), are mainly interested in the local, disciplinary power that those institutions produced, not in the place of insane asylums and penitentiaries within the political system. Similarly, many scholars of midwifery are primarily interested in the professional conflict between female midwives and male obstetricians and general practitioners, not in public administration, and many scholars of library history seem to be more interested in the development of catalogues and subject-classification systems than in political decision-making. One important challenge has thus been to extract information about political decision-making from historical studies that deal mainly with other topics and concerns.

In addition to the data we have compiled on centralization, fusion, and subsidization, we have compiled other types of data that help to give a sense of when and where public services were established and expanded, including data on public spending, bureaucracies, legislation, the hiring and organization of professionals, and the proportion of the population to whom services were provided. We also rely on data from other sources, notably on economic development (Maddison 2011), democracy (Marshall and Jaggers 2012), the religious composition of the population

(Lindert 2004, originally from French statistical yearbooks in the 1920s), the ideological orientation of heads of government (Brambor, Lindvall, and Stjernquist 2017), and urbanization (Banks 2009).

When we analyze the evidence on how public services were governed in different countries, we attempt to strike a balance between giving each policy area and each country's history its due as a contingent moment, with depth and detail, and making broader inferences about the development and organization of public services across time and space. In the policy-specific chapters, we concentrate on descriptive univariate and bivariate evidence and discuss many empirical cases and examples in detail; in the final chapter, we combine all the data from the individual chapters in a more systematic qualitative and quantitative analysis.

The rest of the book investigates seven public services: policing, prisons, schools, libraries, mental institutions, vaccinations, and midwifery. We are interested in why each of these policies mattered to governments, how and why it first expanded, how it was organized with respect to the vertical and horizontal distribution of power, and, finally, why governments organized their services differently. We divide the seven public services into three groups: policies that were meant to maintain order (policing and prisons), policies that were meant to spread knowledge (schools and libraries), and policies that were meant to improve health (asylums, vaccinations, and midwifery).

Part II examines the development of modern systems of public order through the creation of police forces and prisons. Before the nineteenth century, policing was typically a local, informal affair, but in the course of the nineteenth century, many countries established professional police forces, either locally, nationally, or both. The London Metropolitan Police is often regarded as the world's first 'modern' police force. This innovation spread quickly, but the organization of policing varied greatly from country to country; we seek to explain this variation. The idea of two paths to centralization applies to policing: centralized 'state-military' police forces (Emsley 1999b) were typically introduced in authoritarian regimes whereas 'state-civilian' police forces were introduced in both authoritarian and liberal-democratic regimes. We find no fusion of church and state and no subsidization of private police in the nineteenth and early twentieth centuries.

We also analyze another nineteenth-century invention: the prison. Mass incarceration in state-run prisons is, perhaps surprisingly, a modern phenomenon (it was the new institution that de Tocqueville and de Beaumont were sent to study in the United States in the 1830s, resulting, among other things, in de Tocqueville's *Democracy in America*). In the chapter on prisons, as in the chapter on the police, we concentrate on the question of centralization, and we again find support for the idea of two paths to centralization. We also find a few examples of publicly funded private prisons in the nineteenth century.

In Part III, we move from order to knowledge, investigating the development of schools and public libraries in the nineteenth- and early twentieth-century world.

The creation of publicly funded elementary, and often compulsory, schooling in most of the world's independent states in the nineteenth and early twentieth centuries was a major event in the history of government. It created, for the first time, a direct relationship between states and masses. This was a challenge to local and, especially, religious control over the hearts and minds of the young. We examine how political decisions over schooling played out amid the fierce battles and skirmishes of the nineteenth century's *guerres scolaires*. Since schooling was where the conflicts among conservatives, liberals, socialists, fascists, churches, and minority religious sects were the most intense, it is not surprising that we find evidence of all of the ideas we discussed in the previous section – two paths to centralization, liberal–conservative conflicts between church and state, and the subsidization of private schools to alleviate conflicts among religious groups.

The next chapter examines the development of public libraries, another quintessential nineteenth-century institution. For a long time, libraries remained the state's most effective method of shaping the educational progress and values of their citizens after they left school, given the restricted access to universities before the postwar period. When it comes to the vertical dimension, we find that only twentieth-century fascist regimes centralized their public library systems. But libraries is where we find the most widespread development of a 'mixed economy' of public services, since many private libraries received public funding – and since many publicly administered libraries received significant private funding.

In Part IV, we study mental and public health. Historians such as Rosen (1958) and Porter (1999) have shown that the development of state policies for public health in the advanced states in the nineteenth century was a clear break with the past, associated with the social problems that came with industrialization and urbanization and with the need to ensure that the country's male population was fit to fight wars. They also note, however, that public health systems developed very differently in the late nineteenth and early twentieth centuries; we offer a political analysis of this variation.

No analysis of the development of the nineteenth-century state can be complete without a discussion of lunatic asylums, psychiatric hospitals, and other mental institutions. The mass confinement of the insane was a nineteenth- and early twentieth-century phenomenon, and the adoption of lunacy laws and the construction of national systems of insane asylums often preceded the development of other public services. But the great expansion of mental institutions played out in different ways in different countries, with distinct choices made about local versus central control, the role of the church, and whether private asylums were publicly funded. As in the other public health domains, we find examples of both the authoritarian and the liberal-democratic path to centralization, but more examples of the former. Mental institutions are also the clearest example of how the subsidization of private service providers became a solution to the problem of capacity: in most countries outside Lutheran Northern Europe and Oceania, governments could not keep up with the rising demand for mental health care, and therefore paid private institutions to care for 'pauper lunatics' – mentally ill individuals who could not themselves afford private care.

The smallpox vaccine, invented by the British physician Edward Jenner in the 1790s, was the world's first vaccine. We examine the development of vaccination programs from the turn of the nineteenth century onward, demonstrating that most governments began to encourage and administer vaccinations within two decades of Jenner's discovery. As in all other chapters, we examine how politicians fought over whether public vaccination programs should be centralized, should be an area of religious involvement, and should rely on the services of private vaccinators. Centralized vaccination programs were introduced mainly by nineteenth-century monarchies, especially during and after the great smallpox epidemic in Europe in the early 1870s. There is thus considerable support for the idea of an authoritarian path to centralization. We also discuss the origins of antivaccinationism, which emerged already in the nineteenth century.

The last empirical chapter examines the state's initial forays into managing childbirth through midwifery. Already in the eighteenth and early nineteenth centuries, in the beginning of the period we examine, some European countries in our study provided public education for midwives and required parishes to hire them. This means that public investments in midwifery were one of the very first large-scale health interventions of the modern era. Its expansion, and the resulting conflict between female midwives and male doctors and bureaucrats, played out in different ways in different countries. Once more, we find distinct patterns of centralization and combinations of public and private authority. The centralization of midwifery in the twentieth century's fascist regimes is a particularly striking example of the authoritarian path to centralization, and meant, as one historian put it, that the 'arm of the state' now reached into every apartment (Lisner 2006, 259).

In Part V, we bring all the evidence from the empirical chapters together and compare policies, countries, and periods, using both qualitative comparisons and quantitative methods, and thus provide additional tests of our main ideas about centralization and the public–religious–private mix in the provision of public services in modern states. The book concludes by asking how much we can learn from the nineteenth-century experience as we consider the problems of today's world and as we endeavor to understand contemporary conflicts over public services.

PART II

ORDER

punishments if criminals were not apprehended. In some cases, policing, broadly defined, was even an entirely private matter with little oversight from the governing classes.

In fact, such 'in-group' policing has existed from early farming communities onward. Schwartz and Miller (1964), in an analysis of fifty-one traditional societies that were drawn mainly from the famous Freeman-Winch sample, found that twenty societies had some form of armed police *avant la lettre*. A further twenty had some organized form of mediation. In the latter cases, and in societies lacking both rudimentary policing and organized mediation, private citizens had to enforce their own norms and rules, with or without third-party encouragement. In ancient Athens before Solon, for example, private citizens were entirely responsible for pursuing any criminal act. Indeed, the state was not permitted to do so. In Republican Rome, matters were handled similarly, at least before the third century BC (Kunkel 1973).[5]

During the feudal era, public order and the apprehension of criminals were official responsibilities of villages and other local communities. The term hue and cry – now a metaphor for turmoil and uproar – refers to the collective common-law obligation to apprehend the felon once a crime had been committed. One classic example of such a framework is the 'frankpledge,' which was introduced by the Norman rulers in England in the twelfth century. It obliged all communities to 'pursue offenders and to ensure the good behaviour of other members of the community' (Rawlings 2002). The frankpledge was organized around geographic divisions of 'tithings,' to which all men belonged. Oaths were sworn to the king to not commit crime, nor to conceal or protect criminals, and tithings were obliged to pursue offenders and keep them in custody. Every town or city was also required to establish a night watch. In charge of this system was a Norman-imposed 'sheriff' – of Robin-Hood fame – who regulated communities and collected fines for the crown, making them figures of local discontent. The sheriff was also authorized to call out all able-bodied men in a *posse comitatus*.

This type of communal self-policing came under increasing pressure during the early modern period. In particular, growing urbanization, and later industrialization, led to insurmountable problems. The hue-and-cry system was difficult to work in the large towns, and unpaid night watchmen proved unwilling to patrol larger and more anonymous cities. By the

5 Today, private dispute resolution continues among groups outside the purview of the law, most obviously within and among mafias (Varese 2001).

eighteenth century, the roles of 'constable' and 'petty constable' – local officers appointed under the sheriff system – had become deeply unattractive. Daniel Defoe characterized this role as 'an insupportable hardship,' since 'it takes up so much of a man's time that his own affairs are frequently totally neglected, too often to his ruin' (cited in Emsley 1983, 24). The demand for order and security had risen with the growing population, but the supply of constables and watchmen had collapsed; across Europe, crime was rife in the cities.

As a result of unrest in the countryside and the development of national standing armies during the Wars of Religion, the maintenance of public order was gradually professionalized across Europe in the course of the early modern period. In France, this process resulted in the *maréchaussée*, a mounted quasi-military force with medieval roots whose role was to keep highways and rural areas free of bandits. Largely staffed by army veterans, the *maréchaussée* was centralized under the Ministry of War from 1720 (Emsley 1983, 13), making it the most significant precursor of modern state-military police forces.

French cities were also developing more professional forms of policing at the local level, both in Paris and in other major cities (Bayley 1990, 31). These city guards were run by *lieutenants généraux* appointed by the central government – a pattern of centralization in Parisian policing that continues to this day. Rural mounted police and organized city guards became more common all over prerevolutionary Europe, as new forms of crime and social unrest combined with a large supply of military veterans following the massive expansion of early modern armies. Much of early modern policing thus took on a military hue.

3.2 MODERN POLICING

The oldest existing national police forces – belonging to the national-military category in Emsley's typology – are the heirs of the French *maréchaussée*, which was transformed during the French Revolution into the famous *gendarmerie*. National-military forces still exist and continue to play an important role in many European countries. That is the case for the *Carabinieri* in Italy, the *Guardia Civil* in Spain, and, of course, the *Gendarmerie nationale* in France. State-military forces are typically under direct or indirect military control, although they play no part in overseas military activity, and they often have military-style training and recruitment policies. Their functions typically involve the maintenance of

It took another forty years for a new police force to emerge. This happened under then Home Secretary Robert Peel in 1829. Peel had served as Chief Secretary for Ireland between 1812 and 1818, helping to establish a centralized gendarmerie, the Royal Irish Constabulary (Emsley 1983). Although that force had been effective for the British government's security needs, it was an implement of colonial power (Brogden 1987), and the English were not willing to subject themselves to the same coercion they imposed upon the Irish. The reformer Edwin Chadwick claimed that a police force 'must owe its real efficiency to the sympathies and concurrent action of the great body of the people' (Miller 1999).

The new police were centrally controlled by the Home Office, not locally by London politicians. But it was no gendarmerie. The London Metropolitan Police was the first 'state-civilian' force – responsible to the government (as opposed to the city) but staffed by and policing the citizenry. The police officers were consistently uniformed and were charged by their two original Commissioners Charles Rowan and Richard Mayne with securing order without favor. As Miller (1999, 33) notes,

Definition of the force as agents of the legal system made their authority *impersonal*, derived from legal powers and restraints instead of from the local community's informal expectations or the directives of the dominant political party. ...Rowan and Mayne determined that "the force should not only be, in fact, but be believed to be impartial in action, and they should act on principle."

The 'Met' secured a reputation for honesty, at least in the minds of European liberals, and while the English police force outside of London developed along a more decentralized municipal model – first through the Municipal Corporations Act of 1835, which required boroughs to appoint watch committees and police forces, and later through the Police Bill of 1856, which provided government grants and merged some police associations – it was London's model that was emulated internationally. The English 'Bobby' provided a halfway-house between the military and the municipal: an outline for a 'civic police.'

The steady expansion of police numbers in London and beyond can be seen in Figure 3.2, which shows estimates from Fyfe (1991) for England and Wales and from Flora et al. (1983) for France of the total number of police officers in those countries. The difference in levels partly reflects coding choices – and the exclusion of the *gendarmes* in France – but the within-country pattern is clear: a continuous upward rise in police

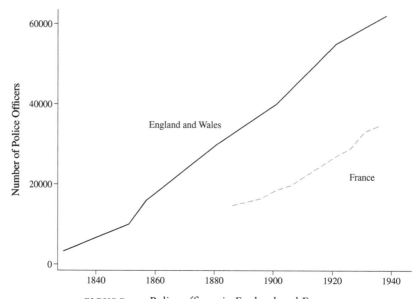

FIGURE 3.2 Police officers in England and France.
Sources: Fyfe (1991) and Flora et al. (1983). *Comment:* 1829 data is size of London
Metropolitan Police at foundation

numbers until the Second World War. In population-share terms, the
number of people served by each police officer in England and Wales
declined from over 1500 in 1851 to 750 in 1901 and to 600 by 1939.
In France, those numbers were approximately twice as large. Of course,
such figures varied dramatically among areas within each country. For
example, in 1844, each policeman served around 350 people in gen-
teel Bath, whereas in industrializing Salford, that figure was almost 2000
(Taylor 1997). Today, the figure stands at around 330, which gives a useful sense of the relative lack of policing in the early days of the modern
police, as compared with contemporary forces.[6]

Along with rising numbers of policemen came organizations that combined their interests and represented them in labor conflicts (Table 3.3).
This was a highly controversial development. Indeed, even today, in a
number of countries that includes the United Kingdom, the police are
banned from striking. Accordingly, police associations typically did not
emerge until the early twentieth century. Many of them date back to the

[6] In some settler colonies with low population density, however, the density of police was
actually higher in the nineteenth century than it is today (Finnane 2005).

TABLE 3.3 *The first police associations*

Country	Association name	Level	Year
Australia	The Police Association of South Australia	Local	1911
	ACT Police Officers' Association	National	1933
Belgium	Le Syndicat National de la Police Belge	National	1922
Canada	Vancouver City Police Association	Local	1918
Denmark	Københavns Politis Selskabelige Forening Rufinus	Local	1898
	Dansk politiforbund	National	1902
Finland	Suomen Poliisikunnan Liitto	National	1906
France	Syndicat géneral de la Police	National	1925
Germany	Bund der Polizeibeamten in Sachsen	Local	1908
	Reichsverband Deutscher Polizeibeamter	National	1919
Italy	Associazione di mutuo soccorso tra carabinieri in congedo	Local	1886
Japan	Japan Police Support Association	National	1900
Netherlands	Rijkspolizei-Vereeniging	National	1900
New Zealand	Police Association Auckland	Local	1913
	New Zealand Police Association	National	1936
Norway	Kristiania politifunksjonaerers forening	Local	1884
	Norsk politiforbund	National	1905
Spain	Sindicato Unificado de Policia	National	1978
Sweden	Poliskonstapelsklubben i Landskrona	Local	1898
	Sveriges Polismannaförbund	National	1902
Switzerland	Vereinigung der Polizeibeamten	Local	1900
	Verband Schweizer Polizei-Beamter	National	1902
United Kingdom	Police Federation of England and Wales	National	1919
United States	Fraternal Order of Police	Local	1915
	Fraternal Order of Police	National	1918

Sources: Kurian (1989) and country-specific sources.

end of the First World War, as in Belgium, Canada, Germany, the United
Kingdom, and the United States.[7]

3.3 CENTRALIZING THE POLICE

We now turn to the main question for this chapter: why police forces
were organized in different ways in different countries. We will devote
most of our attention to civilian police forces, but we begin with the case
of gendarmeries.

As the discussion in Section the previous section showed, most gendarmeries were created in authoritarian or colonial regimes. Indeed, very
often their foundation was explicitly justified with the need to prevent
antimonarchical uprisings, as in the case of the Spanish *Guardía Civil*
in 1844. Similarly, the Piedmontese *Carabinieri* were deployed to crush
republican uprisings in the 1820s, and 'the senior officers of the corps
prided themselves on a personal bond between the *Carabinieri* and the
king' (Emsley 1999a, 193). The Austrian *k.k. Gendarmerie* was founded
by Emperor Franz Joseph to safeguard the Habsburg Monarchy after
the repression of the 1848 uprisings (Emsley 1999a, 224). Gendarmeries
are of interest to us since they are a clear, early example of the authoritarian path to the centralization of public services. State-military forces
that were developed later in the nineteenth century, such as the reformed
Danish *Gendarmerikorps* in 1885, were also often used as political tools
by pro-monarchy forces. As Emsley (1999a, 238) notes concerning the
Danish case,

Concerned about the radical rhetoric of the Left, and the proliferation of patriotic
rifle associations created by the Left, the Right's response was to establish the new
corps of professional soldiers to intimidate its opponents in the countryside.

Table 3.4 describes the overall pattern of the governance of *civilian*
police forces across the countries in our study. It is immediately apparent that the only real difference in the design of police forces concerns
the dimension of centralization. No country in our study had a non-
secular police force. To find one, we would need to either extend the
analysis backward in time to the Counter-Reformation, examine smaller,
now-extinct states such as the Papal States, or cast forward to the contemporary religious police of Saudi Arabia and Iran. We discuss historical

---

7 On police unions in US cities and the history of police unions in that country, see
  especially Levi (1977).

TABLE 3.4 *How the civilian police were governed*

	Public only	Mixed public–private
National	Austria (before 1849, 1853–1861, from 1920), Denmark (from 1919), Finland, Germany (from 1933), Ireland, Italy, Japan (from 1875), New Zealand (from 1877), Norway (from 1936), Spain (from 1931)	
Local or regional	Australia, Austria (1849–1852, 1862–1919), Belgium, Canada, Denmark (before 1919), France, Germany (before 1933), Japan (before 1875), the Netherlands, New Zealand (before 1877), Norway (before 1936), Spain (before 1931), Sweden, Switzerland, United Kingdom, United States	

Notes: In 'national' systems, most civilian policemen were employed by, or otherwise responsive to, the national government, as opposed to regional or local authorities. Italy refers to Piedmont until Italian unification. Spain was governed locally until 1867 and by the regions from 1868 until the Second Republic in 1931. Both the governments of the Second Republic in 1931 and of Franco in 1939 enacted centralizing reforms. Canada has operated a hybrid system since 1873, whereby eight of the ten provinces and all the territories, along with 191 out of 450 municipalities, rely in part on the Royal Canadian Mounted Police (previously the Northwest Mounted Police); however, most police officers are employed at the municipal level.

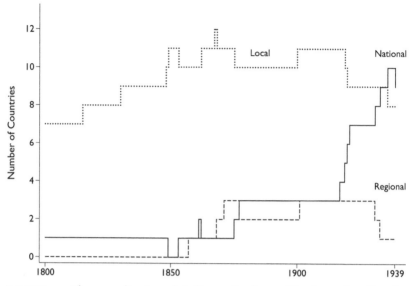

FIGURE 3.3 The centralization of civilian police forces. The figure describes the number of countries in the sample in which the main police forces were governed at the local, regional, and national levels.

connections between religion and policing below, but in the period we study here, all police forces were secular. Nor do we find any examples of subsidization. Again, if we were to extend backward in time to organizations such as the Bow Street Runners, other cases might fit, but not in the period we consider here.

But when it comes to centralization, there was substantial variation both across countries and within countries, with eight countries switching status at some point, particularly in the interwar period. Figure 3.3 demonstrates how common centralization was in the countries in our sample between 1800 and 1939, splitting decentralized systems into those where the police were governed at the local and the regional level. Broadly, we see a general trend upward in centralization, which accelerates in the interwar years, as both social democratic and fascist governments centralized their civilian police forces. The number of regionally governed systems is fairly constant, and while the number of locally governed systems rose in the first half of the nineteenth century – as new countries enter the sample or develop their earliest recognizably modern police forces – it first stabilizes and then starts to decline in the early twentieth century.

The explanation for these cross-national trends in centralization has been a topic of some debate over the past few decades, with David Bayley's work being particularly influential. For Bayley, 'police systems will be decentralized only if state institutions are created without substantial popular resistance, if mobilization demands are slight or produce little popular resistance, and if bureaucratic traditions derived from state-building are decentralized' (Bayley 1975, 365). This is a somewhat complex conjectural approach, and Bayley did not directly test these ideas; he drew these patterns from the experience of four countries: England, France, Italy, and Germany.

Our own analysis suggests that there is considerable support for the idea of an authoritarian and a liberal-democratic path to centralization, particularly the latter.

A number of countries have either always had centralized police administration, ever since their first modern police force, or transitioned to centralized forces early on in our sample.

In the first group, we have countries such as Finland and Ireland. Finland's centralization dated back to the period of Russian rule, with a Chamber of Police appointed by the state and the takeover of town policing by 1904 (Kurian 1989, 115). By the time of Finnish independence in 1917, this legacy of authoritarian rule under the Russian Tsar had solidified into a centralized system for the now sovereign country (Hietaniemi 1992).

A similar experience of colonial absolutism producing centralization occurred in Ireland. Ireland has always had a centralized police force. This derives from the colonial experience of British rule – another authoritarian path to centralized policing, at least from the Irish perspective. The early nineteenth century was a period during which the British were deeply concerned about Irish rebellions in the context of the Napoleonic Wars. Robert Peel, who would famously go on to establish the civilian police for of London, was asked to create a gendarmerie to keep the Irish peace. That body, designed to keep the (military) peace, would become the Irish and then Royal Irish Constabulary over the course of the nineteenth century. Unlike the British police, 'the Irish Constabulary was a national force under the control of government' (Tobias 1972, 217). The British kept decentralization for themselves; when it came to colonial dominions and to the Irish, centralization was considered necessary to effectively coerce peace (Finnane 1981). The long shadow of colonial policing cast into postindependence Ireland: the *Garda Síochána na hÉireann*, created in 1923, retained the centralized structure of its forebears.

We now turn to countries that moved from having decentralized to centralized systems. Here we see strong evidence of our 'two paths to centralization.' The most obvious examples of an authoritarian path to centralization is the Meiji reforms in Japan in the 1870s and the centralization of the German police under the new national-socialist government in 1933.

Japan experienced an extremely rapid period of police centralization between 1869 and 1874. Whereas policing in Tokugawa Japan was essentially conducted along localized, feudal lines by samurai and their assistants, the Meiji-era police reforms were deliberately modeled on centralized continental European practice. Some city forces, such as Tokyo's, were established in 1871, but they were quickly brought under the control of the Home Ministry, which had jurisdiction over a new country-wide centralized system. This model was explictly designed along the centralized lines of parts of French policing by Kawaji Toshiyoshi, who joined the Iwakura mission of Meiji politicians to Europe and the United States between 1871 and 1873.

[Kawaji's] recommendations showed a preference for the French rather than the British or American model of police, reflecting a desire for central control . . . In line with continental European usage tracing back to the *Polizeistaat*, the Meiji founders employed the term "police" in the broad seventeenth and eighteenth century sense of all internal administration, rather than the narrow sense of crime prevention and detection, as adopted by the British and Americans. (Tipton 1990, 38)

Kawaji's successor as Home Minister, Yamagata Aritomo, further increased the control of the Ministry. In short, Japan's move from decentralized, feudal policing to a centralized system reflected an ideological attraction to state-driven absolutism.

German unification in 1871 had led to a regionally based model of police organization in the various *Länder*, including Prussia, and the Bismarckian constitution kept policing under the control of state governments. Attempts in the Weimar era to centralize aspects of policing – including the 1922 *Reichskriminalpolizeiamtgesetz* – met with strong resistance from the *Länder*, with Bavaria refusing to implement that law.

However, the electoral success of the Nazi Party in 1933 was followed almost immediately by the centralization of all aspects of public coercion across the country. In 1934, the *Gesetz über den Neuaufbau des Reichs* made the police a responsibility of the central state, splitting it into a state-military *Ordnungspolizei* and a civilian *Sicherheitspolizei* (Nitschke 1996, 92). Of course, the Nazis also had their party-based militia and paramilitary units of the *Sturmabteilung* and *Schutzstaffel* as means of coercion, but it is notable that they immediately centralized the broader bodies of policing upon winning power.

The colonial path to centralization seen in Ireland also showed up in other English-speaking colonies. The case of Canada is somewhat complex, since it includes both centralized and decentralized forces, hence we discuss it below. But New Zealand provides a more straightforward account of the move from local to nationalized policing in order to suppress indigenous populations, in this case the Maori. The initial Armed Police Force of New Zealand was founded in 1847, after the 1845 Maori insurrection, and was modeled on the Royal Irish Constabulary, but urban policing was left to municipal police. In 1853, following the New Zealand Constitution Act, police forces merged into provincial forces that matched the newly created provinces (Hill 1991, 61). Over the coming decades, the Maori wars intensified and at their conclusion a centralized gendarmerie was formed: the Armed Constabulary. Moreover, the province of Auckland, where ethnic violence was particularly widespread, merged its provincial force with this national force (Hill 1991, 62). After the provincial governments were themselves abolished in 1876, their police forces were merged into the Armed Constabulary in 1877 – one of the few examples of a gendarmerie and civil forces combining. Thus the initial centralization of the New Zealand police was largely a result of the colonial authorities' suppression of the Maori community. But it is also an example of a liberal-democratic path to centralization, for the abolition of the provinces and the general drive to centralize services in New Zealand in the late nineteenth century occurred during a period of liberal hegemony in national politics. Indeed the final creation of the modern New Zealand Police was in 1886 under the relatively liberal Stout-Vogel ministry.

We also find other evidence of a liberal and social-democratic path to centralization in democracies. Norway in 1936 is one good example (Ellefsen 2015). The Norwegian Labour Party competed successfully in elections in 1930, 1933, and 1936, and in 1935 formed a government. As Bayley (1996, 54, 62) notes, the police force was nationalized by the Labour government, which also reduced the number of separate forces, although it refrained from issuing direct operational orders.A similar story can be told about Denmark in 1919 and afterward, also driven by progressive-liberal and social democratic politicians. In both Norway and Denmark, arguments were made that a modern police needed to be centrally controlled to be effective. Conservative politicians were largely opposed in both countries. Interestingly, from our perspective, so too were Denmark's right-wing liberals, *Venstre*, as advocates of limited state power (Furuhagen 2017, 127). This meant that the 1919 reforms only created a state police *alongside* municipal policing in Denmark. It took until 1938 for all policing to be brought completely under national central control (under social democratic and social liberal leadership).

The [social democratic] government argued that policing was a state responsibility, and that nationalization would create a more effective police service. Such a police service could also be effective in defending democratic society against extremist movements. Venstre and the conservatives voted against, presenting the same arguments as before. They also voiced concerns that nationalization would threaten the integrity of traditional local self governance in the municipalities. (Furuhagen 2017, 128)

As the Danish case shows, there was some tension among liberal parties in Europe. On the Continent they tended to be comfortable with full national control of policing; in countries with traditions of local control, such as the Scandinavian and English-speaking countries, right-wing liberals tended to remain supportive of decentralized policing, whereas more progressive liberals favored centralization.

The example of the British 'bobby' demonstrates this tension. Rising industrial and commercial elites – the basis of progressive liberalism in Britain – had much to gain from a centralized police force. Silver (2017, 12–13) notes,

Not only did the manufacturing classes wish to avoid personal danger and inconvenience while protecting their property, but they also saw that – contrary to the social rationale underlying the yeomanry – the use of social and economic superiors as police exacerbated rather than mollified class violence . . . Thus, at a time when the agrarian rich often sought to multiply and reconstruct the traditional means of self-defense against violent uprising and attack, those who sprang from the newer sources of wealth turned toward a bureaucratic police system that insulated them from popular violence, drew attack and animosity upon itself, and seemed to separate the assertion of "constitutional" authority form that of social and economic dominance.

The epitome of this desire was the London Metropolitan police: a centralized, uniformed and professional force that demonstrated centralization was possible without despotism. It was highly influential in Continental Europe among liberal centralizers, including the Cavour government in Piedmont. As Emsley (2013, 206) notes, it had 'a general appeal to continental liberals who approved the concept of an unarmed, nonpolitical police that respected rights and was not bound to enforce scores of pettifogging regulations.' At the same time, however, traditional English liberals remained fearful of a nationally centralized force as reminiscent of a gendarmerie that might crush long-cherished local independence. Along with conservatives, much happier with traditional local responsibilities for law and order, they advocated against full centralization, and hence the organization of the 'Met' remained London-only.

Decentralization, then, had powerful advocates in Britain and elsewhere. Some countries retained mostly decentralized police systems throughout the period we study, including Australia, the United Kingdom, and the United States. Australia developed a police force very early on its state-building process – the South Australia Police were established in 1838, not long after the first modern police forces emerged in Europe. Whereas most decentralized police forces were constructed from municipal policing, the Australian police force began – and remained – led by each province's chief executive. As Finnane (2005, 53) notes, 'for all of the Australian colonies ... the control of police was from the earliest moment vested in the governor.' This intermediate form of centralization presents an interesting contrast to the model that emerged in England at the same time. Australia in the nineteenth century was of course a decentralized set of colonies, so the fact that there was no centralized control over the continent as a whole should not surprise us. But it also had an extremely low-density population, especially thinly spread across the rural interior, and attempts in the middle of the century to raise local funds to secure more local control ran up against the very high costs of doing so (except, interestingly, in the smallest province, Tasmania, which moved from provincial to municipal control between 1856 and 1898; see Finnane 2005, 55).

Canada faced similar difficulties when it came to policing beyond its major urban areas. While Toronto and Montreal had municipally run police forces from the 1830s and 1840s (see Chapter 1), the western provinces were so thinly populated, and hence potentially lawless, that demands were made for some broader force that might aid in policing the frontier. Whereas in Australia those forces remained provincial, in Canada the federal government intervened, through the foundation of the Northwestern, later Royal Canadian, Mounted Police – the famed 'Mounties.' The efficiency and professionalism of the Mounties meant that Canada in fact transitioned to a quasi-federal policing structure from 1873, as everywhere outside of the settled East contracted out

with the Mounties to provide rural and later also some municipal policing (Bayley 1992). The massive expansion of the use of the centrally
run and trained Mounties combined with the fact that the major cities
and eastern provinces retained their decentralized control of municipal policing makes it difficult to adequately categorize Canada's level
of decentralization. Somewhat like France it was a mixed system with
centralized gendarmerie-like forces in the rural areas but with municipalities running their own forces. Since the majority of uniformed officers
remained employed at the municipal or provincial levels we code Canada
as decentralized.

Policing in the United States of America remained decentralized
throughout our period, since its relatively greater population density
meant that locally run policing was viable financially and logistically.
However, even here tensions arose on the frontier and as interjurisdic-
tional crime increased. The solutions to these difficulties were at first
left in private hands, through agencies such as the Pinkertons, but the
creation of the Bureau of Investigation, later the Federal Bureau of Investigation, in 1908 as a federal policing structure reflected the demand
for policing above the state and municipal levels. Unlike in the case of
Canada, though, the FBI operated in a separate domain and was not
used to 'contract out' law enforcement from local authorities.

England retained a decentralized police system throughout the nineteenth and twentieth centuries, despite the fact that the London
Metropolitan Force was controlled by the Home Secretary and hence
by the central government. The expansion of the modern police through
the middle of the nineteenth century occurred through a constant back
and forth between central legislation and local recalcitrance – the County
Police Act of 1839 permitted counties to establish police forces, but did
not require them to do so, and only half of them had chosen to develop
'reformed' police forces twenty years later. Even when the 1856 County
and Borough Police Act attempted to create more uniform policing, the
central hand was weak: Westminster supervised but did not direct police
forces and it funded only around a quarter of the costs (Bayley 1990,
96). Still today, despite the important role of the Home Office in setting
police funding, the police are governed locally in the United Kingdom and
increasingly have their own elected commissioners; no truly centralized
police force has ever developed.

The French case is a particularly interesting example of mixed centralized and decentralized forces, especially since many contemporaries
viewed central control of policing as a defining feature of French

absolutism well before the creation of modern civilian policing. Without wishing to be too anachronistic in our recounting, France had already taken the 'authoritarian path' to centralization as early as the seventeenth century. In 1667, Louis XIV appointed a *lieutenant-général* to supervise policing in Paris under the king's direct control (Emsley 1983, 8). *Lieutenants-généraux* were then diffused through the realm, with many major cities having their police governed in a direct line to the monarchy by 1700 (Bayley 1975, 342–3). In the countryside, a similar centralizing principle had been followed – *intendants* were placed in charge of rural policing, including the *Maréchaussée*, the precursor of the *Gendarmerie*, again under direct instruction from central government. When modern civilian policing emerged in Paris in 1829, it was again under central control, and once more under authoritarian rule: in the dying days of the Bourbon Restoration. Later, centralized police forces also emerged in Lyon, Toulon, and Marseille. However, under our coding France did not develop a fully centralized system before the Second World War, because outside of Paris, a few other major cities, and rural areas, municipalities remained in control of their policing. Each town of 5000 people had at least one police officer and these local police were funded, organized, and appointed by the town councils and from 1884 elected mayors (Berlière and Lévy 2011). Thus the majority of French people lived under a decentralized police system despite the important separate strand of centralization.

During the Second World War France did finally experience the full centralization that its absolutist past had promised but not fulfilled. The puppet Vichy regime centralized policing for all towns with more than 10,000 people in 1941, under the watchful eye of the Nazi occupiers (Berlière and Lévy 2011). Just outside our sample period, then, we find another example of the authoritarian path to centralization.

Continuing with our brief extension past 1939, one particularly interesting natural experiment that demonstrated the power of national ideas about police centralization and decentralization is the organization of the police in occupied Germany after the Second World War (Bayley 1975, 369). It is striking that each occupier hewed closely to its prewar police organizational structure when governing policing in its occupation zone (including the mixed model favored by the French). Bayley (1975, 368–369) describes the main differences:

The Americans created small municipal and communal units, each with elected bodies ... as the basis for police forces ... The British set up district police commands patterned after British counties ... The French, though resisting centralization of police forces across the Allied occupation zones, placed police forces under strict control by the state governments, supervised by French occupation authorities.

Yet, as Bayley notes, when the Allies left, the administrative structure of German policing essentially fell back into its pre-war, Weimar-Republic form. National histories of police organization thus demonstrate sharp qualitative differences, and also reflect long-standing institutional stability.

3.4 RELIGIOUS ANTECEDENTS AND PRIVATE DETECTIVES

Religious policing, in the sense of a fusion of church and state, was largely a phenomenon of the Reformation and the Counter-Reformation, and accordingly it had largely vanished among the countries in our study by the nineteenth century. Nonetheless, it is worth examining this earlier period to understand exactly why secular policing proved near-ubiquitous, for in a number of cases, the most developed police forces in the early-modern era had concerned themselves with imposing, through coercion, the moral codes of the church.

Before the Reformation, as we have seen, communal self-policing dominated, with responsibility for the apprehension and detention of criminals given to the local community at pain of punishment imposed by sheriffs and *intendants*. Under feudalism, the many overlapping authorities did include the Church, whose landholdings across Europe were vast and who operated its own criminal justice system, in which canon law often demanded the prosecution and punishment of those violating religious codes (Brundage 2009). In fourteenth-century Italy, for example, Church courts actively punished sexual misdemeanours, as Brundage (2009, 514) notes:

Both Courts Christian and secular tribunals regularly took action against couples suspected of living in sin. Those convicted – and convictions were routine – were usually punished by fines, sometimes supplemented by public penitential acts, such as offering a candle during Mass or marching barefoot and in penitential garb around the Church during services on Sundays or feast days.

The fusion of state power and religious policing emerged more clearly during and after the Reformation, as moral practices became more politicized. The use of policing to enforce religious codes – often the only real function of police in this era – was most associated with the Catholic

Church in the Counter-Reformation, *in extremis* through the Inquisition. Indeed, many scholars have argued that the Inquisition's shadow casts into contemporary policing. Bayley (1975) notes, 'Where the Inquisition was strong, there police forces active in politics are to be found from an early time.'

To provide one vivid example, the breakaway Calvinist city of La Rochelle was successfully subdued in 1628 by the French government. In re-Catholicising La Rochelle, a police court was established to enforce morality. Robbins (1995, 287) notes that 'verdicts of the municipal police court promulgated an all-encompassing paternalism characteristic of Counter-Reformation theology,' including policing meat sales during Lent, gaming on Sundays, begging, and unauthorized alms-giving. Ultimately, the police could be used as a tool of repression of religious minorities (Robbins 1995, 290–291).

Such religious use, or abuse, of the police was not limited to the agents of the Counter-Reformation. The English Civil War produced similar moral regulation under the Protectorate of Oliver Cromwell. Bayley (1975, 331) argues that 'police in Cromwell's time were required to be preoccupied with prevention of blasphemy and the keeping of the sabbath.'

As the eighteenth century began and religious conflict was stilled, the importance of moral and religious policing declined. While criminal-justice systems continued to enforce moral rules and regulations in line with religious teachings, the religious cast of policing was replaced gradually by a public criminal code in most countries. A few exceptions remained; in particular, until Italian unification, the Papal States operated a papal police (Hughes 2017).

Although the police were not governed by religious institutions, the police themselves were often religious. Indeed, Conway (2013) notes that trainee members of the Irish Garda attended mass every Sunday in uniform, and in 1928, 250 Gardaí marched in uniform through Rome for a meeting with the Pope (and later with Mussolini). In other words, the police in Ireland were influenced by religion (Gryzmala-Busse 2015), but in administrative terms, all countries, also Ireland, had secular police forces during the period we study.

That uniformity also largely holds with regard to the absence of subsidization of private policing. Once public policing existed, private police did not receive public subsidies, as they had in the past. There were private detectives and security forces throughout the nineteenth and twentieth centuries, but they existed alongside public police forces and were not integrated in them.

The study of private policing has had a renaissance in recent years since private security organizations have proliferated since the 1960s, from detective agencies to security guards and neighborhood-watch organizations (see, for example, Johnston 1992 and Zedner 2005). Many authors have noted that this marks a return to the practices of the early modern period, when both self-policing and private policing were common.

The most useful distinction among early forms of private policing is between professionalized and nonprofessionalized private policing. Nonprofessionalized policing was broadly an extension of communal policing from the medieval era, updated to reflect new challenges as urbanization and industrialization progressed. In England, this meant the establishment of voluntary 'felons associations,' where upstanding citizens paid a subscription to collectively enforce the apprehension of criminals. In a sense, this was the functional equivalent of friendly and cooperative societies, albeit for criminal justice. They enforced the protection of property, particularly against horse theft (Philips 1989). Such organizations had largely vanished from England by the 1840s, in part because of their replacement by publicly funded municipal police, but also because subscription-based groups became unwieldy and subject to collective-action problems as cities grew (Johnston 1992).

In the more sparsely populated settler-colony countries, a looser form of private enforcement prevailed: vigilantism. This was particularly pronounced in the United States. Rather than social and economic elites protecting property, vigilantism was based around the whole community self-policing, and it tended to spill over into enforcing moral norms. Some of the best known vigilante groups – such as the South Carolina 'Regulators' and the Missouri 'Bald Knobbers' – extended their purview to curtailing alcohol consumption, adultery, and other vices (Johnston 1992, 14). They thus bore some resemblance with the religious forms of policing that we discussed earlier.

Professional private policing remains common today. Security firms are the most obvious example, but it also provided the framework for early organized policing and hence influenced how public policing developed. We have already mentioned the most well-known private professionalized police in England, London's Bow Street Runners. In the eighteenth century, the magistrates John and Henry Fielding invented a quasi-private form of criminal justice, combining a government stipend with private fees for the resolution of criminal cases (Emsley 1983, 26). Over time, they brought together night-watches, 'thief-takers,' and constables to professionalize the detection and prevention of crime, and other magistrates around London began to employ their services, which included sending out both foot and mounted patrols. They eventually secured a grant of £4,000 from the central government to subsidize their micro police force (Emsley 1983, 27). But this kind of policing proved unable to deal with mounting crime and civil unrest in London. The need for public direction and funding was already clear by the turn of the nineteenth century, when our analysis begins.

The best-known other examples of professional private policing are the private detectives and repressive police forces that were retained by industrialists in the United States, Germany, and elsewhere. The Pinkerton agency, founded in 1850, and the Brinks Incorporated agency, founded in 1859, provided specialized security and detection services to corporations. The Pinkertons became well known for strike breaking in the steel industry as well as for their pursuit of criminals and general detective work. Until the Bureau of Investigation was founded in 1908, they were one of the few security entities working across state boundaries in the United States. O'Toole (1978, 28) notes that the Pinkertons 'provided America with something we have always boasted we didn't need and never had: a national police force' (quoted in Johnston 1992, 20). Still, while industrialists all across America could call on the Pinkertons, that organization does not otherwise meet our definition of a police force, since it was not typically consented to by the public it policed.

In some countries, businesses were able to pay publicly employed policemen privately. In mid-nineteenth-century Prussia, for instance, Emsley (2013, 164) notes that 'industrialists offered benefits to gendarmes in the shape of cheap housing and work for their children, and they took over the full costs of any gendarmes that they could have stationed on their premises.' Even in England, it was possible for businesses to temporarily fund new police officers, should their borough lack them. Hence, private police and privately paid public police both complemented the broader public police force in many countries.

Much rarer, however, was subsidization of private police by *public* monies. The one partial exception we have found was in Switzerland in the early twentieth century. The first private security agency was founded in 1905, and by 1914 the Swiss state had already begun subsidizing them to provide security for the national exhibition. Thereafter, an ever greater number of police tasks were transferred to private security firms, the best known being *Securitas* (Bieri 2015).

3.5 CONCLUSIONS

As urbanization and industrialization created new challenges of rising criminality and weakened communal self-policing in the nineteenth-century world, countries converged on the idea of modern, public, professionalized forms of policing. But the organization of policing varied greatly among countries. Many states retained military-style *gendarmeries*, and civilian police forces could be either local or national.

As we have seen, this was largely a secular story. Religious and moral policing, common during both the Reformation and Counter-Reformation, was a thing of the past by the nineteenth century. But important questions remained about the level of control central governments ought to exert over the police. Liberals, conservatives, and socialists were split apart and asunder by these questions. Liberal fears of an overbearing state were set against a desire for impartial professionalism; conservative preferences for localism had to be weighed against the power to coerce sedition and rebellion, and socialists had to make their peace with police forces that might oppress them, but that were also staffed by working men and effective at reducing crime that harmed the poor.

The main finding of this chapter concerns the nature of the regimes that opted for centralized forms of policing. In Chapter 2, we argued that there were two main paths to the centralization of public services: the authoritarian path and the liberal-democratic path. This conjecture holds in the case of policing. But there is an added twist, for the idea of an authoritarian path to centralization applies mainly, but not only, to state-military police forces, whereas the idea of a liberal-democratic path to centralization applies uniquely to state-civilian police forces.

4

Prisons

My experience is that a fellow never really looks his best just after he's come out of a cell.

P. G. Wodehouse, *The Inimitable Jeeves* (1923)

The publication of Michel Foucault's *Discipline and Punish* (1975) upended scholarship – indeed, popular debate – on the purpose and origins of prisons. Foucault's book is most famous for the idea of 'disciplinary' power: prisons, according to Foucault, were places where the imprisoned were taught to conform to society's demands out of public view. This made modern prison sentences different from executions, which, in the early modern period, were carried out in public.

For Foucault, punishment is a form of power over the body of the condemned, which may have shifted historically in form but remains constant in essence. This idea is different from the more traditional view of the development of punishment that is associated with historical figures such as the Italian social reformer Cesare Beccaria and his many followers. Beccaria was the Enlightenment theorist of punishment *par excellence*. Writing in the late eighteenth century – a time of arbitrary, gruesome, and public punishments – Beccaria argued with moral clarity for a rational, systematic, and more humanistic approach, in which the purpose of punishment was to reform the condemned. He made a clear distinction between this modern approach and earlier punishment practices.

Before the late eighteenth century, those who were convicted of some form of crime – itself a concept that was shifting and opaque – typically faced some form of punishment that shamed them, exiled them, or, *in extremis*, killed them. Our contemporary understanding of prison as a form of punishment for those who are convicted of a crime did not have a clear parallel in the early modern period. Prisons, perhaps better thought of as jails, existed for three main reasons. First, just like a jail run by a small-town sheriff, it was a place where the accused could be stored until the real punishment was meted out. Second, it was a chaotic work-house for the indigent or delinquent, complete with gin, sawmills, and piecework. Third, it was a debt-collection device for creditors, where debtors – and often also their families – were held at the expense of their creditors in 'debtors' prison.'[1]

In other words, punishments typically took place *outside* of prison, and prisons performed roles that were quite distinct from their contemporary functions. The idea of the prison as a place to punish criminals by removing them from society for a period of many years was still not well known.

Cesare Beccaria's writings offered a philosophical basis for the gradual shift to the nineteenth century's mass prison. From the late eighteenth century onward, starting with the development of the Philadelphia and Auburn models of mass imprisonment, a moralistic movement of penal reform spread across North America and Western Europe. For the early prison reformers, the purpose of imprisonment was to bring about the prisoner's redemption and individual salvation. The movement's aim was to draw out the last vestiges of medievalism in modern society by putting an end to torture, cruel and unusual punishment, exile, and the commercialization of jails. By the early twentieth century, the rule-bound, industrial mass prison was ubiquitous.

But were Beccaria's ideas really victorious? Foucault and his followers drew attention to the ways in which the state's power over citizens *grew* during the era of penal reform, and showed that modern, institutionalized, disciplinary punishment could be as fierce as its arbitrary medieval precursors. Indeed, by the early twentieth century, most prison systems had convict populations that were far more numerous than the population of those who were punished in, say, the eighteenth century. Moreover, by that time, the central state had seized control from localities and the church in a much more comprehensive way than was the case for the other social institutions discussed in this book.

---

[1] As always, there are exceptions; see, for instance, Sellin (1944) on Amsterdam's early modern 'houses of correction.'

In this chapter, we examine the development of modern prison systems from their origins in the early nineteenth century until the Second World War. The chapter makes three main points. First of all, we analyze cross-country comparative data on the development of prison populations in most of the states in our sample, documenting the growth and – in some cases – decline of prison populations between 1800 and 1939. We show that prisoner numbers appear to have peaked as industrialization and urbanization developed at their highest rates.

Second, we identify a uniform trend toward centralization, but we also find that moments of centralization were typically associated with either authoritarian governments or with liberal or social-democratic governments in democracies. In other words, the timing of most centralizing reforms confirms the idea of two paths to centralization set out in Chapter 2.

Third, we discuss the role of the church and the role of private prisons. We show that religious authority over prisons, while common in the early modern period, had largely vanished by the nineteenth century, although the church remained influential in certain associated policy areas such as reformatory schools or probation services. But subsidization of private prisons did occur, particularly in the English-speaking world.

4.1 PUNISHMENT BEFORE THE NINETEENTH CENTURY

Dungeons and jails and have existed since antiquity, but the mass prison is a modern institution. Crime, however, is not new. How, then, did communities deal with criminals in the early modern period and earlier? As Beccaria's work suggests, the answer is, rather inhumanely, by contemporary standards. In medieval Europe (Spierenburg 1995, 53), Tokugawa Japan (Botsman 2013, 169), the Ottoman Empire (Peters 2005, 101), and elsewhere between 1500 and 1750, the chief forms of punishment were private torture, public shaming, execution, and exile. Jails existed as holding pens for the accused, not as instruments of punishment in their own right. Spierenburg (1995) distinguishes between corporal and capital punishments that were inflicted on the bodies of the condemned, typically in public, and the 'lesser punishments,' which, as the Enlightenment wore on, became increasingly common. The lesser punishments either involved physically sending away the condemned or confining them in penal bondage.

Banishment was originally a local phenomenon: a means of removing vagrants or punishing those who transgressed moral norms by committing offences such as adultery or bigamy. It was enacted by local courts and restricted to parishes or counties – and, in seventeenth-century Holland, also to the provinces (Spierenburg 1995, 62). In an era of restricted mobility, due to feudal rules on agricultural servitude and the fear of vagrancy, such geographically limited bans could be effective, but as internal migration became more free, and more common, the threat of banishment had to be implemented at a *national* level.

Conveniently for those who were charged with meting out punishments, this process coincided, in some countries, with the development of overseas empires, with their far-flung and undermanned colonies. The condemned were particularly useful as workers since they lacked basic rights. Thus began the era of 'transportation,' which became a mass solution to the problem of growing criminal populations, particularly in Britain. Transportation was far less expensive than setting up and staffing penal systems at home. As the British reformer and later prime minister, Robert Peel, remarked in 1826,

I admit the inefficiency of transportation to Botany Bay, but the whole subject of what is called secondary punishment is full of difficulty ... The real truth is the number of convicts is too overwhelming for the means of proper and effectual punishment. (quoted in McGowen 1995)

Fulfilling the dual aims of punishment and colonial profit, transportation began first to the American colonies in the seventeenth century before expanding greatly in magnitude with the opening of the Australian continent to European settlement. Once arrived, convicts were under a form of long-distance bondage, working for settlers or the colonial government for a fixed, typically lengthy, period (Hughes 1987).

Penal bondage also existed domestically, albeit in a variety of chaotic, organic forms. One of these forms involved the largest guardable constructions of the era: naval vessels. In Continental Europe, and particularly on the Mediterranean littoral, convicts were typically sentenced to row the galleys (Spierenburg 1995, 66). In Britain, some of the earliest 'prison-like' entities were naval hulks moored off-coast, made famous by Dickens's *Great Expectations*. These prison hulks in fact counted as parishes in nineteenth-century censuses.

The more obvious physical predecessors of modern prisons were debtors' jails and early modern 'houses of correction.' In Britain in the late eighteenth century, there were, along with small parish and county jails, more than 300 such small-scale penal institutions, confining a wide array of individuals, often in the same rooms, despite nominal distinctions among debtors, felons, and the indigent poor (McGowen 1995). Debtors were often kept with their families, with subsistence paid by creditors.[2] The presence of debtors in prisons was controversial among reformers, but it did have the ancillary benefit of providing a clear source of private funds for running prisons. Indeed, most jailers before the nineteenth century supplemented their incomes by selling ale to prisoners and charging visitors' fees to their acquaintances. Such behavior raised the ire of both reformers and government, but it substituted for parish funds.

As debtors became a smaller share of the prison population – with recorded criminal behavior rising and felons becoming the predominant group – new sources of funding were needed if the convicted were to be confined domestically without relying on sales of alcohol and other dubious income streams. One possibility emerged from 'houses of correction,' elsewhere referred to as 'bridewells' or 'workhouses.' These institutions were created to house vagrants, minor felons, and other able-bodied poor. Inmates were set to work in such institutions, often to provide resources for industrial and mercantile production. Male inmates were often set to 'rasping' – sawing dyewood to create color powder – and female inmates to spinning and weaving. The proceeds from such onerous tasks were often enough to sustain the construction and staffing of the workhouse, and indeed typically led to complaints about undercutting the wages of local workers (a complaint frequently heard about prison labor to this day).

Prison reformers had concerns about the exploitation of convicts. During the early nineteenth century, work was increasingly valued for its corrective effect on prisoners, not for its economic benefits. The most infamous of all the pointless and mundane activities of the times was the treadwheel – a giant cylindrical staircase on which convicts walked ceaselessly for six hours a day. Although these ascetic punishments may have been effective deterrents and, more debatably, catalysts of reform, they were certainly not profitable. Workhouses in short order required public support; indeed, the great nineteenth-century expansion of administrative boundaries and local taxation in Britain was built around the Poor Law Unions, the geographical entities that were responsible for the maintenance of local poorhouses.

---

[2] The famous prison reformer John Howard counted 242 debtors and 475 wives and children in the Fleet prison in London (McGowen 1995, 81).

Although houses of correction contained a mix of noncriminals and felons, they provided a template for later mass institutions of imprisonment for convicted criminals – the modern, publicly financed prisons. As the feudal system collapsed across Europe in the early modern period, traditional forms of punishment quite simply struggled to keep up with the growing numbers of convicted criminals. Urbanization and industrialization, in particular, produced great societal strain, pushing the question of punishment out of the hands of localities. Once the central state became involved in the business of punishment, it opted for the creation of domestic mass confinement systems, often funded by a mix of prison labor and public funds. By the middle of the nineteenth century, prison finally became a systematic and viable alternative to preexisting means of punishment.

Table 4.1 compares the use of imprisonment with its main alternatives in Britain between 1806 and 1833, drawing on data collected by Ducpetiaux (1835). One fairly striking observation is that almost all forms of punishment became more frequent in an absolute sense – capital punishment more than tripled and transportation sextupled. Imprisonment also became more common, making up the lion's share of all punishment, but it is clear that even at the time of the Great Reform Bill, England's prisons did not hold prisoners for longer than for short custodial sentences. For longer terms, transportation was still the solution. To find out more about how long-term imprisonment eventually won out against other forms of punishment, our gaze must turn to the other side of the Atlantic.

4.2 THE GROWTH OF PRISONS

The development of the modern prison during the nineteenth century is a paradigmatic example of policy diffusion through architectural design. As Foucault argued, the modern state impressed its control over the confined through literal oversight, *in extremis* through prisons designed according to the 'panopticon' model developed by Jeremy Bentham. In reality, the circular panopticon was replaced, in most cases, by the so-call 'radial' design – with a hub in the center and long prison wings as 'spokes' heading outward (Johnston 2000). Prison design was meaningful beyond purely architectural concerns. Radial prisons, along the lines of the Eastern State Penitentiary in Philadelphia, permitted easy monitoring of convicts from the central hub, while allowing prisoners to be placed in rows of single cells, removed from the distractions of fellow inmates.

TABLE 4.1 *Forms of punishment in early nineteenth-century England*

	1806–1812	1813–1819	1820–1826	1826–1833
Capital punishment	2,800	6,584	7,659	9,457
Transportation for life	76	564	1,000	2,979
Transportation for 21–35 years				13
Transportation for 14 years	291	1,012	1,196	4,287
Transportation for 7 years	3,660	7,823	10,828	16,221
Prison for 3–5 years		99	79	46
Prison for 1–2 years	13,413	1,698	2,343	1,673
Prison for 0.5–1 years		5,644	8,088	9,050
Prison for fewer than 6 months		21,737	31,988	47,620
Whipping and fines	1,027	1,487	1,832	2,225
Total	21,277	46,651	65,015	93,579

Sources: Ducpetiaux (1835)

The radial design was part and parcel of the early prison reform movement, which was typically led by religious groups such as the Quakers. Early reformers, inspired by Beccaria's rationalism and their own religious beliefs, argued that punishment in the early nineteenth century reflected atavistic desires for vengeance on the convicted rather than seeking to reform the criminal. For those motivated by religion, reform had a spiritual dimension: imprisonment would force the convict to face God and repent his, or occasionally her, sinful behavior. This religious conversion, in turn, would convert convicts back into law-abiding citizens upon release.

Ecclesiastical jails had long existed, so religious motivations in prisons were not new (see Peters 1995, 30–32, on inquisition jails and Spierenburg 1995, 50, on the separate domains of ecclesiastical and lay courts). But ecclesiastical jails largely existed to punish heresy or to contain wayward priests; the use of prisons to indoctrinate or reinforce religious learning and practice is a nineteenth-century phenomenon.

Two models of mass prison management developed in early nineteenth-century America, both of which were meant to produce this salutary effect on prisoners. The Pennsylvania Model, developed at the Eastern State Penitentiary in Philadelphia, kept prisoners in individual cells in permanent solitary confinement (the exercise area was at the back of the cell). The Auburn Model, developed in the state of New York, had the prisoners engage in group activity outside of their cells, but in absolute silence. Ultimately the second model won out for cost reasons, but both types of prison reform found a way to develop mass institutions without the chaos and corruption and profit-making of eighteenth-century jails.

Of course, the absence of profit-making required substantial public funding, and the development of mass prisons increasingly became a public expense in Europe, its settler colonies, and Japan.

Depending on their penal codes, countries faced strikingly different demands on their emergent national prison systems. Unfortunately, therefore, cross-national evidence on imprisonment rates is difficult to assemble and are beset by problems of measurement error and comparability. For example, given that many prisoners served less than a full year and were regular entrants into the penal system, distinguishing gross conviction rates and net imprisonment rates is typically important, to avoid double-counting. Moreover, in a number of countries, separate data were collected for different types of prisons – consider, for example, the distinction in France between short-term *maisons d'arrêt*

FIGURE 4.1 Prisoners in England, France, and Italy.
Source: Rusche and Kirchheimer (1939); Melossi (2001)

and long-term *maisons centrales*. Finally, there is no central source for estimating imprisonment numbers in the nineteenth century.

Nevertheless, we have collected data from ten countries in Europe and beyond, normalizing prisoner numbers by 100,000 population as is standard in the literature. Across various data sources, we do see a common pattern: for the most part, countries experienced an inverted-U-shaped pattern of imprisonment, with a peak reached during each country's main period of urbanization.

Figure 4.1 begins with data collected by Rusche and Kirchheimer (1939) on imprisonment rates in England and France, and by Melossi (2001) on imprisonment rates in Italy, over the period between 1870 and 1940. In these countries, there was a general decline in imprisonment numbers during the late nineteenth and early twentieth centuries (the Italian data also shows a rise in the 1870s and a peak around 1880). It is notable that Italy had far higher imprisonment rates than England or France – despite having more decrepit prisons.

The question is whether prisoner numbers were lower in England and France in the era before the data collected by Rusche and Kirchheimer (1939). Evidence from Table 4.1 suggests this was the case for England, with around 150 prisoners per 100,000 population in 1811 (during the Napoleonic Wars) and a strikingly high 486 prisoners per

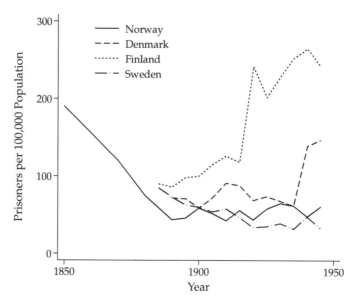

FIGURE 4.2 Prisoners in the Nordic countries.
Source: Christie (1968)

100,000 population in 1831. This strongly suggests that there was a surge in imprisonment beyond the rate of population growth in the early nineteenth century, followed by a decline from 1880 onward. Historical accounts also suggest that the early nineteenth century saw an unprecedented growth in crime and in societal concern about criminality – it is no coincidence that it was also the era of the founding of the modern British police force, as we explained in Chapter 3. Rusche and Kirchheimer (1939, 97) also have data on conviction rates in France in the early nineteenth century – these doubled from 35,214 in 1825 to 72,940 in 1842, although the population increased by just 10 percent.

The suggestion, then, is that the prison population was largest in the middle of the nineteenth century in England and France, perhaps slightly earlier in England, whereas in Italy imprisonment rates peaked in the second half of the nineteenth century. Not coincidentally, the 1840s and 1850s in France, the period after the Napoleonic wars in England, and the 1860s and 1870s in Italy were periods of especially high population growth and rapid industrialization.

Data for the Nordic countries, collected by Christie (1968), reveal similar patterns, albeit in the early twentieth century, which was when those countries experienced rapid urbanization and high population growth (particularly as emigration to the United States declined). In Finland,

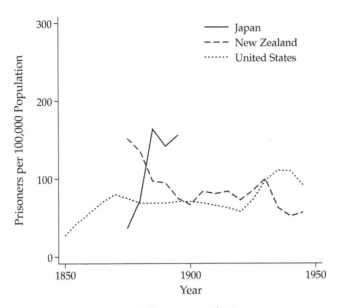

FIGURE 4.3 Prisoners outside Europe.
Source: Botsman (2013); Melossi (2001); (Newbold 2007)

imprisonment rates increased greatly in the 1920s and 1930s, which is likely to be an effect of the political situation in the first decades of independent Finland. Sweden and Norway appear to have had declining imprisonment rates since the late nineteenth century – indeed, in Norway, for which we have data from Christie going back to 1850, there appears to have been a dramatic decline. What is perhaps most surprising to contemporary eyes is that generally the Scandinavian countries had higher imprisonment rates than England or France in the early twentieth century.

Finally, we examine three countries beyond the European core: Japan, New Zealand and the United States of America. Data from Japan, for a few years in the late nineteenth century, come from Botsman (2013). Data on New Zealand come from Newbold (2007), and data for the United States come from Melossi (2001). Here we see somewhat different patterns. In the United States, there was a gradual rise in imprisonment rates, with only a brief dip in the 1920s.[3] In New Zealand, by contrast, there

---

[3] Since the 1960s, as is well known, imprisonment rates in the United States have sky-rocketed to around 750 people per 100,000 population – a level that makes early nineteenth-century Britain seem lenient.

was a secular decline throughout the period, from double the rate of the United States in 1880 to substantially lower in the 1940s.[4] In Japan, finally, there was a very steep rise in imprisonment rates in the beginning of the Meiji period, following a massive expansion of the national prison system and the replacement of the Tokugawa justice system with a modern penal code.[5]

4.3 CENTRALIZING PRISON SYSTEMS

As in other chapters, our core measurement strategy when describing the level of centralization in different countries is to determine which level of government was responsible for the hiring, firing, and payment of prison employees. Table 4.2 demonstrates how our sample of countries fits into the vertical and horizontal dimensions of administration.

In most cases, prisons were originally run locally, although in a few smaller countries – such as Belgium and Denmark – there was in fact a tradition of national control of prisons that dates back to the beginning of the period we study. Some federal countries, such as Australia, Switzerland, and the United States, remained committed to decentralized prisons throughout the period we examine, excluding the occasional national-level institution for extreme or political crimes. With these exceptions, at a higher rate than in any other comparable case in this book, countries tended to move from decentralized to centralized institutions over time. Figure 4.4, which counts the number of countries in our sample where prisons were governed nationally, locally, and regionally, shows clearly that there was a broad wave of centralization beginning around 1870. By 1900, most countries had centralized their prisons.

We begin our analysis of individual country experiences of prison administration by examining some of those countries where prisons were always centralized, at least from the start of our period: Belgium, Denmark, and France. The French experience is directly connected to the centralizing initiatives of the Revolutionary and Napoleonic eras. The

---

[4] Like the United States, New Zealand has experienced an increase since the 1960s, but the imprisonment rate has returned only to the level of the 1870s.

[5] In contrast to the United States and New Zealand, Japan's incarceration rate today is very low (around 40 people per 100,000), suggesting that just like the continental European countries, Japan has had an inverted-U-shaped pattern of imprisonment over time.

TABLE 4.2 *How prisons were governed*

	Public only	Subsidies for private prisons
National	Austria, Belgium, Canada (from 1896 from 1868), Denmark, Finland, Germany (from 1936), Ireland, Italy (from 1891), Japan (from 1876), Netherlands (from 1886), New Zealand (from 1880), Norway (from 1903), Spain (from 1834), Sweden (from 1825), United Kingdom (from 1877)	Canada (1868–1895), France
Local or regional	Australia (*regional*), Germany (*regional*: before 1936), Italy (*local*: before 1891), Japan (*local*: before 1876), Netherlands (*local*: before 1886), New Zealand (*regional*: before 1880), Norway (*local*: before 1903), Spain (*local*: before 1834), Sweden (*local*: before 1825), Switzerland (*regional*), United Kingdom (*local*: 1823–1877), United States (*regional*: from 1923)	Canada (*regional*: before 1868), United Kingdom (*local*: before 1823), United States (*regional*: before 1923)

Notes: In 'national' systems, most prisons were administered by agencies of the national government, as opposed to regional or local authorities. In systems with 'subsidies,' at least some privately run prisons received public funding.
Sources: Own categorization based on literature cited in the text

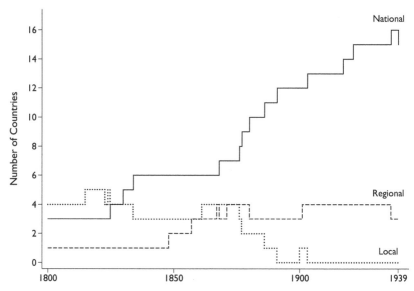

FIGURE 4.4 The centralization of prisons. The figure describes the number of countries in the sample in which prisons were governed at the local, regional, and national levels.

first major wave of penal reform took place from 1790 through the 1820s. As O'Brien (2014, 20) notes,

penal legislation was part of the social welfare program of the Great Revolution, as well as part of the expansion of the repressive forces of the central state, including the creation of a modern police force and the codification of the law ... [and] the establishment of central prisons.

While the process of central control began toward the end of the eighteenth century, for O'Brien, the key date is 1810, during the Napoleonic Empire, 'when an imperial decree set aside 11 million francs for the organization of a centralized prison system in France' (O'Brien 2014, 21).

The Napoleonic influence largely explains the case of Belgium, under the sway of French control from 1794 and adopting the centralizing Napoleonic penal code in 1810. On independence in 1830, Belgium retained this centralized administration; indeed in 1832, the central government reduced the influence of local members of prison committees by rotating them and shortening their terms of office (Vanhulle 2010, 121). The small size of Belgium meant that centralized prison governance was especially advantageous.

A similar principle applied in Denmark, with penal legislation and prison administration led from the center – indeed the Danish king himself was inspired by Beccaria's liberal approach to prison reform, legislating in 1789 that criminal law should 'determine a reasonable and fitting relationship between the crime's various degrees and its punishment' (Smith 2004, 216, fn7). Here we see an early example of the liberal desire to rationalize and moralize imprisonment – although the reform it led to was implemented in an absolute monarchy.[6] In the Danish case, ambitions did not always meet reality – a plan to construct centrally controlled prisons in every major town in 1802 was delayed by the Napoleonic Wars (Smith 2004, 210). Nonetheless, direction clearly came from the center.

We now turn to examine the lion's share of cases – those countries that began the nineteenth century with decentralized prisons but where the central state took control. Most of these transitions took place in the last few decades of the nineteenth century.

The late nineteenth-century drive to centralization followed from the process of diffusion and learning we discussed earlier. In particular, prison architecture converged on a number of 'modern' models that were replicated throughout Europe, wealthier settler colonies, and in poorer countries as diverse as Cuba, Brazil, Russia, and China (Johnston 2000). Mass prisons conformed to Victorian ideas about reducing the chaotic environment in earlier jails, while maximizing oversight by guards, and carefully segregated individual prisoners, to promote their religious salvation. Despite these moral goals, often centered on the individual, the mass design meant that building prisons required huge economies of scale. Centralization made sense in technical and economic terms, for mass prisons required large numbers of prisoners and large amounts of capital, both of which were easier to assemble at the national rather than local level.

We see some of the patterns we noted in Chapter 3 on policing, and will see in other areas, since centralization often occurred under either an authoritarian government (as in the cases of Meiji Japan or Nazi Germany), to control subjugated imperial populations (as in Ireland and New Zealand), or under liberal governments (as in Norway). Unlike in policing, we do not see examples of socialist centralization, but in

---

[6] It might appear unusual that these initiatives came from a monarch, but in neighboring Sweden, too, prison reform was a key interest of the king. The future king Oskar I wrote an anonymous treatise on the topic in 1834 that inspired 1840s prison legislation.

the case of prisons this is largely because the main wave of centralization happened in the late nineteenth century, before socialist parties had reached the pinnacles of power.

As with policing, the advent of the Meiji restoration led to a rapid centralization of prisons in Japan. The Meiji's combination of authoritarianism with a rationalizing spirit meant an active early seizure of central control over the state's coercive apparatus. It is important not to confuse the fact that Japan pursued an authoritarian centralizing path in the 1870s with a worsening of prison conditions for inmates – punishment in Tokugawa Japan was notoriously bloodthirsty, and, indeed, it was the Meiji government in 1879 that ended the practice of public displaying severed heads (Botsman 2013, 169). Moreover, as with policing and other public services, the Meiji Restoration led to an international mission by Ohara Shigechika to study prisons in European countries and colonies. Since the 1870s also marked a period of prison centralization in Europe – including England, Ireland, and Italy– part of the move to centralization was a process of diffusion.

Indeed, rhetoric jumped ahead of action. According to (Botsman 2013, 160),

'When the new "Prison Rules" were first circulated to officials in 1872, they were prefaced with a statement explaining that it was not yet possible for the government to build new prisons in all parts of the country ... soon afterward regional authorities were ordered to suspend all attempts to implement the new "Prison Rules" until proper investigations had been made into the costs they were likely to entail ... In spite of these setbacks the new "Prison Rules" were not abandoned. They remained on the books as national law.'

In 1876, the new Home Ministry finally took charge of funding and monitoring a centralized prison system that could actually be operated as such (Hiramatsu 1973, 30). Prison centralization was led by the international-mission leader Ohara Shigechika, and fit neatly into broader Meiji goals.

'Ohara's emphasis on the need to clear away barriers and obstacles that might impede a sweeping, central gaze can also be linked to the Meiji government's efforts to restructure and streamline the Japanese polity as a whole' (Botsman 2013, 156).

Centralization of prisons also occurred under the fascist regimes of the 1930s, though in the cases of Italy and Spain prisons had already been nominally centralized before further fascist consolidation. The case of Nazi Germany is one of a sharp transition, however, from regionally decentralized governance in the Weimar Republic to extreme state centralization by 1935. According to Cantor (1934, 85), in the Weimar era 'each one of the German states has jealously guarded its independence in penal affairs.' There had been moves to create a centralized penal code but these typically met with resistance from the Länder. Thus German prisons had remained emphatically decentralized from unification onward. However, following Hitler's accession to power, authority was quickly stripped from the German regions. Per Wachsmann (2015, 74),

The first, and most thorough, process of centralization occurred in the legal sphere, between February 1934 and April 1935. Only now, in the Third Reich, did the Reich Minister of Justice gain full authority over the administration of justice in Germany.

There are also examples of a liberal path to centralization of prisons though perhaps less commonly than in other public services and not always under fully democratic rule. We begin with the Italian case, where centralization occurred in 1891 under the liberal Crispi government, albeit in a country where political rights were still limited. In the land of Cesare Beccaria, before unification some regions had experienced profound prison reform movements and had abandoned capital punishment and introduced separate confinement (for example, Tuscany), whereas in the South capital punishment remained common and conditions were poor. Clearly this meant a 'wide diversity in penal legislation' (Wines 1873, 17). Following unification a series of attempts were made to rationalize and centralize prisons in Italy but it was not until the penal code reforms between 1889 and 1891 that Italy could finally be said to have a unified prison system. This was an emphatically liberal agenda under Francesco Crispi: Gibson (2019, 68) notes that Crispi

'became prime minister with the intent of constructing a national social policy for Italy ... the passage of unified legislation for all penal institutions signalled Italy's commitment to the international consensus that, at least in rhetoric, condemned corporal punishment and promoted rehabilitation of convicted criminals.'

In order to accomplish these goals, Crispi needed to centralize the administration and financing of prisons, which was accomplished by the liberal Minister of Justice Giuseppe Zanardelli. Dondici (2017, 36) notes that there had been some attempt at uniform rules prior to this date but until 1891

'the Italian penal apparatus was characterized by lack of consistency and fragmentation ... warders, for example, did not have standard wages, and their contracts varied according to changes in local government ... a national prison system can only be reasonably talked about from 1891 onwards.'

Italy is thus an emblematic case of prison centralization driven by liberals, with the goal of standardizing and humanizing treatment. It is notable that while liberals were often a key force in centralizing prisons, it did not necessarily require a fully democratic system for them to be able to achieve these goals, largely because unlike the case of say education, conservatives were not strongly opposed to centralization and hence did not feel compelled to use antidemocratic institutions to prevent these reforms. This in turn helps to explain the general trend toward centralization even before mass enfranchisement.

The Dutch also followed a liberal route to centralization – one that occurred gradually over the course of the nineteenth century as the prison reform movement took hold. Even in 1775 the English penal reformer John Howard had been impressed with the condition of prisons in the Netherlands, where separate confinement was already common even at that time. That practice was made universal in 1851, and physical and capital punishments had been outlawed by 1870. However, the final step of prison centralization was accomplished in the Penal Code of 1886: 'At that time, the entire system of penal establishments was put under the control of the Minister of Justice, appointed by the King' (Teeters 1944, 83–84). The Penal Code was the culmination of a legislative process that had begun five years earlier but crucial to note is that this occurred under a series of governments dominated by liberal parties and was led by two Independent Liberal ministers of justice: Hendrik Jan Smidt and Anthony Modderman (Bonger 1933, 260).

That the Netherlands centralized prisons despite the general trend toward decentralization in almost all other public services in that country, including civilian policing, is notable. Timasheff (1957, 609) notes that

'This centralized direction is considered by the Dutch criminologists to be a functional requisite of a rational and efficient prison system. The adoption of centralization is the more remarkable as Holland, like England, possesses a long and glorious tradition of local self-government. But the Dutchmen are firmly convinced that the prison system cannot be managed locally.'

As we shall see, the English too were to centralize their prisons at a similar time and for similar reasons emphasizing efficiency.

The English case shows the importance of spiralling prison costs in pushing governments of authoritarian and democratic hue, and of liberal and conservative bent, toward the centralization of prisons. The key moment in England was the Prisons Act of 1877. As Fox (1952, 47–48) notes, by 1865,

The foundations of a coherent and uniform system of imprisonment had now been laid. ... What still lacked was the means of enforcing them in the local prisons. The Act of 1865 had stripped the local authorities of almost the last vestige of discretion in the management of their prisons, and gave the Secretary of State power to enforce compliance by withholding the Grant in Aid ... but even this was not enough. ... There were still too many local prisons: they were already expensive and to put them all into a state to comply with the law ... would have imposed an intolerable burden on the county rates. ... The General Election of 1874 brought into power a government pledged not to increase but actually relieve the burden of rates ... and in 1877 Parliament took the plunge. By the Prison Act of that year the ownership and control of all local prisons ... were vested in the Secretary of State, and the cost of their maintenance was transferred to public funds.

The quote is worth dwelling on. It may have been a rationalizing liberal government that initially planned to centralize the prisons in the spirit of Beccaria in 1865, creating mandatory regulations, separate cells for prisoners, and reduced hard labour; but it was a conservative government in 1877 that finally fully centralized the system, largely to reduce the tax burden on rural rate payers. It is notable that both political parties were largely supportive of the Bill's passing and that opposition came largely from Radicals and Irish Parliamentarians who were concerned about centralization leading to 'despotism' and that 'it would be followed by the centralisation of the police, on the similar premise that crime was a national rather than a local problem' (McConville 1981, 478). There were also some concerns from Conservative members who 'grieved for the loss of local patronage' (McConville 1981, 478–9). Thus some similar mixed motivations across political ideologies as we saw with policing did occur with respect to prisons, but the conservative financial motivation for centralization, along with liberal concerns about universal regulations, won out.

In a number of cases, a centralized system was accompanied by a locally operated prison system that dealt with lower-level criminal activity. Perhaps the best example is Canada, where provincial and local prisons are used for sentences of less than two years and federal prisons for longer sentences. We categorize Canada as having federal prisons from after the North America Act of 1867, when this structure was imposed and provincial prisons such as that at Kingston, Ontario were taken over by the federal government (Archambault 1938). For small-scale crime, the system remained decentralized.

We conclude by examining those few countries where prisons remained largely decentralized across our period of analysis: Australia, Switzerland, and the United States. As we noted above, the key commonality across these countries is that they had federal systems of government and that prisons were controlled by sub-national regions (states in Australia and the United States and cantons in Switzerland).

The Australian prison system was governed by its states and territories from independence. Of course prison plays a special role in the Australian imagination given Australia's colonial settlement as a destination for transported convicts from the United Kingdom. The early states were founded by free settlers leaving the original penal colony and they found quickly that they too would require a system of punishment and imprisonment, although they too developed their own system of transportation to Van Diemen's Land (Tasmania) and Norfolk Island (Hirst 1995, 290). Whereas in the United States, towns and cities often founded their own prisons, the low density of Australian settlement recommended a higher level of government that might be able to handle the fiscal burden (O'Toole 2006, 44). Thus we see some of the drive to centralization for fiscal reasons that dominates in other countries occur even in the Australian case where the federal government itself never took a role.

The United States provides the widest ranging example of prison governance with local jails, state penitentiaries and federal institutions all dealing with different criminals. Like the Canadian case, the United States reserved federal penitentiaries for the more hardened criminals but with a much higher 'cutoff' point. Moreover federal prisons came quite late in American history, with Fort Leavenworth becoming the first federal penitentiary in 1895. The majority of criminals remained in local or state prison. In 1930, over 100,000 prisoners were in state prisons with just over 12,000 in federal penitentiaries (Langan et al. 1988, 5). Indeed, it was not until 1929 that the Federal Bureau of Prisons was even established. Thus for our period, and indeed up to today, imprisonment in America has been largely decentralized.

The Swiss prison system is an example of extreme decentralization, with cantons having administrative control of prisons throughout our period. Indeed it was not until 1942, after the end of our sample period, that Switzerland even had a unified penal code (Eisner and Killias 2004, 260). In the 1871 International Penitentiary Congress, Switzerland described the arrangement as follows:

Each canton is sovereign. It has its own special penal system and its own places of imprisonment. Its prisons are thus placed under the control of the cantonal executive authority or of the council of state. (Wines 1873, 33)

What all three decentralized prison systems have in common, of course, is that they developed in countries with federal structures of government. This is not to say that centralization is impossible in federal systems – witness Canada for example. But in our sample, it is only in federal countries that prisons remained decentralized throughout the whole of our period. Elsewhere, the fiscal and reform pressures for centralization eventually overwhelmed local interests.

4.4 A MIXED ECONOMY OF PRISONS

The church played a minimal role in the administration of prisons in the nineteenth and early twentieth centuries. It was common for prisons to employ priests and ministers as chaplains for the prisoners, but the prisons were controlled by secular authorities, not by ecclesiastical institutions or religious orders.[7]

Ecclesiastical prisons did exist in medieval times. One prominent example were the inquisitorial prisons, which were run by the Catholic church and funded by the seizure of property from presumed heretics (Peters 1995). Despite conventional wisdom, these prisons predated the Counter-Reformation, dating back to the twelfth and thirteenth centuries in countries such as France and Sicily. Their particular method of financing proved successful, and Peters (1995, 31) observes that 'from the fourteenth century on, inquisitorial prisons were probably the best-maintained prisons in Europe.'

Over time, these religious institutions, which at first confined errant religious members, such as those accused of heresy, began to imprison lay people, especially for crimes against morality, such as incest. This practice was long lasting. As Peters (1995, 31) notes, the jurisdiction of ecclesiastical courts over both monks, clergy, and laymen was not challenged before the Reformation, and it continued to be source of conflict as broader movements for the elimination of clerical privileges emerged in the eighteenth and nineteenth centuries.

As was common in the premodern era, church courts typically prescribed various forms of public shaming for noncapital offences. But prison sentences did happen, and there is considerable evidence that the modern idea of imprisonment, as a punishment distinct from capital or corporal punishment, originated within eccliastical institutions. As Johnston, Finkel, and Cohen note, the idea came into favor gradually, 'first by the Christian church for those under its direct jurisdiction and later by

---

[7] On the role of prison chaplains in Sweden, to take one example, see Nilsson (1999, Chapter 10).

civil authorities for minor offenders' (1994, 21). But ecclesiastical prisons were largely wound down before the era of mass imprisonment, and it was not of great interest to the church to maintain large numbers of prisoners, particularly as Enlightenment-era liberalism mellowed religious doctrine during the eighteenth and nineteenth centuries.

But it is worth recalling the importance of religious motivations behind the design of modern prisons. In particular, the Quaker movement was an important force behind early prison reforms in the United States. Just as imprisonment had been considered by early modern religious authorities to be a form of punishment that permitted redemption – unlike exile or execution – modern prisons came to be seen as having broader redemptive qualities. Led by figures such as William Penn in the United States and Elizabeth Fry in England, Quaker prison reformers argued that the chaotic and profit-driven private jails of the eighteenth century ought to be replaced by well-ordered, publicly run penitentiaries that sought to educate and redeem the prisoner – often through methods we might now, perhaps ironically, view as 'cruel and unusual.'

Eastern State Penitentiary in Philadelphia was emblematic of this design (Johnston, Finkel, and Cohen 1994), isolating prisoners in single cells with their own individual outdoor exercise areas accessed through a door in the back of the cell, with complete silence being required at all times (Guards even wore slippers, so their steps would go unheard). In this solitary environment, the prisoner was expected to come closer to God, repent, and reform. Thus, while churches left the prison business already in the eighteenth century, early nineteenth-century prisons were typically meant to achieve religious goals: the mass prison was designed by, though not run by, the godly.

The fact that the prison reformers of the late eighteenth century were so dismayed by the riotous, privately financed prisons of the era suggests that there is a long tradition of private monies and ownership in the history of prisons. Moreover, prison labor was ubiquitous in nineteenth-century Europe, which might suggest that subsidization was common, since there was a mix of private and public funds.

For the most part, however, monies travelled in the opposite direction to the way we conceptualize subsidization in this book. Our definition involves privately run institutions receiving public monies. In the world of prisons, it was quite often the case that publicly run institutions were supplemented by private monies – the profits from prison labor, the payments of creditors to keep debtors in prison, and the sale of foodstuffs to

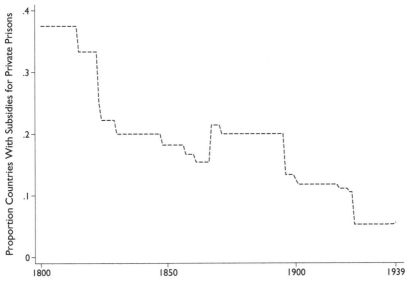

FIGURE 4.5 Public funding for private prisons.

the prisoners (a financing method used in many Swiss cantons, as noted by Howard 1777).

While the mix of private and public responsibility typical of prisons led to some of the same political and management challenges that were faced by institutions in other areas we think of as subsidized, such as schools, it did so in a rather different manner. Rather than private entities trying to capture state resources in order maintain institutions that were typically desired and beloved, we have public institutions trying to capture private money in order to maintain institutions that few individuals saw as more than a necessary evil.

Thus, subsidization, under our definition, occurred in a fairly small group of countries. Nonetheless, a number of English-speaking countries did experiment with subsidized systems in the nineteenth century – a pattern that can be seen in Figure 4.5.

These countries were mostly religiously mixed. In other words, the limited evidence we have on the subsidization of prisons points to a pattern that is similar to what we will observe in other chapters: subsidization of public services is most common in religiously diverse societies. However, it was not the case that religious organizations remained in charge of prisons – as in the cases of schools or asylums.

Given the coercive nature of imprisonment, that is perhaps unsurprising. Subsidization instead meant state support for private gaols.

The clearest example of subsidization comes from the case of France and here it reflected an attempt to reduce the fiscal burden of prisons, essentially by outsourcing their management to private enterprise. While prison administration remained broadly centralized, considerable latitude was granted to local prisons in terms of how they might use their prisoners in essentially forced industrial employment. O'Brien (2014, (156) argues,

'As a producer and a consumer, the French prison system was under the influence of business interests throughout the nineteenth century ... The productive system in the French prison system was organized in two ways: *entreprise*, which was control of the system of production by an outside entrepreneur; or the far less common *régie*, in which the state supervised production. Under the *entreprise* system, the entrepreneur was charged with the provisioning and maintenance of the prison in return for which he had total control over the organization of work.'

This is, to be sure, an unusual form of subsidization. The government still *de jure* ran the prisons and provided funding – a fixed price per prisoner – but the private entrepreneur both provided day to day funding and profited from prisoner labor. The system lasted throughout the nineteenth century and dominated the entire prison system – just four prisons were outside the *entreprise* system by 1890 (O'Brien 2014, 156). The system was not uncontroversial and was particularly opposed by workers and their parliamentary representatives who saw it as an attack on free labor.

Private prisons receiving government backing were also common in eighteenth- and early nineteenth-century Britain and nineteenth-century Canada and the United States. In the case of Britain this developed out of a long tradition of profit-making private prisons, which only gradually came under government control, until the 1823 Gaols Act which began standardization of prisons and the 1835 Prisons Act which began public funding of prisons. In the United States, private prisons were particularly common away from the more densely populated eastern seaboard. Kentucky in the 1820s constructed and ran its own public prison before turning it over in 1825 to a private contractor who financed the operation through convict labour (Feeley 2002, 333). Similar models appeared in Tennessee, Nebraska, Kansas and Oregon over the nineteenth century. In California, construction of the famous San Quentin prison was privately contracted in order to run it as a brick factory. This mix of public and private funding lasted through to the early twentieth century. The most pronounced version was the 'convict leasing' system that dominated in the South, whereby the state leased out prisoners to private corporations, receiving substantial revenues in return. The system expanded rapidly in the Jim Crow era as southern states imprisoned newly freed slaves and profited from their work as convicts. This practice, – essentially a perverse continuation of slavery –, persisted until the mid 1920s (Shichor 1995, 42).

Although for the most part the mixed economy of prisons meant for-profit use of prison labour, there are some examples of services that were connected with the prison system where religious organizations in religiously mixed societies received subsidies, however. Swiss correctional houses for young offenders, for example, were subsidized and in Ireland, youth offenders were typically housed in religiously run establishments (the so-called Industrial Schools), distinct for Protestants and Catholics (see Arnold and Laskey 2012, xix; O'Sullivan and O'Donnell 2007, 37).

Perhaps the most interesting such example is the governance of probation services in the Netherlands. Heijder (1973, 106) notes that from 1905 onward, the Dutch government began to subsidize religious and private organizations that worked with ex-prisoners, including the Salvation Army, the Roman Catholic Rehabilitation Society, and a corresponding Protestant probation society. Bonger (1933, 265) notes that

'the costs are partly paid out of its own resources, but mostly by the Department of Justice ... The religious discord in the Netherlands is, unhappily enough, very great. Every important church organization (Calvinists, Roman Catholics, etc.) has its own institutes. There is also a very large neutral organization.'

It is noteworthy that Dutch 'pillarization' occurred even in probation services – though not when it came to imprisonment itself.

4.5 CONCLUSIONS

According to Cesare Beccaria and the liberal reformers who followed him, the very authority of the state to confine and punish its citizens must be brought into question. And it is true that the crueller punishments of the early modern era were largely eliminated – at least outside the fascist states – by the 1930s. Yet, the replacement of arbitrary physical punishment by the rationalized and allegedly reformed system of mass imprisonment did not bring about a system that was free from tyranny. As imprisonment rates soared above one individual per thousand population in the middle of the nineteenth century, the state had more direct physical control over its population than ever before.

Moreover, unlike schools, midwifery, and other more benign social institutions that are also examined in this book, there was, in the case of imprisonment, a near-universal convergence around a central, public, secular form of governance. It was a form of governance that gave the nation-state near – dare one say – tyrannical powers over its population, while depriving religious and local authorities of their long-held moral and punitive power. It is with the prison that we see the clearest example of the defining centripetal mode of state power in the golden age of state-building.

PART III

KNOWLEDGE

5

Schools

The children learn to cipher and to sing,
To study reading-books and history,
To cut and sew, be neat in everything
In the best modern way ...
                William Butler Yeats, 'Among School Children' (1926)

Of all the social institutions we examine in this book, primary education was the most pervasive. By the Second World War, rare was the
child who had not been influenced, directly or indirectly, by the state's
interventions in learning. In most of the countries in our study, primary
education was compulsory for all children under eleven, and the state
had committed to substantial public investments in the construction of
schools, the payment of teachers, and a powerful school inspectorate.

That broad description of the state's growing influence over education belies the radically different ways in which education was governed
and provided, and the heated political battles that surrounded these decisions. Before the nineteenth century – a few exceptions, such as the
famous case of Prussia, aside – elementary education, if it was provided
at all, was delivered through churches, in the home, or by local private
or community-run schools. The idea that the central state might bother
itself greatly with schooling and the upbringing of children was foreign
to most people in the eighteenth century. If the state had such a role, it
was simply to ensure obedience to the writ of the church and the hand of
the monarch.

In feudal and early modern societies, where the vast majority of all
subjects were peasants, it would not have been entirely clear to the

authorities what extra learning was meant to achieve, except to encourage sedition or generate undesirable expectations of advancement. Elites, of course, were educated in the classics and divinity, sometimes also in the art of government, even perhaps in natural sciences. But this learning was imparted privately by tutors and by the few ancient universities. Skilled workers in towns and cities were educated under the purview of guilds and journeymen.

And still – even before industrialization and urbanization presented new opportunities for a literate and skilled workforce – early stirrings of state-led mass education could be seen in the eighteenth century. In particular, Prussia and Austria, under monarchical leadership, both developed national systems of primary schooling. Prussia, in particular, became a model for reformers across Europe, as it married a rationalist, organized and uniform model of schooling to a conservative and nationalist state-building agenda. For rulers concerned about the strength of their standing armies in an era of European wars, the Prussian model became a lodestone of educational efficiency in the nineteenth century.

Elsewhere, as in England, education was left entirely in the hands of the voluntary sector – typically through churches – or, as in the United States, to towns and villages in an entirely decentralized fashion. Still today, those early organizational choices (if they can even be viewed as active choices) shape patterns of educational administration around the world. They have fundamentally shaped conflicts between church and layman, nation-state and local institutions, and majority religions and minority sects.

By the end of the period we investigate, despite political conflicts over education broiling over several decades, the state's remit largely remained in primary education. Even in places where secondary education had become a state responsibility, enrollment rates were low (less than 10 percent in many cases). Meanwhile, higher education remained an entirely elite enterprise. Accordingly, in this chapter we focus our attention on primary education – sometimes referred to as elementary education – which typically reached children between the ages of five to six and ten to twelve.

We find strong evidence for the idea of two paths to centralization in the domain of schooling. Centralized schooling was often imposed by authoritarian governments, starting with Meiji Japan and continuing with the twentieth century's fascist regimes. Because of education's crucial role in shaping the minds and behavior of young citizens, leaders with the desire and ability to control the citizenry have often found education a key instrument. But we also find evidence of the liberal and socialist paths to centralization in democracies. Sometimes, governments centralized schools to wrest control from traditional authorities, particularly the church, driven by liberals, as in France and Belgium in the 1870s and 1880s, or by social democrats, as in Norway.

When it comes to the choice between public and mixed modes of governance, we also find strong support for the conjectures in Chapter 2. Education was the site of fierce battles between the secular state and religious authorities over its governance. In general, the forces of secularism were led by liberals, although there was a second wave of secularization in the 1930s, especially in Scandinavia and Spain, which was driven by socialists and social democrats.

With primary education, there is also an important role for private, typically religious, providers. Subsidization was relatively common in education, albeit not as common as for some of the other public services we examine in this book. Its prevalence typically depended on two factors: a preexisting network of providers and a religiously heterogeneous population which mitigated against a fully fused system where the majority church took control. Education provides a paradigmatic example of how subsidization could be used to assuage the concerns of minority religious groups that the state's expansion of education might promote single religious forms of authority.

5.1 EDUCATION BEFORE THE NINETEENTH CENTURY

There is nothing modern *per se* about educating the next generation. Indeed, at least since the invention of written language, settled societies have needed to pass on the basic skill of literacy. What distinguishes education in the nineteenth century from previous periods is that educating the young was now seen as a universal goal, and not limited to a small elite. This is not to say that there were no earlier attempts at universal education. But it was not a cross-national norm until the middle of the nineteenth century, and even then it would take another fifty years until primary education enrollments were more or less universal in the countries in our study.

The origins of demands for mass education lie in late-Enlightenment debates. Thinkers from Locke to Rousseau and from Condorcet to Paine argued that education ought to be viewed through the same rationalist lens that Enlightenment thinkers had brought to the natural sciences, and increasingly to the art of government. This meant a more rigorous analysis of how education might be structured to enhance individual capacities and encourage self-improvement. Most famous, of course, was Jean Jacques Rousseau's *Émile* (1762), which set off a grand debate about education as individual emancipation, out of the purview of church learning and catechism. But, perhaps ironically, Rousseau did not prove to be the harbinger of reform in nineteenth-century education. *Émile* imagined an individualized process of self-education, outside of formal schools and essentially limited to the elite. Rousseau was not alone in opposing formal education; indeed, many *philosophes* regarded the extension of formal education to the masses as undesirable and self-defeating. Voltaire wrote, 'It seems to me to be essential to have ignorant beggars ... to give the meanest of people an education beyond the station that Providence has assigned for them, is doing real injury' (cited in Stone 1969, 86–87).

But this elitist, self-improvement view of education was not the only path that was drawn out of Enlightenment thought. Other thinkers, typically those who believed in universal rights and were inspired by the American and French Revolutions, argued on moral grounds for universal, compulsory education. Most famous were the Marquis de Condorcet and Thomas Paine. They both reasoned that education was a good in itself and that it would make it possible for the masses to read the very pamphlets that argued for the universal rights of man. Stone (1969, 85) quotes commentators at the end of the eighteenth century remarking that the 'peasantry now read the *Rights of Man* on mountains and moorside and by the wayside.'

While this possibility recommended itself to radicals, it is not surprising that it aroused elite suspicion and opposition. This reaction recalled similar tensions during and after the Reformation. Protestant teaching recommended individual study of the Bible, and hence literacy, yet the ability to read also raised elite concerns about susceptibility to sedition.

It was indeed in a Protestant country – Prussia in the eighteenth century – that broad-based primary education first emerged. But the threat of sedition was attenuated because mass education could also be structured to embed the seeds of nationalism. For two centuries, Prussia's harnessing of education to the demands of military expansionism was envied across Europe. Even in 1870, ten years before the passage of the famed Ferry Laws in their own country, the defeated French blamed the 'Prussian schoolmaster' for their military failings (Halls 1976, 7). Indeed, when one studies education in the late eighteenth and early nineteenth centuries, one immediately notes the massive contrast in the educational

must address itself' (cited in Green 1990, 153). The 'double thought' would have the restored Bourbon monarchy replace the Emperor after 1815, but broadly speaking, unlike their Prussian rivals, French absolutists ignored primary education in anything beyond its ability to teach the catechism and national loyalty.

England was, if anything, even more neglectful of primary education than France. This in fact reflected a regression over the eighteenth and nineteenth centuries. Many reasons have been given for England's decline in education – the lack of demand during low-skill industrialization, the fear of literacy producing sedition during the French Revolution, and the stultifying role of the English aristocracy. In part, though, it also reflects the religious conflicts that dominated British politics at the time – the exclusion of Catholics and Dissenters from public life spilled over into attitudes toward educating their young. It was only in 1833 that the British government even legislated to grant public money to schooling, and school development was largely handled by the Anglican 'National Society' and the dissenters' 'British and Foreign Schools Society,' both of which were entirely voluntarist. In the end, as we shall see, state intervention after 1870 built off this voluntarist framework to eventually achieve universal education, but until that time the state barely deigned to treat education as worthy of its interest.

Thus across the Great Powers, there was enormous variation in the seriousness and stability with which primary education was treated until the middle of the nineteenth century. It is only at that point that we see the wave of modernization occur across countries, as the importance of schooling for both industrialization and national identity became apparent and as political leaders realized that domestic struggles over the control of education were very much worth fighting.

In the settler colonies of the English-speaking world, education advanced much faster than in the mother country, but here it depended a great deal on the density of settlement and the growth of the economy. The United States raced ahead of most other countries in literacy and primary enrollment during the early nineteenth century, but even here this was a largely northwestern and midwestern phenomenon, with the slave states lagging dramatically even in the education of white citizens (Green 1990, 12). Australia and New Zealand, for their part, struggled to expand education effectively due to their low population densities. Australia could not rely on the network of voluntary religious education that prevailed in England, since churches were too thin on the ground to supply sustainable schooling (Partridge 1973, 11).

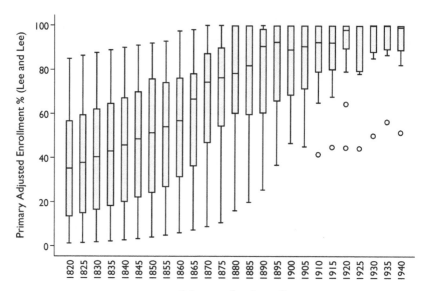

FIGURE 5.1 Primary school enrollment.
Note: Each year's boxplot displays the distribution in enrollment across countries.
Sources: Lee and Lee (2016)

5.2 THE EMERGENCE OF MODERN SCHOOLING

At the end of the Napoleonic Wars, there was thus already substantial variation in state involvement in education, from universalism in Prussia to benign neglect in England. By 1939, however, when we end our analysis, compulsory primary schooling was near-universal among the countries in our study, and indeed political battles had largely moved on to the provision and governance of secondary schools. While there were leaps and bounds in primary enrollment – particularly between 1860 and 1890 – the trend toward more public involvement in primary education, higher enrollments, and more years of education began in the early nineteenth century and increased fairly constantly until 1900.

Figure 5.1 gives a good overview of this historical pattern. The data in this analysis come from Lee and Lee (2016), drawing on the authors' cross-referencing with censuses and statistical yearbooks. They thus represent the best historical data on the extent of education in the nineteenth century that are currently available. Two things are particularly striking. First, the median level of enrollment in our study expanded across the nineteenth century – from under 40 percent in 1820 to over 90 percent by 1900, though it took until the interwar years for the median to be universal primary education. The largest jump in the median was between

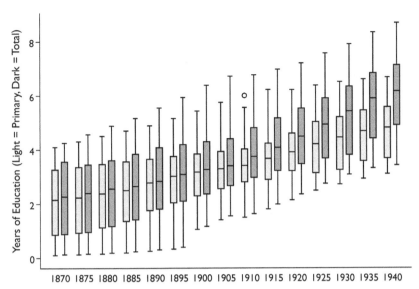

FIGURE 5.2 Average years of education. Light gray bars are primary education; dark gray bars are total education.
Source: Lee and Lee (2016)

1860 and 1890, which in part reflects a number of major education laws being passed – including the Forster Act in England and the Ferry Laws in France. Second, there is great variation in enrollment rates in the countries in our study through all of the nineteenth century. In 1820, primary enrollment rates varied from minuscule (Finland and Japan) to over 80 percent (Denmark and Sweden), and the variation in enrollment outcomes across countries barely declines – even as the median rises – before the year 1900. The standard deviation is almost identical (around 25) between 1820 and 1880; it then declines fairly steadily to fifteen by the start of the First World War and drops to ten by the mid 1930s. Hence, only by the end of our period of analysis is there consistent cross-country convergence in primary enrollment, and even at that time there were still some notable laggards – in particular Spain, where a majority of students were enrolled only by the 1930s.

That primary education was the crucial building block for state expansion in control and direction of the minds of its young citizens can be seen clearly in Figure 5.2, which also uses data from Lee and Lee (2016). This figure shows the average estimated years of education in the working-age population. It thus represents the stock of education rather than the flow (which means that major reforms to primary education are slower to show up in this data than in the enrollment statistics). Unfortunately, we are limited here to data from 1870 onward.

The data are split into those years of education that come from primary education and those that come from all forms of education (including primary). Again, we see the trend from Figure 5.1 of gradual increases in education provision across the late nineteenth century, with an acceleration in the early twentieth century, in part because of the major growth in primary enrollments from the 1870s onward. In terms of the average 'stock' of primary education in the workforce, the median country moved from two years of primary education in 1870 to around five years in 1940.

Although the distribution across countries of their educational 'stock' declines slightly over the period, it is much less dramatic than in the enrollment figures, which suggests that some of the expansion in primary enrollments was fairly minimal in terms of the amount of education children actually received. The figure also demonstrates trends in the stock of *all* years of education. As can be seen, in 1870, this was barely different from primary education; there was precious little by way of secondary education and those who received it were such a small minority (under 2 percent on average by 1870 and under 5 percent until 1910) that they hardly mattered for the overall stock of education in the workforce. By the end of the period we study, though, we do see a separation of the two distributions: the average country had around one year of extra education stock coming from postprimary education, largely because the mean secondary enrollment rate had hit 15 percent by 1940.

Broadly, though, secondary education is a post–World War II phenomenon – all the action, and hence the politics, in the prewar era lay in the control of primary education.

Along with pupil numbers, the forces of teachers that educated the young expanded dramatically during the nineteenth century. With greater numbers of teachers came organizations that claimed to act on their behalf: teachers' associations and, eventually, unions. These began as early as 1842 with the Dutch Education Society and spread at a clip so that by 1920 all countries in our study had a national teachers' association. Table 5.2 describes this expansion. Quite notable is the fact that even in countries where education remained locally controlled throughout our period, national teachers' organizations soon emerged. Their ability to organize at scale, even when governance was fragmented, helps to explain the enormous success of teachers, relative to many other professionals, in managing entry into the profession and, later, wage bargaining.

TABLE 5.2 *The first teachers' organizations*

Country	Name	Membership	Level	Year
Australia	Queensland Teacher Union	Individual	Local	1889
Austria	Die Mittelschule	Individual	National	1861
Belgium	Onderwijzenbond Mechelen	Individual	Local	1857
Belgium	Fédération générale des instituteurs belges	Individual	National	1869
Canada	Canadian Teacher Federation	Institutional	National	1920
Denmark	Danmarks Lærerforening	Individual	National	1874
Finland	Suomen Kansakoulunopettajayhdistys	Individual	National	1893
France	Fédération nationale des syndicats d'instituteurs	Individual	National	1905
Germany	Allgemeiner Deutscher Lehrerverein	Individual	National	1848
Ireland	Irish National Teacher's Organisation	Individual	National	1868
Italy	Federazioni Nazionale degli Insegnanti	Individual	National	1901
Japan	Japan Teachers Union	Individual	National	1947
Netherlands	Onderwijs Genootschap (Dutch Education Society)	Individual	National	1842
New Zealand	New Zealand Educational Institute	Individual	National	1883
Norway	Norges Lærerforening	Individual	National	1892
Spain	Asociación general de maestro	Individual	National	1912
Sweden	Sveriges Allmänna Folkskollärarförening	Individual	National	1880
Switzerland	Schweizerischer Lehrerverein	Individual	National	1849
United Kingdom	Educational Institute of Scotland	Individual	National	1847
United Kingdom	National Association of Head Teachers (England)	Individual	National	1897
United Kingdom	Ulster Teacher's Union	Individual	National	1919
United States	National Education Association	Individual	National	1857

Sources: Country-specific studies.

5.3 CENTRALIZING EDUCATION

The varying power of church and state, liberals and conservatives, and socialists and fascists produced a wide array of forms of school governance between 1800 and 1939. Indeed, the variation we find in the governance of schools is wider – and longer-lasting – than for any of the other public services in our study, which is perhaps a reflection both of the perceived political importance of schools and of deep ideological conflicts over how they should be governed. As Lipset and Rokkan (1967) observed long ago, the struggle between the 'centralizing, standardizing, and mobilizing *Nation-State*' and the 'historically established corporate privileges of the *Church*' was one of the nineteenth century's defining political conflicts, and 'the fundamental issue between church and state was the *control of education*' (Lipset and Rokkan 1967, 14–15, emphasis in original).

Table 5.3 describes the variation in the governance of primary education in our sample. This table is similar to the one presented in Ansell and Lindvall (2013), but varies in several important ways. First, while that article focused solely on the 1870 to 1939 period, we now extend our coding back in time to 1800 where appropriate. Second, following the logic of the other chapters, we look at the vertical and horizontal dimensions *in toto* rather than splitting out secularization and subsidization (although we discuss those differences in the text). Third, following further research we have altered the coding of a few cases. These changes are important for accuracy's sake, but they do not in fact alter substantially any of the findings in the earlier paper.[1]

The most striking pattern in Table 5.3 is the high degree of variation in school governance across our sample, which persists into the interwar years. While there was a trend toward centralization and public monopoly on average, many countries remained distinctly governed throughout the period we study, and indeed until today. There was no inevitable progression toward a convergent 'modern' model of schooling.

---

[1] To be specific, we note that there was much more back-and-forth in the secularization of the Spanish school system than our earlier coding captured, that German education remained partly religious in the Weimar Republic (Lamberti 2002), that Japan briefly decentralized its school system following widespread protests to the first wave of centralizing reforms before centralizing it once more (Platt 2004), that Canadian schools cannot accurately be described as secular (see Chapter 1 on Montreal), that the subsidization of private, religious schools in the nineteenth-century United States was a marginal phenomenon (Katznelson and Weir 1985, 37–41), and that Belgium combined a fusion of state and church with subsidies for so-called adoptable schools (Mallinson 1963; see also Depaepe et al. 1998).

TABLE 5.3 *How schools were governed*

	Public only	Mix public–church–private
National	Austria (from 1934), Belgium (1879–1884), France (from 1880), Germany (late 1930s), Italy (from 1923), Japan (1871–1878, from 1880), New Zealand (from 1901), Spain (1931–1933, from 1936), Sweden (from 1930)	Germany (1934 to late 1930s) Spain (1901–1930, 1934–1935), Sweden (1914–1929)
Local or regional	Australia, Austria (1868–1933), Finland, Italy (before 1871, before 1923), Japan (before 1879), Netherlands (before 1890), New Zealand (1877–1901), Norway, Switzerland (from 1880), United States	Austria (before 1868), Australia (before 1880), Belgium (before 1879, from 1885), Canada, Denmark, Finland France (before 1880), Germany (before 1934), Ireland, Netherlands (from 1890), New Zealand (before 1877), Spain (before 1901), Sweden (before 1914), Switzerland (before 1880), United Kingdom

Notes: In 'national' systems, schools were administered by the national government, as opposed to regional or local authorities. In systems that had a mix of public, church, and private schools, religious authorities – or the clergy – were directly involved in running at least some public schools, at least some private schools received public funding, or both.
Sources: Own categorization based on literature cited in the text

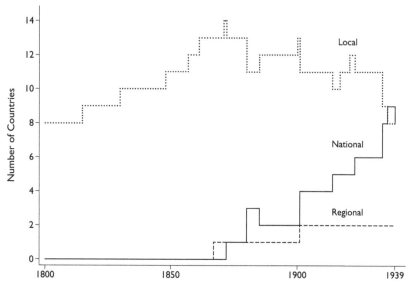

FIGURE 5.3 The centralization of schools. The figure describes the number of countries in the sample that administered primary schools at the local, regional, and national levels.

These general trends can be seen in Figure 5.3 in this section, and in Figure 5.4 in the next section. Let us begin with the historical development of centralization. There is a trend away from local control and toward national and regional control of schooling. No country begins our sample period with a nationalized schooling system, but a number of countries did centralize their school governance in the 1870s and 1880s (Japan, France, and briefly Belgium), with New Zealand and Spain following at the turn of the century (the centralization of the New Zealand school system occurred gradually over the period between the 1870s and the 1900s). A second major wave of centralization occurred in fascist and social democratic regimes in the 1930s (Austria, Germany, Italy, and Norway). Centralization typically accompanied either major nation-building efforts or the victory of ideologically driven political parties.

That said, many countries retained entirely decentralized education systems for the whole period, and indeed continue to do so today – for example Canada, where schools are governed by provincial authorities, and United Kingdom and the United States, where schools are predominantly local institutions.

We find two main paths to centralization of school governance. First, there is a path associated with liberal or social democratic parties coming to power in at least relatively democratic states. These parties had ideologies that placed uniform and universalizing principles above the traditional customs and interests of long-standing local elites, assemblies, ecclesiastical institutions, and religious orders. In other words, they argued for broadly consistent treatment of school students in a compulsory and centrally led educational system that would be directed by the government rather than churches or traditional authorities.

Second, there is a path associated with authoritarian governments that were engaged in coercive state-building, led by fascist parties or authoritarian modernizers. These governments were also determined to displace existing traditional systems of school governance, but for reasons of state and party rather than universal liberal or social democratic principles.

Decentralization, by contrast, remained common where such totalizing movements were unable to secure consistent control of government – where democratic reforms were slower and local notables and assemblies were able to retain their long-standing privileges.

Third-Republic France is a classic case of liberal centralization. Just a few years after the creation of the Third Republic and France's democratization in the 1870s, the Chamber of Deputies adopted the so-called Ferry Laws, named after the republican politician Jules Ferry, between 1880 and 1882. These laws both centralized and secularized France's primary education system, as well as making education compulsory and free of charge. The central government took on the lion's share of spending, and took full responsibility for paying primary school teachers by 1889 (Grew and Harrigan 1991, 212; Saville Muzzey 1911, 257). It is worth noting that while the Ferry Laws marked the final takeover of education by central authorities, during an earlier liberal era, that of the July Monarchy, there had been steps in this direction with the Guizot Law of 1833, though which the central government obliged municipalities to create schools and indeed sent national inspectors to visit them. But it is not until the liberal-democratic era of the 1880s that we see the central state itself taking responsibility for the hiring and payment of teachers, which was previously handled by the municipalities, often in tandem with the local priest.

The brief victory of Belgian liberals during the Belgian *guerre scolaire* a few years earlier had also led to rapid, though reversed, centralization of schools: the teachers became state functionaries and the central government decided the quantity of schools in the municipalities and the quantity of teachers and classes in each school (Mallinson 1963,

85–86). As in France, the Belgian liberals also made primary schooling compulsory in 1883, further extending the central state's remit over the nation's children (Kalyvas 1998, 303).

In terms of liberal- and socialist-led centralization, an indicative case is Sweden in the first third of the twentieth century. In this period, as Sweden was becoming fully democratic and increasingly dominated by centrist and social democratic parties, there were a series of centralizing reforms involving national funding, control over curricula, the expansion of school inspectorates, and training and wage-setting for teachers (Tegborg 1969). 1914 is a particularly important year in this gradual process of centralization, for from that year onward, all hiring decisions had to be approved by national school inspectors (Jägerskiöld 1959, 82). The reform in 1914 was sent to parliament by K. G. Westman, an education minister who represented the agrarian party, but it had been prepared by his predecessor Fridtjuv Berg, a liberal who was one of Sweden's main proponents of centralized education (Gralén 1955, 172–173).

In Norway, a social-democratic-led government in 1936 introduced legislation that centralized many functions of the elementary school system. Concerning the hiring of teachers, a carefully struck balance was established between local and national concerns: the district school director, who was directly responsible to the Ministry of Education in Oslo, could refer a hiring matter to the Ministry if he disagreed with the school boards decision, but only if the school board was split (Lindegren 1941, 42). As Telhaug and Mediås (2003, 122) note, the 1936 laws were characterized by a 'central ambition of greater uniformity.'

At the right-wing authoritarian end of the spectrum, the Meiji Restoration marked a sharp centralizing moment in Japanese education history, as the Meiji rulers sought to speedily transition Japan to compete with Western powers. Platt (2004) shows that education in the pre-Meiji Edo period was largely carried out at the local level, and identifies the Meiji-era Fundamental Code of 1872 as a major event in the history of Japan. The reform replaced village-level administration with national school districts controlled by centrally appointed prefects. Although funding was still locally sourced, governance was now managed centrally (Platt 2004, 131–141). These centralizing reforms were contentious, and power shifted back and forth between center and periphery over the 1870s and 1880s, but ultimately the forces of consolidation and centralization won out (Platt 2004, 234).[2]

---

[2] But, Platt questions Passin's (1982 [1965]) earlier interpretation of the 1880s as a period when there was a shift from a liberal to a conservative educational system in Japan.

The Fascist regimes in interwar Europe also provide particularly clear examples of the authoritarian route to centralization: in both Italy, through the 1923 Gentile reforms, Austria, and Germany, the new fascist governments centralized education within one or two years of taking power. In Germany's Weimar Republic, the Social Democrats had also tried to centralize education – which suggests that socialists and fascists sometimes had similar preferences over centralization – but where the Social Democrats failed because of opposition from the German states, the Nazis, who abolished both federalism and democracy, succeeded. Pine (2010, 14–21) emphasizes the role of the National Socialist Teachers League, which, by 1936, organized approximately 97 percent of all teachers and whose function was to 'provide reports on the political reliability of teachers for appointments and promotions' (15). Pine also notes that the Ministry for Education and Science established centralized control over the appointment of all teachers in August 1937. But the centralization of the school system began already in 1933; for example, a 1934 law 'removed the autonomy of the *Länder* (states) in order to achieve centralized state control over education' (Pine 2010, 27).[3]

This pattern played out more broadly across the fascist states. In Austria, after the fall of the First Republic and the rise of Austro-Fascism in the 1930s, a program of centralization and politicization of bureaucracies was carried out, as in Germany. The new constitution gave high authority to the Federal government and arranged for its commands to be carried out by state governments (Scheipl and Seel 1985, 102; see also Engelbrecht 1982–1988, Volume 5, Chapter 9, especially Section 9.3). In Italy, centralization happened earlier, soon after Mussolini's march on Rome: in the early years of Fascist government, the Gentile reform (1923) centralized the school system and introduced national examination system (Tannenbaum 1974, 239). The first major steps toward centralization were taken some ten years earlier with the adoption of the Daneo-Credaro Act under a liberal government in 1911, but this legislation was subsequently watered down and not effectively implemented, in part because of the outbreak of the First World War (Dal Passo and Laurenti 2017, 24–25).

---

[3] Anticipating our later discussion of the role of religious schools, we also note that the Nazis eventually sought to secularize church-run schools and shut down private religious schools, contrary to the *Reichskonkordat* with the Vatican that Hitler's regime had entered into in 1933. By mid-1939, 'all denominational schools in Germany had been replaced with nonreligious 'community schools' and all private Church-run schools had been shut down' (Pine 2010, 29).

But many of the countries in our sample retained decentralized schooling systems. Because schools had usually been run by local religious authorities, in a number of countries where the established church remained powerful, for example England and Denmark, the inertia of local control proved impossible for liberals to override, and they ultimately concentrated their efforts not on creating a national system but rather on ensuring that the majority church did not fully dominate all provision and that a system of decentralized secular schools be created alongside existing religious providers. In England and Wales, the first Liberal government of William Gladstone expanded primary education by developing local school boards elected by taxpayers alongside existing Anglican and minority religious schools. In other words, where liberals could not centralize, they aimed to supplement existing provision and to make education compulsory, as indeed the Liberal Party achieved in England and Wales during Gladstone's second government in 1880.

The stability of decentralized systems in many other countries was related to political federalism. For example, the federal countries of Australia, Canada, Switzerland, and the United States have always had decentralized education systems, which persist today. Education became the responsibility of the Canadian provinces as a result of the 1867 British North American Act, which was an important part of the new Canadian constitution. This division of powers has persisted (Johnson 1968, 105; Sandiford 1918, 348). But funding for schools was provided for the greatest part – over 90 percent – by municipalities, through local school taxes (Sandiford 1918, 381).

Likewise in Switzerland, the cantonal governments jealously guarded their 'almost exclusive authority in educational matters' (Poslethwaite 1995, 638). This authority was enshrined in the federal constitution of 1874 (Guyer 1936, 102). Each canton had its own school law, and these laws varied considerably from one canton to another (see the case studies in Guyer 1936, 233–364). To the extent that conflicts over the level of authority existed, they were between municipality and canton: in many large cities, such as Zurich, Lucerne, and Berne, although formal authority remained with the canton, funding and administration were delegated to municipalities.

But decentralized governance of schools was also, and perhaps to an even greater extent, a result of countries following neither of the paths to centralization that we describe in this book: they were led neither by modernizing authoritarian governments nor by democratically elected liberal or social democratic governments.

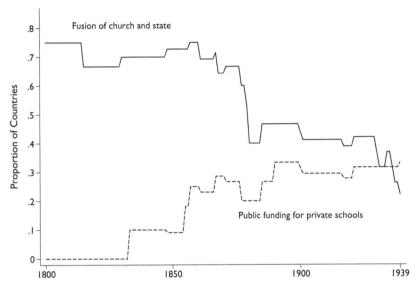

FIGURE 5.4 Church schools and private schools. The figure describes the proportion of countries in the sample in which public schools were governed, at least in part, by church authorities or religious orders and the proportion of countries in which private schools received public funding.

5.4 RELIGIOUS AND PRIVATE SCHOOLS

How did the mixed economy models of schooling develop that we see in Table 5.3? Why was there a long-run trend toward secular control of schooling, but stasis in the balance between public and private provision? Since education demonstrates variation both in religious control and in the public subsidization of privately run schools, we split our analysis of the mixed economy of schooling into analyses first of secularization and then of subsidization, as in Ansell and Lindvall (2013).

Turning to the data on the fusion of church and state in Figure 5.4, the pattern is quite clear: in most countries, churches lost control of school governance over our the period we study, but their influence was more durable than in any other policy area discussed in this book. The process did not, however, occur smoothly through the nineteenth century.

In 1800, only around a quarter of the countries in our study had secular schooling, notably the Netherlands and the United States, and that number had hardly shifted by 1870. From that point onward, however, we see a rapid drop in the proportion of countries with a fusion of church and state in the domain of schooling. In some cases, this is because new countries enter the sample (for example Italy), but for the most part it reflects real changes in religious versus secular governance, as in Austria in the 1860s, New Zealand and Belgium in the 1870s (although the reforms were reversed in Belgium), and France and Switzerland around 1880. The striking wave of secularization stands out in Figure 5.4 as a step-change from a world in which only a quarter of countries had secular schooling to one in which more than half did.[4]

A second wave of secularization occurred toward the end of our period, during the 1930s, accompanying the wave of centralization in that era. It is notable that both secularization waves occurred during highly contentious political debates between the Old Regime alliance of local notables and the church on the one hand and modernizing ideological governments of liberal, socialist and, later, fascist stripes on the other. Some countries, however, remained entirely untouched by the wave of secularization – notably England.

When it comes to the subsidization of private schools – the second important trend in Figure 5.4 – there is slightly less variation over time, and subsidization has never been a chosen solution for the majority of states.

This is not to say there were never changes – Australia and New Zealand abandoned subsidization in the 1870s and 1880s, whereas the Netherlands adopted it gradually in the late nineteenth and early twentieth centuries – but for the most part, subsidization was relatively uncommon but fairly stable where it existed, as in Canada, Denmark, Ireland, and the United Kingdom.[5] In all these cases, its merits were to assuage domestic religious conflicts between majority churches and dissenting minority religions and sects. Schooling is thus a clear example of the religious-compromise path to a mixed economy of public services that we discussed in Chapter 2 – indeed, it is the clearest example among all the policy areas in our study.

Secularization in schooling, as we saw in Figure 5.4, occurred in a solid wave around the 1870s in many countries. As with centralization, this in part reflects the success of liberal governments in taking power during this era. In some cases, especially Belgium, liberal successes in

---

[4] Passin (1982 [1965], 27, n. 27) notes that although the Japanese term for local schools for commoners in the Edo period is typically translated 'temple school' or 'parish school,' there was in fact no religious element in the governance of local schools in Japan in the Edo period (or later). But Passin (1982 [1965], 30) does point out that Shinto and Buddhist priests represented approximately one-fourth of the teachers in local schools.

[5] On subsidies for nongovernment schools in Australia, see Wilkinson et al. (2007).

secularizing schools were short-lived, whereas in most others, such as France and New Zealand, the governance reforms held. Secularization occurred later in countries with established churches, and there were important reforms in Norway in 1889 and Denmark and Sweden during the 1930s.

The French case of secularization is perhaps the best known, given its important role in the ensuing debates over *laïcité*. In the mid-nineteenth century, Rabbis, Protestant ministers, and Catholic bishops and priests were represented on the academic councils that governed schooling within the *départements*. Since local authorities answered to these academic councils, the whole school system was put under clerical supervision, and in many public schools, the teachers were nuns or priests. In particular, Catholic public schools proliferated after the adoption of the so-called Falloux Law in 1850. By 1876, when Catholic school attendance reached its peak, 44 percent of all primary school students attended Catholic schools (private or public) (Grew and Harrigan 1991, 95–97).

The Ferry Laws, passed in 1880–1882, made education free of charge, compulsory, and secular (Kusters and Depaepe 2011; Saville Muzzey 1911). The number of secular state supervisors increased, and the number of students attending Catholic schools decreased rapidly between 1881 and 1901 – primarily because of the reduction of Catholic public schools. The secularization of the school system paved the way for the formal separation of church and state in 1905 (Kusters and Depaepe 2011, 23). The sharpest decline in Catholic school attendance took place between 1901 and 1906 (Grew and Harrigan 1991, 108, 280), and by 1906 only 1 percent of all pupils attended Catholic public schools. After the separation of church and state, the Catholic schools turned into independent schools outside the public school system (Teese 1986, 248). Figure 5.5 describes the dramatic decline in teachers in religious schools in France, first slowly after the adoption of the Ferry Laws and then quickly in the early twentieth century.

Belgium in the 1870s and 1880s is another good example of how liberalism led to the secularization of education. The second premiership of Walthère Frère-Orban in 1878–1884 was the only significant liberal premiership in the late nineteenth and early twentieth centuries (the country was otherwise dominated by Catholic parties in this period). During Frère-Orban's time in office, there was a great showdown between the Catholic Church and the secular state. Immediately after winning office, the liberals nationalized primary education and banned the practice of

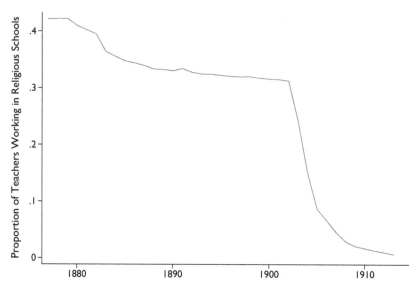

FIGURE 5.5 Teachers in French religious schools.
Source: Ministère de l'Agriculture et du Commerce (Various years)

letting municipalities 'adopt' Catholic schools instead of creating their own, secular schools (the Belgian reform was in many ways similar to the Ferry reforms in France a few years later). The church was no longer allowed to intervene in school affairs (Mallinson 1963, 85–86, 96). The Catholics rebelled against the new law, and within months, 30 percent of pupils and 20 percent of teachers had left the public schools in favor of private religious schools. Moreover, as Kalyvas (1996, 1998) has documented, the liberal education reforms were met with an unprecedented Catholic political mobilization; the Catholics won the 1884 elections and soon proceeded to undo the previous government's policies (Mallinson 1963, 101).

An even more fraught debate between secularists and the church happened in Spain during the Second Republic. The leftist government was adamantly opposed to the role of the church within the school system. Prime Minister Azaña claimed:

At no moment, under no condition, at no time, will either my party, or I in its name, subscribe to a cause by which education can be entrusted to the religious orders. That, never. I am very sorry: but this is the true defence of the Republic. (quoted in McNair 1984, 27)

The anticlerical tilt of education policy was at least a contributory factor to the political tensions that ultimately resulted in the Spanish Civil War. Once Franco seized power he quickly reestablished the authority of the church to create schools and de-emphasized the importance of mass literacy and primary education, which was tasked with securing 'the religious, moral and patriotic principles which are the driving force of the glorious National Movement' (quoted in McNair 1984, 29).

In countries that had established churches, liberal and social democratic parties took much longer to secularize education. In both Denmark and Sweden, for instance, liberal and social democratic parties were dominant from the 1900s (Denmark) and the 1910s (Sweden); yet, the secularization of education was slow and gradual, for by our reckoning, these systems were not secularized until the 1930s. In Denmark, a Social Democratic–Social Liberal coalition government cut the bond between the national church and the public school system in the 1930s (Korsgaard 2004, 423; Bugge 1982, 69). In Sweden, school reforms in 1927 and 1929 moved the responsibility for schools from church municipalities to secular municipalities, and through the municipal reform of 1930, parish priests lost their permanent status as members of school councils (Jägerskiöld 1959, 62–63, 83). But the church retained a formal role: in both countries, vestiges of the church's old power remained until after the Second World War.

A number of countries did retain religious schooling throughout our whole period of study, and indeed in many cases continue to do so. One obvious example was Belgium, where the liberal anticlericalists discussed above were unable to make their reforms stick once they had lost electorally to conservative parties (Depaepe et al. 1998). But more broadly, the English-speaking countries of Canada, Ireland, and the United Kingdom are where religious schooling held out the longest.

For the latter two countries, this relates in part to the political importance that the established Churches of England and Ireland had in the nineteenth century. The United Kingdom barely had any form of nonreligiously run public schooling until the 1870 Forster Education Act and even thereafter operated a 'dual system' of religious and secular ('board') schools, both of which received public funding (on the dual system, see, for example, Cruickshank 1963, Chapter 2).

Though post independence Ireland was able to more clearly legislate along the lines of the Catholic Church (Gryzmala-Busse 2015), the preexisting system of the Irish National System of Education, dating back to 1831, was retained. The schools that were associated with the National System were meant to be religious but nondenominational, and the commissioners on the national School Board therefore represented the Church of Ireland, the Roman Catholic Church, and the Presbyterian Church, sharing power between the main churches and their affiliates. The schools supported by the Board were known as 'vested' schools, and were meant to follow a number of rules, including open admission for all children, separate religious instruction, and the employment of lay school teachers. As the school system expanded, however, the Board became more and more unable to control local schools effectively. Over time, therefore, the National System evolved into a denominational system (Raftery and Nowlan-Roebuck 2007, 356–367; Akenson 1970, 3, 353, 385). In neither England nor post-independence Ireland were secular, anticlerical political parties major players – debates revolved around how to treat dissenting minority religious groups, which was resolved through subsidization, and not the conflict between church and layman.

As we argued above, the subsidization of private schools tended to emerge as a compromise solution to the governance of education where religious minorities felt threatened by a system run by the state in partnership with the mainstream religion and were also numerous enough to successfully advocate for their interests. That solution meant minority religious governed schools would be able to receive public funds but remain direct outside state control. Typically, the mainstream religion received similar treatment in this compromise and oftentimes a third secular system of schools would also develop. This pattern emerged in countries with considerable religious heterogeneity, as Table 5.3 suggests: England, the Netherlands, Canada, Australia and New Zealand (before the 1880s), and Ireland. Even the case of Denmark, an otherwise homogeneously Protestant country, meets this criterion.

The Netherlands is the paradigmatic case for our argument about the relationship between religious heterogeneity and subsidization. The constitution of 1848 guaranteed the freedom to provide education, enabling Catholics and Protestants to start their own schools, but there was not, at this time, any public funding for private schools. Since religious schools had to secure their own funding, many of them were unable to meet new education standards that were introduced by a liberal government in 1878, and many religious schools had to close. In the 1887 elections, an antiliberal coalition came to power, and passed the School Act of 1889, which ruled that private schools would receive state subsidies that covered approximately one third of their costs. This was only the first step,

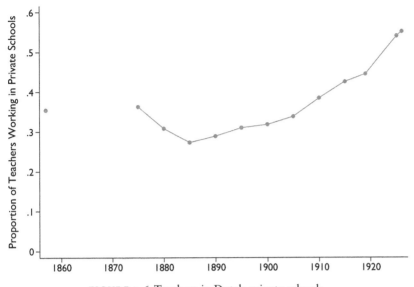

FIGURE 5.6 Teachers in Dutch private schools.
Source: Centraal Bureau voor de Statistiek (Various years)

however; the so called school dispute (*schoolstrijd*) was finally resolved through the *Pacificatie van 1917*, or 'Pacification of 1917,' when the constitution was amended and by 1920 all primary schools, public or private, were guaranteed equal financial support (Knippenberg and van der Wusten 1984, 179; see also Dekker, Amsing, and Wichgers 2019). As (Lijphart 1968) and many others have argued, this was a crucial event not only in the democratization of the Netherlands but also in the emergence of that country's 'consociational' politics. Figure 5.6 describes the great increase in the proportion of teachers who worked in private schools after these reforms.

The slow, piecemeal development of education in Britain, mentioned above, has often been attributed to these religious conflicts and arguably it was only once they were resolved in Forster's Education Act of 1870 that mass expansion of primary education actually occurred, despite Britain's status as the wealthiest Great Power of its age. As Andy Green notes,

Anglicans were reluctant to cede control over education which they considered the hereditary and natural prerogative of the established Church ... Dissent ... were equally suspicious of state intervention because they recognized the dominance of the Anglicans within the establishment and believed that this would lead to unequal state support for Anglican education. (Green 1990, 210)

Support for Anglican schools – which was in place from 1834 onward – predated the creation of state schools and local school boards through the 1870 Education Act. Nonconformist and Catholic schools also received state support, although their subsidies were less generous. As in many other European countries in this period, state support for religious institutions was politically contentious. Nonconformists and secularists lobbied hard during the passage of the 1870 Act to remove state support for denominational teaching and to essentially secularize primary education. Their efforts were not successful, however. The government did create new, nominally secular, schools to be controlled by local school boards. However, the government also permitted the established Anglican church and other religious organizations to found new schools eligible for government subsidization during a 'grace period.' The Church of England rapidly established subsidized church schools throughout England, and in many rural areas such schools in fact monopolized local education provision (Cruickshank 1963). Indeed, state schools ended up filling a somewhat residual role (Arthur 1995, 18).

In the British case, there was thus some subsidization for denominational schools, recognizing in part the demands of religious minorities for non-Anglican control, but all within a system that maintained the traditional role of the Church of England. As Loss (2013, 10) notes, 'While the 1870 act did establish the first state-funded schools under government control, it also formalized the parallel system of church and state schools that still survives.' As in the Netherlands, subsidization was used to bridge conflicts between majority and minority religions. Unlike the Netherlands, however, where different religious denominations were treated equally from 1917, this was done in a way that privileged the majority religion at least until the Second World War.

Subsidization also occurred in others countries with religious divides *within* Protestantism. A closer examination of the Danish case reveals that the so-called free schools (*friskoler*) were often operated by organized groups within the Danish Lutheran church (Kaspersen and Lindvall 2008, 127–128, 133–135; see also Korsgaard 2004, 334). In that sense, subsidization was a solution to religious conflict also in Denmark, albeit not the conflict between Catholicism and Protestantism. In Denmark, in 1855, a new law created these 'free' (private) schools and made it possible for parents to start and run their own schools with significant state support. The principles of the 1855 law and the ideas of parental school freedom that they were based on were given constitutional status in 1915 (Korsgaard 2004, 336, 382). In 1919, a system of equal treatment for private schools was implemented, whereby 'free' schools were given an amount of money per child that was equivalent to the expenses of public schools (Christensen 1987, 50).

We should be careful, however, not to overemphasize the political benefits of subsidization. After all, throughout our sample it remains a distinctly minority choice – around 25 percent of countries had subsidized education in any given year. And thinking through what subsidization really implied politically, this should not surprise us. It meant the tolerance of a parallel system of private schooling that nonetheless received public funds. The state lacked both control of and accountability for this sector in anything other than an indirect way. For liberals, socialists, and later fascists this was hardly in keeping with universalist views of what education might accomplish on behalf of the state. Subsidization was a particular solution to a particularly intractable political problem – the coexistence of religious groups who were strong enough to survive but not strong enough to overpower dissenting sects. That type of political problem called for a form of power-sharing, which of course meant power dissolution from the perspective of the central state. For those politicians interested in nation building and state making, giving up real control over education was a sacrifice indeed and hence it only occurred where minority religious groups were strong.

There were also alternatives to subsidization that could resolve the dilemma of schooling in religiously heterogenous countries. In both Imperial and Weimar Germany, religious schooling operated separately for Catholic and Protestant pupils, but not because schools were run privately and then publicly subsidized. The German approach was instead the creation of separate *public* schools for different denominations (Lamberti 1989). In the Weimar Republic, religious schools existed alongside secular schools, which were meant to be the baseline school provision. In practice, however, Article 146 of the Weimar Constitution permitted public religious schools for different denominations 'insofar as a proper school organization ... would not be adversely affected,' a stipulation that rarely proved prohibitory (Lamberti 2002, 61). Furthermore, religious authorities were granted seats on the local school boards (Lamberti 2002, 172), meaning that the governance of religiously heterogeneous schools was essentially guaranteed at the school-board level of publicly run schools, rather than through public subsidization of private schools. As we saw in Chapter 1, the governance of religious heterogeneity through separate school boards was also a solution adopted in Quebec, and as we noted above, in Ireland, different denominations were represented on the National School Board. Thus, subsidization was not the sole solution to the problem of minority religious schooling, although it was more prevalent than managing it through public school boards.

While subsidization was a stable equilibrium in many cases, it was abandoned in the Australian colonies around 1880. Here the problem lay in the incapacity of the voluntary and religious sector to provide effective schooling at scale given the very low population density of Australia. Simply put, the English model could not be effectively stretched over a continent-size country with a small population. Many of the same tensions between Catholic and Protestant (both Anglican and dissenting) adherents still existed in Australia but the Anglican church lacked the size to impose its own network, although it was able to block the idea of a National Board comprising different religious backgrounds, as held in predominantly Catholic Ireland (Partridge 1973, 13). A dual system of provincially run schools and religious schools operated through the mid-nineteenth century, with the latter receiving subsidization. It proved too expensive to run effectively and was replaced by fully provincial control around 1880.

In the United States, as we have noted, public support for private schools, especially Catholic schools, was a marginal phenomenon in the nineteenth century. But there were intense political debates over schooling that were motivated by the conflict between Protestants and Catholics, especially in the 1870s–1880s, as noted by Kleppner (1979, 221–237) in his study of the third party system in the United States. Kleppner describes that period as a 'paroxysm of political antipopery' which 'owed more to the 'school question' than to any other single factor' (221). The "school question" had many dimensions, but one of them was the Catholic hierarchy's 'demands that a share of the public-school fund be diverted to support their church schools.'

5.5 CONCLUSIONS

Education was perhaps the most fiercely debated of all social institutions during the nineteenth century, and in certain countries, including Belgium and Spain, it was the key divide shaping the party system and even contributed to the Spanish Civil War. Who was to control hearts and minds? The church or the state? The center or the periphery? The public or the private sector? Countries varied dramatically across the nineteenth and early twentieth centuries in how they answered these questions. Ultimately there were two paths to central control – through liberals and socialists in democracies or through nation-building authoritarians, particularly the fascists. What was in common in both cases was a totalizing ideology that saw a single national way to govern hearts and minds. Battles with the church too were fierce – secularism was largely though not solely a liberal fight and it varied depending on the degree of fusion of church and state. Finally we have seen that subsidization varied in as much as it provided a mechanism to defuse religious conflict. Still, it was an expensive solution that cost the state both money and power.

6

Libraries

Why is there not a Majesty's library in every county town? There is a Majesty's jail and gallows in every one.

Journal entry by Thomas Carlyle (1832)

The Boston Public Library was the first free, tax-funded city library in the world. It was founded in 1848, opened to the public in 1854, and moved to its current location in Copley Square in Boston's Back Bay in 1895.[1] On its grand facade, it is written in capital letters, as if on a temple of old, 'The Commonwealth Requires the Education of the People as the Safeguard of Order and Liberty.' But not all libraries are as grand as Boston's: big city libraries are one form of public library, but there have been many others, including parish libraries, school libraries, and libraries run by voluntary associations. The political history of public libraries is just as varied as that of other public services, if not more so.

There have been libraries for as long as there have been books. What concerns us here, however, is the nineteenth-century idea that governments should establish, or at least pay for, libraries that are open to the general public. The diffusion of this idea a century and a half ago is in many ways typical of the nineteenth century's revolution in government: at the turn of the nineteenth century, when we begin our story, the idea of public libraries for all was a fringe, radical notion associated with French revolutionaries; by the interwar period, when our story ends, public libraries were taken for granted in most parts of

---

[1] On the history of the Boston Public Library, see especially Whitehill (1956).

Western Europe and North America, and governments regulated and financed complex systems of libraries within their jurisdictions.[2]

But the development of public libraries was also uneven: public libraries were established earlier in some countries than in others, and they have been governed differently in different political systems. We begin our analysis of the governance of public libraries with the distribution of power among local, regional, and central authorities. Unlike other services, which were often governed by national authorities and sometimes even brought into being through national initiatives, public libraries have always been predominantly local institutions. Local, often philanthropic initiatives came first; national regulation and funding came later. There are a few isolated examples of outright centralization, but only in twentieth-century authoritarian regimes. In democracies, liberal and progressive reformers sometimes sought to raise the status of regional libraries vis-à-vis local ones, but they stopped short of establishing centrally administered national library systems. Our findings thus provide some support for the idea of an authoritarian path to centralization, but only weak support for the idea of a liberal-democratic path.

We then examine the distribution of power over libraries among public authorities, religious institutions, and private organizations. Concerning the 'fusion' of church and state, we note that parish libraries played a significant role in some parts of Europe before the emergence of modern public libraries in the second half of the nineteenth century. We also note that some of the very earliest public library initiatives resulted from political confrontations over church property. When it comes to the role of private associations, we find that most countries opted for a mix of public and private libraries once modern public libraries did emerge. Even in parts of the world where public support of privately provided public services was rare, such as the Nordic countries, libraries that were run by private foundations and voluntary associations received significant public funding.

We end by noting that many countries also have a history of what one might call subsidies in reverse – private funding for public institutions: the first city libraries were often established by wealthy citizens,

---

[2] After the Second World War, the promotion of public libraries was high on the agenda of the United Nations Educational, Scientific and Cultural Organisation, UNESCO, which released its manifesto 'The Public Library' in 1949. UNESCO advanced the view that public libraries are 'a product of modern democracy and a practical demonstration of democracy's faith in universal education as a life-long process' and commenced a decades-long global public library campaign (Laugesen 2014).

and large, philanthropic foundations long funded new libraries in cities and towns around the world. The most famous example is the so-called Carnegie libraries, which were funded by a late nineteenth-century bequest from the American steel magnate Andrew Carnegie.[3]

6.1 BOOKS BEFORE THE NINETEENTH CENTURY

A library, according to the *Oxford English Dictionary*, is a 'building, room, or set of rooms, containing a collection of books for the use of the public or of some particular portion of it, or of the members of some society or the like.' A *public* library is 'maintained for the use of the public, usually out of public funds.'

But who are the public, and how may the public use the book collections? Since we wish to include as many countries and periods as possible in our analysis, we define public libraries broadly. We therefore include libraries that were unavailable to some citizens, such as the segregated libraries of the American South. We also include some fee-charging libraries, notably those in Australia and New Zealand, since this makes our definition congruent with our definitions of other public services (for instance, we treat midwives as public service providers even if their services were often copaid by the mothers and families they assisted). In the postwar period, it has usually been taken for granted that library services should be nondiscriminatory and free of charge: according to the UNESCO's 1949 manifesto on public libraries, for example, a public library must not only be '[e]stablished and maintained under clear authority of law' and '[s]upported wholly or mainly from public funds,' but also '[o]pen for free use on equal terms to all members of the community regardless of occupation, creed, class or race.'[4] For the purposes of historical inquiry, however, it is best to adopt a broader definition, if only because it then becomes possible to analyze the process through which libraries eventually welcomed broader groups and made books available free of charge.

The idea of public libraries did not emerge out of thin air in the nineteenth century; it was a result of broad social changes in the eighteenth

---

[3] On the history of the Carnegie libraries, see especially Bobinski (1969) and Van Slyck (1995).

[4] Similarly, the International Federation of Library Associations and Institutions defines a public library not only as 'established and financed by a local – or in some cases, central – government body, or by some other organization authorized to act on its behalf,' but also as 'available without bias or discrimination to all who wish to use it' (Murison 1988, 5).

century, which was when a large and diverse reading public emerged in Western Europe and North America (Habermas 1989 [1962]). One important precursor of the modern public library, the subscription library, dates back to this period. Subscription libraries were private organizations that lent books to fee paying members and shareholders. The first subscription libraries were established in the seventeenth century, but they were especially popular in the eighteenth and early nineteenth centuries; some still exist today.[5]

Another precursor of the modern public library was the parish library. The often small parish libraries were established by churches and managed by local priests or other church officials, and they made books available to parishioners. In countries with established churches, such as England, Denmark, and Sweden, we count parish libraries as public libraries, since there was no clear distinction between church and state at the local level in these countries during the period we are studying.

Voluntary associations also began to operate public libraries in the nineteenth century. In some countries, especially in the German-speaking parts of Europe, new voluntary associations were formed for the specific purpose of making books available to the public. In other countries, libraries were established by voluntary associations that had other purposes, notably by temperance organizations – who regarded a visit to the library as a healthy pastime for the urban working class – and by trade unions. In the English-speaking countries, the Mechanics' Institutes in industrial towns and cities also played an important role in the nineteenth century's library movement. We count libraries run by voluntary associations as public libraries if they were funded and regulated by either local, regional, or national governments.

In countries with an early development of schooling, finally, school libraries were sometimes made open to the general public, not only to teachers and school children. For example, the state of New York adopted a law already in the first half of the nineteenth century that made it possible to open up school libraries for the general public's use (Bobinski 1969, 4; see also Du Mont 1977, 15–17). By 1835, the libraries of the New York school district libraries contained some 1.5 million volumes.

---

5 Subscription libraries have been called different things in different countries. In the United States, they were known as 'social' libraries, which provided 'a circulating collection of materials and frequently a reading room for the use of any person meeting the established criteria, which usually involved a fee or subscription, or a payment to become a joint owner' (Davis and Tucker 1989, 1). In Australia and New Zealand, most 'public' libraries were in effect publicly subsidized subscription libraries well into the twentieth century.

Combined school libraries and public libraries are common to this day, which testifies to the old and deep connections between two of the public services we examine in this book: schools and libraries.

With the coming of modern tax-funded public libraries, earlier forms of semi-public libraries – often operated on a voluntary or philanthropic basis – went into decline. Many of them were simply absorbed by the growing national public library systems. Seavey (1994, 519) notes, for instance, that many public libraries in the United States were once 'social' libraries, as subscription libraries were known in America. In this respect, the public library has a lot in common with social insurances: it is a service that was once provided by private associations that was later absorbed by public bureaucracies. As economies of scale become more important and public demand increased, small-scale, privately funded organizations were replaced by larger tax-financed institutions.

Long before the eighteenth and nineteenth centuries, there were many other forms of libraries than those we have discussed here, but they were typically only available to specific institutions, such as universities, monasteries, and academies. Since those libraries were never meant for the general public, we do not include them in our study. Nor do we include national libraries such as the Bibliothèque nationale in Paris, the British Library in London, or the Library of Congress in Washington, DC, even if some of these institutions were in fact opened to the public in the nineteenth century. For example, the British Library's reading room, where Karl Marx once wrote *Capital*, was opened to the public in 1867.[6]

6.2 LIBRARY REFORMS AND LIBRARY REFORMERS

It is often said that modern, tax-funded public libraries emerged in the United States and England in the middle of the nineteenth century, with the adoption of library legislation by the Massachusetts legislature in 1848 and the passage of the Public Libraries Act 1850 for England and Wales (extended to Scotland and Ireland in 1853–1855). Because of the pioneering efforts of American and English library reformers, later generations of library reformers in other countries typically looked to the United States and England for inspiration, and many of them were educated and trained in the United States.

---

[6] The year 1867 was also the year the first volume of *Capital* was published.

TABLE 6.1 *The first laws on public libraries*

Country	Year
France	1794
Spain	1835
United Kingdom	1850
(Ireland)	1853
Italy	1866
New Zealand	1869
Japan	1899
Sweden	1912
Denmark	1920
Belgium and the Netherlands	1921
Finland	1928
Norway	1933
Australia	1939

Notes: Ireland was not independent when the English Public Libraries Act was extended to Ireland. Neither Austria, Canada, Germany, Switzerland, nor the United States introduced national legislation on public libraries before 1939, but many of the constituent states of these five federal countries did adopt library legislation. The Austrian government had adopted a national *Bibliotheksinstruktion* already in 1778, but there were no public libraries at that time.
Sources: Barnett (1987, 415–416), Bartolomé Martínez (1989, 272), Dean (1983, 402), Harvey (2015, 187), Ketelaar et al. (2010, 14), Liesen (2014, 32), Minto and Hutt (1932, 99), Thorsen (1972, 26), Traue (2007, 153), and Welch (1976, 58)

But the idea that governments should be responsible for making books available to the public was not new to the middle of the nineteenth century, and the library laws that Massachusetts and England adopted around 1850 were not the first laws that were based on this idea. Table 6.1 lists the years in which some form of national library legislation was first introduced in each of the countries in our study. As the table shows, the library laws of revolutionary France (1794) and Carlist War Spain (1835) predate the English Public Libraries Act 1850. Since the list in Table 6.1 is a little unfair to the public library pioneers in federal countries such as the United States, we provide a list of the years in which statewide library laws were adopted in the nineteenth-century United States in Table 6.2, using data from Bobinski (1969).

In both France and Spain – and in Italy, which adopted its first national library legislation during unification – the idea of making books available to the public was a direct consequence of the dissolution of Catholic monasteries. In France, the revolutionary government decided to make the book collections of the dissolved monasteries available to

TABLE 6.2 *Public library laws in US States before 1900*

States	Year
Massachusetts	1848–1851
New Hampshire	1849
Maine	1854
Vermont	1865
Ohio	1867
Colorado, Illinois, and New York	1872
Indiana and Iowa	1873
Texas	1874
Connecticut and Rhode Island	1875
Nebraska	1877
California and New Jersey	1879
Montana	1883
New Mexico	1884
Missouri	1885
Kansas and Wyoming	1886
The Dakotas and Pennsylvania	1887
Washington	1890
Utah and Washington, DC	1896

Source: Bobinski (1969, 6)

the public, and therefore authorized local governments to set up public libraries (Hassenforder 1967, 34). In Spain, the liberal government that served under the child-queen Isabella II in the 1830s pursued a policy of *desamortización*, expropriating the property of religious orders, including their book collections, which were used to set up provincial libraries (Bartolomé Martínez 1989, 272). The first decree on public libraries in the Italian lands, in 1860, suppressed religious organizations in Umbria and transferred ownership of all books to government libraries; in 1866, similar provisions were extended to all of Italy, and in 1873 they were extended to Rome, which had become the capital of united Italy in 1870 (Dean 1983, 401–402). The parallels with the development of schooling are striking (see Chapter 5). In Catholic Southern Europe, we observed a direct confrontation between church and state that was quite unlike the gradual secularization in Protestant countries and quite unlike the combination of religious, voluntary, and secular services in religiously mixed societies.

What France, Spain, and Italy also have in common, however, is that these early library laws were not effectively implemented. The monasteries were dissolved, and their book collections confiscated, but the resources devoted to making the book collections publicly available were meagre. The main period of growth in the French public library system was in the Third Republic, there is broad agreement that Spanish provincial and local libraries in the nineteenth century did not receive adequate institutional or financial support (Gómez Hernández 1993, 57), and the government of unified Italy soon determined that the library system needed to be reorganized.[7]

Mid-nineteenth-century efforts in the English-speaking countries to create modern public libraries proved to be more enduring, even if the legislation they adopted was enabling, not mandatory: national and state governments did not fund libraries, nor did they require local governments to do so; they merely authorized local governments to establish libraries if they wished. One clear example of such 'enabling' provisions is the English Public Libraries Act, which, in 1850, permitted boroughs with a population of over 10,000 to raise local taxes to fund public libraries if at least two thirds of the local taxpayers approved.

On the British Isles and in the United States, local governments established their own libraries from the middle of the nineteenth century. In other countries – where public library legislation was typically adopted later, in the late nineteenth or early twentieth century – local and national governments instead often supported libraries that were run by voluntary associations and other private organizations. In one public library pioneer, New Zealand, this was the main model well into the twentieth century. Only rarely did municipalities in New Zealand set up libraries of their own; instead, they supported the fee-charging libraries of voluntary associations, especially those of Mechanics' Institutes. That did not mean that libraries were few, however. In 1878, there was one public library for every 1,529 people in New Zealand and in 1906 one for every 2,099 (Traue 2007, 152), making New Zealand the country with the world's highest ratio of libraries to population at the turn of the twentieth century (McEldowney 1994).

By the end of the nineteenth century and in the beginning of the twentieth, many national governments became more directly involved in the provision of library services – by adopting new laws, by providing direct financial support to libraries instead of relying on local-government funding, and by reorganizing national library systems and assigning different responsibilities to local circulating libraries and larger regional libraries.

---

7 A committee for the 'reorganization of the libraries of the kingdom' was set up in July 1869 (Traniello 1997, 96).

In most countries, however, national governments continued to have an enabling role: they supported existing city libraries and other forms of public libraries, but they did not require local governments to have libraries, as some countries did after the Second World War; nor did they establish libraries of their own or absorb local libraries into national bureaucracies. There were a few important exceptions, however, to which we will now turn.

6.3 THE LOCAL CHARACTER OF PUBLIC LIBRARIES

Table 6.3 describes how public libraries were governed in the countries in our sample between the beginning of the nineteenth century and the beginning of the Second World War.

The first thing that stands out is that public library systems have rarely been centralized. There are three examples of the centralization of libraries to the national level, and they are all twentieth-century authoritarian states: interwar Germany, Italy, and Japan. In other words, we find evidence of the first path to centralization that we identify in this book – the authoritarian path – but it is important to note that only fascist or fascist-like states attempted to control the dissemination of knowledge and ideas in society by creating a nationally administered system of libraries.

There is little evidence of a second, liberal-democratic path to centralization in the domain of libraries. As shown in Figure 6.1, however, there were a few countries that shifted the responsibility for libraries from the local to the regional level in the late nineteenth and early twentieth centuries, and those were typically democratic countries with liberal or, later, social democratic governments. This suggests that there is some evidence for the liberal-democratic path to centralization after all, albeit only partial centralization to the regional level.

In 1926, Italy's fascist government established a new institution called the General Directorate of Academies and Libraries, which was responsible to the Ministry of National Education and controlled a total of 4000 libraries, whether they were governmental, nongovernmental, or so-called popular libraries (Dean 1983, 413). A few years later, in 1932, the fascist government also established an organization called the National Body for Popular and Scholastic Libraries, which was set up to promote school libraries and popular libraries throughout Italy. It grew out of the old Catholic Association for School Libraries, which was first renamed the National Fascist Association for Italian School Libraries and then

TABLE 6.3 *How libraries were governed*

	Public only	Mix public–church–private
National	Germany (from 1934), Italy (from 1932)	Japan (from 1933)
Local or regional	Australia (interwar period), Belgium (before 1863), Canada (before 1888), England and Wales (from 1850), France (before 1861), Ireland, Japan (before 1928), New Zealand (from 1930), Spain, United States	*Subsidies for private libraries:* Australia (before First World War), Austria, Belgium (from 1863), Canada (from 1888), Finland, France (from 1861), Germany (before 1934), Italy (1870s to early 1930s), Japan (1928–1932), the Netherlands, New Zealand (before 1930), Norway, Switzerland; *parish libraries:* Denmark (before 1880s), England and Wales (before 1850), Sweden (before 1912); *both parish libraries and subsidies:* Denmark (from 1880s), Italy (late 1860s, early 1870s), Sweden (from 1912)

Notes: In 'national' systems, libraries were governed by the national government, as opposed to regional or local authorities. In countries that had subsidies for private libraries, at least some libraries that were run by voluntary associations or other private organizations received public funding. In a few countries in northwestern Europe, an established state church operated parish libraries, as indicated in the table.
Sources: Own categorization based on literature cited in the text

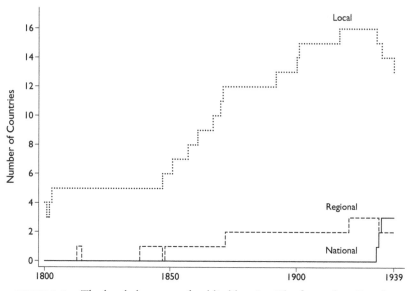

FIGURE 6.1 The local character of public libraries. The figure describes the number of countries in the sample that administered public libraries at the local, regional, and national levels.

turned into a state bureaucracy (Dean 1983, 416). The 1932 reform appears to be a clearer example of centralization than the 1926 reform (see Traniello 2002, 169–176), which is why we draw the line in 1932 in Table 6.3.

The Nazi government in Germany also centralized libraries after coming to power in 1933 (Thauer and Vodosek 1978, 101): all existing public libraries, most of which were *Volksbiliotheken* run by voluntary associations, were centralized under the Ministry for Science and Education (Koch 2003, 71), which we encountered in the previous chapter on schools (Chapter 5). Soon after the establishment of the new National-Socialist regime in Germany, all libraries became subject to detailed new regulations, not only concerning their collections, through the 'cleansing of book collections,' but also concerning staffing (Koch 2003, 73–74). In 1937, the government also issued guidelines about the creation of a new system of public and private popular libraries (Thauer and Vodosek 1978, 131).

In Japan, Meiji-era reformers such as the education minister Fujimori Tanaka had long seen libraries and schools as important instruments of social change (Welch 1997, 16), but Japan did not introduce a centralized national library system in the Meiji era. Instead, nineteenth- and early twentieth-century Japan had a mix of municipal (local) and prefectural (regional) libraries. Under the Meiji-era Library Statutes, *Toshokanrei*, more and more libraries were established, and by 1911, toward the end of the Meiji Era, there were 541 public libraries in Japan (Welch 1997, 73). Under Emperor Taishō, the library system expanded further, with the regional level playing an increasingly important role. When the Japanese regime became more authoritarian in the early Showa period, however, central authorities became more influential (Welch 1976, 241). In 1929, two new agencies were established in the Education Ministry: the Bureau of Student Control – later the Bureau of Thought Supervision – and the Bureau of Social Education, which supervised all libraries in Japan (Tung 1956, 207–208).

There is thus a great deal of evidence for the first, authoritarian path to centralization when it comes to the twentieth century's most authoritarian regimes.

We have found no examples of outright centralization in democratic regimes. As mentioned earlier, however, there are a few examples of partial centralization to the regional level in democratic countries. As in other policy areas considered in this book, notably midwifery and vaccinations, there were many twentieth-century states that sought to expand and standardize the provision of public services by increasing the authority of regional governments, and this pattern of reform was especially common in democratic regimes with liberal or social democratic governments.

One example is the United Kingdom, which pioneered tax-funded local public libraries in the 1850s. A new act on public libraries in 1919 – adopted just after the introduction of universal suffrage – allowed existing library authorities at the local level to relinquish their powers to the County Councils, although most libraries remained local institutions (Kelly 1973, 217).[8] The new legislation that was adopted in 1919 also removed the cap on how much local governments could spend on libraries (Minto and Hutt 1932, 125–126).[9]

---

[8] A few years later, Baker (1922) wanted to go further, calling for a National Library Service as a part of post–World War I reconstruction. Libraries in Ireland, always a more centralized country than England and Wales, were governed at the regional level starting in 1902, when new library legislation made Irish District Councils responsible for libraries within their jurisdictions (Minto and Hutt 1932, 145, 351).

[9] The Public Libraries Act was extended to Ireland in 1853 (Minto and Hutt 1932, 99). Since local governments in Ireland were smaller than in England, new legislation adopted in 1855 allowed smaller towns to raise taxes to pay for libraries (Hoare and Black 2006,

In Second-Republic Spain, left-wing governments also sought to centralize libraries to the regional level. The first republican government created two new library agencies, the Board of Pedagogical Missions and the Board of Exchange and Acquisition of Books, or JIAL (*Junta de Intercambio y Adquisición de Libros*), and the 1932 Municipal Libraries Decree provided that any municipality without a library could request one directly from JIAL (Fonseca Ruiz 1977, 11–12). Toward the end of the Second Republic, library reformers countenanced an even more ambitious program of centralization to the national level; in 1939, the year Barcelona and Madrid fell, María Moliner – a member of JIAL and a prominent linguist – proposed a national library policy, called the General Plan for the Organization of State Libraries (Gómez Hernández 1993, 87).

In the Progressive Era United States, in the 1890s and early 1900s, many states also established state agencies – usually called State Library Commissions – to promote public libraries (Bobinski 1969, 8–9). By 1935, six states had passed legislation 'requiring the state library agencies to prepare state-wide plans for setting up regional libraries' and thirty-one states had 'some provision for contracts between library agencies or for regional library agencies' (deGruyter 1980, 519). There was also some discussion within Franklin D. Roosevelt's administration in the 1930s of establishing a federal office for library affairs (Munthe 1964, 89). In spite of these initiatives, however, libraries in the United States remained predominantly local.[10]

As these English, Spanish, and American examples show, twentieth-century library reformers in democracies sometimes sought to consolidate and improve library services by encouraging regional library development and centralizing some functions to regional institutions, but fully centralized library systems were never implemented in democracies.

The main insight offered by Table 6.3, therefore, is that public libraries were very rarely centralized in the first place. Throughout the period we study, and still today, public libraries are predominantly local institutions. Some scholars even include the local character of public libraries in the very definition of the public library concept. The International

---

253). Compared to England, however, the public library network in Ireland expanded slowly (Hoare and Black 2006, 475; Wiegand and Davis 1994, 296).

[10] During the Great Depression, the Work Progress Administration, the WPA, funded many library-related projects, but even during the Depression, 'public library development in the country was still a local community driven phenomenon'(Seavey 2003, 373).

Federation of Library Associations and Institutions, for instance, defines a public library as 'established and financed by a local – or in some cases, central – government body' (cited in Murison 1988, 5). As this definition suggests, local administration is the norm when it comes to public libraries.

Even in a country like France, with its long history of centralization, public libraries have always been local institutions. When the French revolutionary government adopted legislation on public libraries in 1794, they assigned the task to the districts – a small administrative unit – and when the legislation was revised under Napoleon, in 1803, libraries became the responsibility of the municipalities (Barnett 1987, 415–416; Hassenforder 1967, 34).[11]

In the United States, which developed some of the world's first modern public libraries in the middle of the nineteenth century, public libraries have always been predominantly local. As Munthe (1964, 16) noted, the credit for the development of libraries 'belongs neither to the federal nor the state governments,' since libraries 'have been left entirely to local initiative.'[12]

In Australia and New Zealand, most libraries before the Great Depression were fee-charging libraries operated by Mechanics' Institutes – an institution that European settlers had brought with them from England. These libraries were also predominantly local. In Australia, local fee-charging libraries were supported by larger public libraries in the capital cities, which, unlike local libraries, were government-run, open to all free of charge, and in fact called 'public libraries' (Jones 2001, 157–158). But most Australians frequented local lending libraries (Horrock 1968–2003), which were responsible to local councils under territorial legislation (Biskup and Goodman 1982, 22).

---

[11] These laws were not implemented effectively throughout the country, but there were public libraries in many French towns even before the expansion of public libraries in the Third Republic; in the 1850s, the English library reformer Edward Edwards observed, for instance, that French municipal councils had 'an enlightened appreciation of the store-houses of learning' (Sessa 1968–2003, 269).

[12] There are examples of small American public libraries from the very first decades of the nineteenth century. In 1803, a man called Caleb Bingham donated a book collection to the town of Salisbury, Connecticut, which was maintained by the town; in 1827, the town of Castine, Maine, turned a small social library into a free public library; and in 1833, Peterborough, New Hampshire set up a library inside a store that also housed the post office (Seavey 1994, 519). After the adoption of state laws authorizing towns and villages to raise taxes for public libraries – see Table 6.2 – the library movement spread much more widely (Wiegand 2015, 83).

The first fee-charging libraries in New Zealand opened in Auckland and Nelson in 1842 (Millen 2014). Until well into the twentieth century, the library system was dominated by this form of subscription libraries (Traue 2007, 153). With the Public Libraries Act of 1869, local governments were authorized to support libraries financially (Traue 1998). The absence of centralization in New Zealand – a country whose public services were otherwise highly centralized – is another indication of the local nature of public libraries.

In the Nordic countries, most nineteenth-century libraries were either parish libraries or, later on, run by voluntary associations. In the twentieth century, all types of libraries were eventually absorbed by the growing municipal library systems. In Denmark, municipal public libraries were first established in Copenhagen in the 1870s and 1880s and spread throughout the country in the early twentieth century (Thorsen 1972, 22). In Finland, Eskola (2001, 74) notes that by 1928, 52 percent of the 1705 public libraries were run by municipalities and towns; the remainder were run by 'youth associations, labour associations and other organizations.' The largest public library in the Nordic countries in the early twentieth century was the Deichman library in Kristiania (Oslo), which was based on a donation to the city from Carl Deichman in the first half of the nineteenth century (Ringdal 1985). Starting as a private library, it became a modern public city library with a 1898 reorganization, which was inspired by the American public library movement. In Sweden, modern public libraries also emerged from several different types of libraries that existed in the nineteenth century, including parish libraries in the countryside, philanthropic city libraries such as the Dickson library in Gothenburg (see Chapter 1, school libraries, and the libraries of working men's associations and temperance organizations. Most of these libraries were eventually absorbed by public city libraries.[13]

In Continental Europe, voluntary associations also played an important role in the nineteenth and early twentieth centuries. In Austria and Germany, municipal public libraries began to emerge in the late nineteenth century (Unterkircher, Fiedler, and Stickler 1981, 171), but for a long time, voluntary popular libraries, *Volksbibliotheken*, played a more important role (Vodosek 2001, 197), including parish libraries, school libraries, and reading societies. In smaller towns and in the countryside, associations such as the *Gesellschaft für Verbreitung von*

---

[13] For a comparative study of public libraries and librarianship in the Nordic countries, see Dyrbye et al. (2009).

Volksbildung and various Catholic associations provided library services. Beginning in the 1890s, the so-called Book Hall Movement in Germany promoted public libraries modelled after those in the United Kingdom and the United States (Vodosek 2001, 200), but only in the larger cities were municipal public libraries established (Thauer and Vodosek 1978, 45–49). During the Weimar Republic, many popular libraries were absorbed by municipal libraries, as in the Nordic countries (Wiegand and Davis 1994, 241), but libraries remained local institutions until Hitler's National Socialists gained power in the 1930s.

Belgian municipalities began to found public libraries, and to subsidize other publicly accessible libraries, in the second half of the nineteenth century (Liesen 2014, 30), and when Belgium adopted its first national public library law in 1921, local governments and private associations remained predominant (Vervliet 1977, 9–10). In the Netherlands, the entire library sector was dominated by private associations, which often received grants from city councils for their work (Schneiders 1998, 153). The first public libraries emerged in Utrecht and Dordrecht in the late nineteenth century; as late as 1906, there were only five public libraries in the country. In Switzerland, the public library system was diverse, with cantonal public libraries existing alongside popular libraries funded by private associations or municipalities (Senser 1991, 23–24; see also Schneider 2012). The 1848 constitution made it clear that the cantons were responsible for cultural institutions, but they could delegate that responsibility to the communes.

6.4 PARISH LIBRARIES AND PRIVATE LIBRARIES

When it comes to centralization, there is thus some support for the idea of an authoritarian path to centralization, but little evidence of a liberal-democratic path. We now turn to the role of the church and the relationship between political authorities and libraries run by private organizations. Figure 6.2 describes the proportion of countries in our sample in which parishes or ecclesiastical institutions governed libraries (a 'fusion' of church and state) and the proportion of countries in our sample in which private libraries received public funding.

As we discussed earlier, some of the very first public library laws ever adopted were introduced to regulate the use of book collections expropriated from dissolved religious orders. In that sense, the early history of public libraries is a history of secularization.

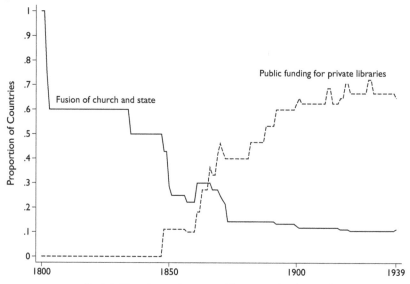

FIGURE 6.2 Parish libraries and private libraries. The figure describes the proportion of countries in the sample in which libraries were governed, at least in part, by church authorities and the proportion of countries in which private libraries received public funding. Note that countries only become part of the sample once the first public libraries are established; the high proportion of countries with a fusion of church and state in the very beginning of the nineteenth century is explained by the fact that only countries with parish libraries are included in the sample at that time.

The most important examples of a fusion of church and state in more modern times were the parish libraries that existed in countries with established Protestant churches: Denmark, Sweden, and England (by the time Finland and Norway became independent, parish libraries appear to have become largely irrelevant in those two countries, but they existed there too in the nineteenth century).[14] In French-speaking parts of Canada, religious libraries also remained important for a long time, but the church in Quebec was not a state church, and with one exception – as discussed in the section on Montreal in Chapter 1 – the parochial libraries there did not evolve into public libraries (Peel 1982, 80).

Danish parish book collections, *sognebogsamlinger*, which were at times a form of subscription libraries (Hvenegaard Lassen 1962, 10–13),

---

[14] In Finland, the influence of the church over libraries declined quickly when the new municipalities were created in the local government reform of 1865; the overview of Finnish public libraries in Schadewitz (1903, 30) lists no parish libraries.

date back to the eighteenth century. So did parish libraries in Sweden (Tynell 1931, Chapter 1). In 1842, Sweden's Education Ordinance, which introduced the compulsory school system (see Chapter 5), instructed local priests to provide parish libraries, which therefore expanded greatly in the 1850s and 1860s, before going into decline in the 1870s and 1880s. Some parish libraries still existed in the early twentieth century, however. In 1867, the Swedish government decided that unlike primary education – which was controlled by the parishes until the beginning of the twentieth century – parish libraries fell under the purview of the secular municipalities. But parish libraries existed for long after that, particularly in the capital, Stockholm (Palmgren 1911, 4, 11–12), and the 1867 decision was not implemented throughout the country – in parts of Sweden, the school authorities, which fell under the domain of the church, continued to administer local libraries (Söderberg 1901, 24).

In England, parish libraries were also common early on, particularly before the 1850 Public Libraries Act. But '[w]ith the advent of institutional libraries, circulating libraries, and later public libraries,' Humphreys (1994, 142) notes, 'parish libraries fell into disuse. As a result, many were sold or destroyed.' After the dissolution of the monasteries in Southern Europe, religiously governed public libraries thus existed mainly in countries with Protestant state churches, where the presence of a local administrative unit within the church hierarchy made local library services feasible earlier than in most other countries. But even in those countries, the church libraries were superseded by other forms of public libraries in the course of the nineteenth and early twentieth centuries.

Figure 6.2 also describes the proportion of countries in our sample in which privately operated public libraries received some form of public funding. As the figure shows, the subsidization of private libraries became an increasingly popular option in many countries as the idea of public libraries spread across the world in the second half of the nineteenth century. Indeed, several countries that did not subsidize other public-service providers – such as Finland and Sweden – nevertheless subsidized libraries that were operated by private foundations and voluntary associations, which represented a significant proportion of public libraries in the Nordic region.

In other words, although the parish libraries of established churches became increasingly irrelevant over time, local, regional, and central governments did necessarily not take over. What we find in the area of libraries, instead, is a more mixed economy than in all other policy areas. The fact that governments often subsidized the libraries of private organizations, as shown in Figure 6.2, is not the only reason for this. Another reason is that governments themselves relied greatly on philanthropy – donations from private individuals and corporations (Murison 1950). The Carnegie libraries in the United States are the clearest example. Andrew Carnegie, a steel magnate, 'offered giving a building (library) free to every town that would tax itself annually for a tenth of the building's value for operating expenses' (Munthe 1964, 18). Philanthropy was particularly important, in the United States, in the first thirty years after the Civil War (Bobinski 1969, 7). Carnegie libraries in the 1930s; were also important in England and Ireland (Murison 1988, 56–58), as well as in other parts of the world.

Over the period between 1800 and 1939, libraries were second only to insane asylums in the proportion of countries that subsidized private service providers, and by the end of the period, the economy of public libraries was even more mixed then that of mental health care. Approximately three fourths of the countries in our study subsidized libraries in the 1930s; by then, the proportion of countries that subsidized private psychiatric hospitals had declined to less than half.

Interestingly, England and the United States are among the countries in which private libraries were not subsidized, which is probably a consequence of the fact that public libraries in cities and towns were established so early.[15]

In Australia and New Zealand, by contrast, subsidization was the main way in which political authorities supported public libraries. In Australia, the Mechanics' Institutes were supported early on by colonial governments, first by giving them free land and building grants, and then, later, through direct subsidies – typically on the condition that the reading rooms were open to nonmembers (Biskup and Goodman 1982, 19).[16] As Hubber (1994, 92) notes, 'In 1890 when there was no library profession, no library associations, and no organized lobbying for library subsidies, the government of the day was making a substantial investment

---

[15] The only evidence of subsidization in the United States that we have found is a study by Dain (1996, 61), who writes that in New York City, 'privately sponsored free libraries operating essentially as charities after the Civil War accepted public funds.' But we have found no other examples of such arrangements. In Ireland, libraries were not subsidized either. Moran and Quinn (2006, 259) note that a Catholic library association applied for public funding twice in the 1920s but were rejected because of the association's denominational character.

[16] On public libraries in Australia, see also Jones (2001).

in colonial library services.' In New Zealand between 1869 and the 1930s, libraries were partly funded by municipal governments, and the central government provided grants between 1877 and the beginning of the Great Depression in 1929 (Traue 2007, 153–154).

In Continental Europe, subsidization was also very common. In Austria, for instance, the public library movement was dominated by so-called public education associations, *Volksbildungsvereine*, which established private libraries that were open to the general public and often subsidized by the municipalities (Unterkircher, Fiedler, and Stickler 1981, 158; Thauer and Vodosek 1978, 59). In Germany, there are records of individual states supporting public libraries as far back as 1851 (Vodosek 2001, 199), but subsidies for public libraries were rare before 1918. Belgium is another country where public authorities supported 'popular' libraries on a large scale. By the early 1860s, some municipalities did so, notably Liège in 1863 (Liesen 2014, 8), and from 1921, the central government did. The library law of 1921 distinguished between three categories of libraries: 'communal' (founded and administered by the communal administration), 'adopted' (privately operated but subsidized by the municipality and state), and 'free' libraries (not publicly funded at all) (Liesen 2014, 32; Wiegand and Davis 1994, 62). In France, private public libraries began to emerge in the 1860s, and already at that time, so-called popular libraries were subsidized by the city of Paris and by other authorities (Richter 1977). A decree adopted in the early days of the Third Republic, in 1874, separated private libraries into 'free popular libraries' and 'municipal popular libraries,' the latter being subsidized by municipalities and subject to state regulation (Hassenforder 1967, 50–54). In the Netherlands, municipalities started to finance libraries at the turn of the twentieth century (Ketelaar et al. 2010, 14), and from 1909 on, whenever a city council agreed to support a library, the central government also provided a matching grant (Schneiders 1998, 153). There was a comprehensive settlement on public funding for libraries when the national library law was adopted in 1921, just a few years after the major agreement on schooling that we discussed in the previous chapter. Under this law, libraries were financed and partly regulated by national government. The so-called Government Grant Condition Act distributed grants that were proportional to population (Ketelaar et al. 2010, 14; Schneiders 1998, 153–154). Many private, subsidized libraries were confessional (Schneiders 1998, 153). The Dutch model of schooling thus applied to libraries as well.[17]

The subsidization of private service providers was common in Continental Europe in most policy areas. What is unusual about libraries is that subsidization was common also in the Nordic countries. In Denmark, central government support for local libraries was first approved with the adoption of the 1882–1883 budget bill. The policy of supporting public as well as private libraries was later enshrined in Denmark's first library law in 1920 (Thorsen 1972, 26). In Norway, there was irregular support for libraries even earlier, from 1836, but more regular support from 1876 (Oyler 1968–2003). In Sweden, working men's libraries and temperance libraries began receiving central government support in 1905 (Palmgren 1911, 36–42), and then more broadly in 1912. In the cities, some libraries were operated by associations and supported by the municipality (as in Stockholm), whereas some libraries were supported by philanthropy (as in Gothenburg; see Chapter 1).

6.5 CONCLUSIONS

To conclude, we find some things in the area of libraries that are reminiscent of our findings concerning other policy areas. First of all, the twentieth century's most authoritarian governments centralized their library systems, as one would expect, given their strong tendency to centralize most public services. Indeed, the fact that those regimes even centralized libraries, which have otherwise been locally anchored institutions in all political systems, is evidence of their strong desire to centralize the institutions that were ideologically useful to them.

We also find that countries with established churches had parochial libraries early on. They were important institutions in the nineteenth century, but in most countries, they were later superseded by other forms of libraries. Nevertheless, parish libraries remained in some countries with state churches, as one type of public library among many. In other words, the capacity of local church institutions mattered greatly to the establishment of libraries in the nineteenth century.The desire of churches to influence the dissemination of knowledge (see also Chapter 5) arguably explains why those libraries remained in some countries even

---

[17] In Switzerland, the government of the canton of Bern began to support private, so-called popular libraries in 1832 (Wirz 1933, 91), and by the 1860s, most popular libraries in Switzerland were subsidized in some way (Heitz 1872, 73).

as the capacity of other institutions and organizations to provide library services increased.

But we also find things that are distinctive about libraries. There is little evidence of a liberal-democratic path to centralization, for example, since public libraries have been predominantly local institutions. Many of the first library reformers were liberals, including William Ewart, the prominent advocate of new library legislation in England in the middle of the nineteenth century. Ewart was not only a liberal member of parliament, but also a Chartist (Greenwood 1902) at a time when many liberals in Europe had grave doubts about the idea of extending the right to vote to the working class (Kahan 2003). But not all library reformers were liberals, and the centralization of national library systems was not on the agenda of liberal parties.

In democratic countries, public libraries typically only served as instruments of national propaganda in wartime. Wiegand (1989) analyzes the role of public libraries in the United States during the First World War. There, for a time, libraries, which were otherwise governed more by local interests and considerations, became more important institutions of national policy. During the war, Wiegand (1989, 136) notes, 'for a brief moment in history ... the public library community could claim an authority delegated by the state.' Indeed, he concludes, 'public librarians seemed blissfully unaware that many of their actions actually reflected the antithesis of democracy, a form of government they were pledged to support.'

We have found many different ways of mixing public and private funding, regulation, and provision of public libraries. Even in regions where the subsidization of privately provided services was uncommon, such as the Nordic countries, private libraries received a great deal of public funding in the late nineteenth and early twentieth centuries. This means that the is little support for our idea that the provision of public funding for private services was a solution to the problem of religious conflict: unlike in other areas, the subsidization of private service providers was the main governance model in almost all countries before the Second World War. Modern library systems are the result of a unique combination of early church involvement, philanthropy, initiatives by voluntary associations, and initiatives by local, regional, and central governments.

Libraries have meant many different things to different people. Consider the following list, which is cited from the introduction to the collected volume *The Meaning of the Library* (2015):

It is a collection of books, a center for scholarship, a universal memory, a maze or labyrinth, a repository of hidden or occulted knowledge, a sanctum, an archive for stories, a fortress, a space of transcendence, a focus of wealth and display, a vehicle of spirituality, an emblem of wisdom and learning, a mind or brain, an ordainer of the universe, a mausoleum, a time machine, a temple, a utopia, a gathering place, an antidote to fanaticism, a silent repository of countless unread books, a place for the pursuit of truth. (Crawford 2015, xvii)

To this we would only add that the idea of *public* libraries – making books available for free to the reading public – was a defining part of the nineteenth century's revolution in government.

PART IV

HEALTH

7

Asylums

I have watched patients stand and gaze longingly toward the city
they in all likelihood will never enter again. It means liberty and
life; it seems so near, and yet heaven is not further from hell.

Nellie Bly, *Ten Days in a Mad-House* (1887)

On January 1, 1890, 86,067 individuals in England and Wales were
registered as insane. More than two thirds, 58,636 individuals, were
committed to lunatic asylums operated by counties, boroughs, or the
London Metropolitan District. 12,126 lived in ordinary workhouses.
8,428 resided in private asylums or hospitals. 620 were confined to the
Broadmoor Criminal Lunatic Asylum in Berkshire. Only 6,257, or 7 percent, were not committed to any institution at all; most of those were
so-called outdoor paupers, a few were private patients (Burdett 1891).
In the beginning of the nineteenth century, by contrast, the population of
the English and Welsh mental institutions had numbered at most a few
thousand individuals (Porter 1987a, 118).

Across the English Channel, in France, the population of the insane
asylums also multiplied during the nineteenth century. In 1889, more
than 55,000 individuals were confined to the 108 French institutions that
were devoted to the mentally ill, including the Bicêtre and the Salpêtrière,
the two Paris hospitals where the physician Philippe Pinel – the father
of curative care for the mentally ill – once served in the late eighteenth
century. As late as 1834, a few years into the July Monarchy and four
years before the adoption of the landmark *Loi sur les aliénés* in 1838, the
population of France's insane asylums had only numbered some 10,000
individuals.

England and France were not unique. Across Western Europe, North America, and Oceania, the large-scale institutionalization of the mentally ill was a nineteenth- and early twentieth-century phenomenon. Historians have offered several different explanations for the expansion of lunatic asylums and psychiatric hospitals in the nineteenth and early twentieth centuries. One plausible explanation is that urbanization and, especially, industrialization, made older forms of parish- and family-based care difficult to sustain. As Wright (1997) has shown, in support of that idea, a large proportion of the asylum inmates in England in the nineteenth and early twentieth centuries were committed at the request of their families, not at the request of public authorities. Another plausible – and complementary – explanation is that the emergence of psychiatry (and its precursors) as a profession and scholarly discipline enabled political and medical authorities to distinguish the 'insane' from other marginal groups, such as criminals and vagabonds, and to suggest new ways of treating them.

We are not only interested in the sheer expansion of mental institutions; we also want to explain how political authorities governed institutions for the mentally ill. All of the countries in our study expanded their systems of mental institutions in the nineteenth and early twentieth centuries, but they governed those institutions differently. Concerning centralization, we find, interestingly, that mental institutions were centralized more often than all other services, except prisons. But they were not centralized everywhere. We find that the idea of two paths to centralization – one authoritarian, one liberal-democratic – holds for mental institutions: between the late eighteenth and early twentieth centuries, insane asylums and mental hospitals were most likely to be centralized in absolute monarchies, in modernizing authoritarian regimes, and in more democratic systems with liberal governments.

When it comes to the roles played by secular authorities, churches, and private asylums and mental hospitals, we find, first of all, that most countries provided public funding for private mental hospitals, although the expansion of public mental hospitals in the nineteenth century and early twentieth centuries often meant that the private sector shrank in relative terms over time. One important reason for the provision of funding for private institutions is that there was an overflow of 'pauper lunatics' or 'indigent insane' from public institutions (that is, patients and inmates who could not pay for themselves), but there were also countries where the subsidization of private institutions was a more permanent feature of mental-health policy. Many private institutions were run by churches or religious orders; in Belgium and French-speaking Canada, for instance, governments relied mainly on subsidized religious mental hospitals to provide mental health care. But the 'fusion' of church and state – that is, a mix of religious and political authority within public institutions – typically ended early on, already in the beginning of the nineteenth century. These findings are consistent with the idea that secularization happened early, and uncontroversially, in the domain of mental and public health. The findings are also consistent with the idea that outside the education system, the subsidization of privately provided services was largely a matter of capacity, not a matter of religious conflict.

Most earlier studies of national lunacy laws and mental institutions are based on longitudinal analyses of individual countries, not on cross-country comparisons. Moreover, many historical studies of mental illness and mental institutions are not primarily motivated by questions about legislation and public administration, but by medical and moral concerns about the effectiveness and legitimacy of confinement and psychiatric care. Several of the classics in the field were written against the backdrop of wide-ranging debates over the deinstitutionalization of the mentally ill in the 1970s and 1980s. Consider, for example, the vast literature on mental institutions in England and Wales. For authors such as Andrew Scull (1979), the history of insane asylums revealed the dark side of institutional care for the mentally ill. For earlier authors, such as Kathleen Jones (1955, 1972), the history of the mental health services was more benign. The history of mental institutions has typically been studied by cultural, intellectual, and social historians, not by political historians; but one notes, when reading this literature, that many intellectual historians are also great historians of politics and institutions.

7.1 MENTAL ILLNESS BEFORE THE NINETEENTH CENTURY

Before the nineteenth century, political authorities in Europe and North America made no clear distinction between the mentally ill – or 'lunatics' – and other groups that were regarded as threats to social order. Consider, for example, the Vagrancy Laws that were adopted in England in 1744. Although these laws made special mention of 'those who by Lunacy or otherwise are so far disordered in their Senses that they may be dangerous to be permitted to go Abroad,' such 'lunatics' were listed among several groups that were believed to threaten the common good, including 'Persons who threaten to run away and leave their Wives and Children to the Parish,' 'Jugglers,' and 'All Persons ... wandering about in the Habit or Form of Egyptians' (the Vagrancy Act of 1744 is cited in Jones 1955, Chapter 3). 'Abroad,' at the time, meant something like 'outside of the home,' not a foreign country. 'Egyptians' referred to the Romani people, which was once erroneously believed to stem from Egypt (the term gypsy is short for 'Egyptian').

In France, legislation under the Old Regime also made few distinctions between the mentally ill, the poor, criminals, and vagrants (Shorter 1998, 5–6). Indeed, when Foucault (1961, Chapter 2) wrote of the 'great confinement' of the seventeenth and eighteenth centuries in his *History of Madness*, what he had in mind was the *indiscriminate* confinement of beggars, criminals, lunatics, and vagrants. As Porter (1987a, 17–21, 118) notes, in terms of sheer numbers, Foucault got the timing wrong: in most countries, and also in France, the confinement of the insane only became a mass phenomenon in the middle of the nineteenth century.

More generally, mental illness in the early modern world was not regarded as a distinct medical or psychological condition that needed to be treated through special methods, requiring special expertise. For example, early modern ideas of madness often grew out of religious thinking, in ways that mattered greatly to the manner in which political authorities approached the problem of lunacy (Lederer 2006).

To the extent that the mentally ill were confined or cared for at all before the nineteenth century, they were typically the responsibility of local authorities and housed in local poorhouses, jails, or madhouses. Then came the age of the insane asylum, which was when the mentally ill were identified as a group with special needs and posing special threats to public order and welfare. Starting in the early to mid-nineteenth century, the mentally ill were increasingly confined to large, separate institutions, called *asylums* in English, *asiles* in French, and *Irrenanstalten* in German.

Many of these institutions are gone now, but the grand edifices remain scattered all over the urban, suburban, and rural landscapes of Europe and North America. Some of them have been converted to open psychiatric wards or general hospitals, others have been repurposed as apartment complexes or business parks or even tourist attractions. Because of the so-called deinstitutionalization of mental health care in the second half of the twentieth century, it is easy to forget how big the old mental hospitals were and how many were confined to them. The great expansion of mental health care in the nineteenth century is one of the first major policy interventions by the modern state in the lives of communities, families, and individuals.

7.2 THE AGE OF THE ASYLUM

More or less concurrently, in the middle of the nineteenth century, all countries in our sample, except Japan, adopted so-called 'lunacy laws.' Those laws typically provided rules for the administration of public asylums, established a state inspectorate for all mental institutions, and regulated procedures of confinement, whether voluntary or involuntary. Prior to the adoption of the lunacy laws, admission to mental institutions was usually unregulated or only lightly regulated. A well-known example was the French Old Regime practice of *lettres de cachet* – sealed letters from the Crown that authorized the confinement of the mentally ill, and others, without legal recourse (Goldstein 1987, 107). One of the main purposes of nineteenth-century legislation was to introduce medical and legal procedures that were meant to make involuntary confinement less arbitrary.

Beginning in the middle of the nineteenth century, when the lunacy laws were being adopted, the population of the insane asylums grew at a high rate in most countries in Western Europe, North America, and Oceania. Figure 7.1 describes the growth of the asylum population in three countries for which we have been able to track down long time series: the Netherlands, Sweden, and the United States. The asylum population grew at an increasing rate throughout the late eighteenth and early twentieth centuries, and in the 1930s, it exceeded 0.3 percent of the population in each country. In countries such as Australia, Ireland, and the New Zealand, an even greater proportion of the population was institutionalized.

The middle of the nineteenth century was also the period in which psychiatry emerged as a distinct profession and scholarly discipline, although the term psychiatry, invented in the early 1820s, was little used at the time. In England, the Association of Medical Officers of Asylums and Hospitals for the Insane, later renamed the Royal College of Psychiatrists, was formed in 1841. A few years later, in 1844, what is now called the American Psychiatric Association was established under the name of the Association of Medical Superintendents of American Institutions for the Insane.[1] In Germany, a psychiatric section of the *Gesellschaft*

[1] The current name, the American Psychiatric Association, was adopted in 1921.

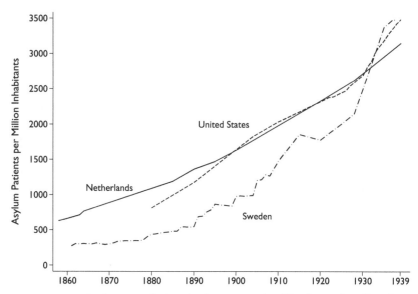

FIGURE 7.1 Asylum populations in three countries. The figure describes the number of asylum inmates per million inhabitants in the Netherlands, Sweden, and the United States from the late 1850s onward. In some cases, different editions of national statistical yearbooks disagreed on the numbers for particular years; we report the latest numbers available, on the assumption that later revisions are more accurate.

Sources: Centraal Bureau voor de Statistiek (Various years) (Netherlands), Statistiska centralbyrån (Various years) (Sweden), and Bureau of Statistics, US Treasury Department (Various years) (United States)

Deutscher Naturforscher und Ärzte was established in 1846; a separate organization for psychiatrists was formed in 1860 and renamed *Deutscher Verein für Psychiatrie* in 1903.[2] These organizations, which are now defined by their links to a particular *profession*, were thus once defined by their links to a particular type of *institution* ('Asylums and Hospitals for the Insane'). With time, because of the close links between asylums (as institutions) and psychiatry (as a profession and a discipline), the term psychiatric hospital came to be preferred over the term asylum, and the terms *hôpital psychiatrique* and *Psychiatrische Klinik* were increasingly used instead of *asile* and *Irrenanstalt* in French and German (on these changes in terminology, see, for instance, Goodwin 1997).

[2] The current name, in English translation, is the German Association of Psychiatry, Psychotherapy, and Psychosomatics.

But even as the names of the institutions changed, the basic model of care – the confinement of the insane in large institutions that were controlled by professionals who sought to apply medical knowledge to mental illness – remained the same, at least until the first decades after the Second World War. Then, beginning in the 1960s and 1970s, a process of 'deinstitutionalization' began all over the West. As a result of several factors, including the widespread critique of large mental institutions in academic circles (see, for example, Foucault 1961; Goffman 1961; Szasz 1961; and Laing 1967), damning depictions of mental hospitals in popular culture (such as Miloš Forman's Academy Award-winning *One Flew over the Cuckoo's Nest*), a desire to save money, and the wide availability of new forms of medication, many, if not most, of the large institutions for the mentally ill were closed. Community care and medication were increasingly preferred over confinement.

This makes the insane asylum unique among the institutions that we examine in this book. In many countries, the creation of a system of asylums was one of the very first major interventions by governments in social life. Consider Ireland, for example, where the creation of a state-mandated asylum system in 1817, under English rule, preceded the creation of most other types of services, including primary education (Brennan 2014, 2).[3] Thus, national systems of asylums were created in the beginning of the period that we examine – in the early nineteenth century – and reached their apogee around the time of the Second World War, when our story ends, but they have now all but disappeared.[4]

---

[3] Regarding France, Castel (1988, 14) notes that the Law of June 30, 1838 concerning the insane was 'the first great legislative measure that recognized a *right of assistance and treatment for a category of the sick or those in need*' (emphasis in original).

[4] Today, there are prominent scholars who argue that the asylum model should be brought back in some altered form (see, for instance, Sacks 2009). Although institutionalization went too far, the argument goes, and although many of the abuses that critics of mental institutions identified in the 1970s and 1980s were real, the asylum model had many virtues, now lost. The mentally ill were often treated neglectfully and cruelly in times past. Referring to the famous nickname of the most well-known insane asylum in England – the Hospital of St. Mary of Bethlehem in London – the historian Roy Porter once noted that 'Bedlam became a byword for man's inhumanity to man' (Porter 1987b, 123). Today, the word bedlam is typically used figuratively, denoting confusion and chaos; that figurative meaning is derived from the nickname of the Bethlehem Hospital in London. But just as the nineteenth century's asylum model of mental health care rarely delivered on its promise to provide compassionate care for the mentally ill, due to overcrowding and underfunding, the pharmacological and community-care model of the late twentieth century has arguably failed to live up to the hopes of postwar psychiatry reformers.

TABLE 7.1 *Early mental hospitals*

Country	First asylum	Year	Type
Australia	Castle Hill Lunatic Asylum, New South Wales	1811	Public
Austria	Narrenturm (Fool's Tower), Vienna	1784	Public
Belgium	The city of Geel, outside Antwerp	1532	Religious
Canada	Hôpital-des-Sœurs-Grises, Montreal	1747	Religious
Denmark	Sct. Hans Hospital, Roskilde	1816	Public
England	Bethlem Royal Hospital, London	1547	Public/rel.
Finland	Själö hospital, outside Åbo	1785	Public
France	Charenton, Val-de-Marne	1701	Religious
Germany	Landes-Irrenanstalt, New Ruppin	1801	Public
Ireland	Magdalen Asylum, Dublin	1765	Religious
Italy	Ospedale di Sant'Orsola, Bologna	1710	Religious
Japan	Metropolitan Matsuzawa Hospital, Tokyo	1879	Public
Netherlands	The madhouse at Zutphen	c.1500	Public
New Zealand	Wellington Lunatic Asylum	1854	Public
Norway	Gaustad Asylum, Oslo	1855	Public
Spain	Hospital de los Inocentes, Valencia	1409	Religious
Sweden	Danviks dårhus, Stockholm	1788	Public
Switzerland	Les Vernets, Geneva	1838	Public
United States	Public Hospital for Persons of Insane and Disordered Minds, Williamsburg, Virginia	1773	Public

Notes: The table lists the first establishment we have found in each country that was devoted exclusively to persons categorized as insane. Some of these establishments existed earlier, for other or for broader purposes; the year given in the table is when the purpose was exclusively to care for and confine the mentally ill.

Sources: Dowbiggin (2011), Earle (1841, 1854), Engstrom (2003), Esquirol (1838), Finnane (1981), Gijswijt-Hofstra (2005), Kringlen (2004), LaBrum (1992), Marx (2008), McCarthy (2010), Moreno and Calixto (2013), Patel et al. (2013), Pylkkänen (2012), Qvarsell (1982), Rosen (1958), Smith (1999a), Stevenson (1988), Sussman (1998), Suzuki (2003a, 2003b), Villasante (2003), Wetterberg (2012), Zalewski (2008), and the contributions to Howells and Osborn (1975)

In Table 7.1, we list some of the earliest institutions that were fully dedicated to the care for and confinement of the mentally ill among the countries in our study, the year in which those institutions were established, and whether they were established as public or private institutions. Determining which establishment came first is not straightforward, since mental hospitals typically emerged through a gradual process of differentiation. First, other institutions – such as prisons, alms houses, and early modern hospitals, which were very different from modern hospitals – began to identify the insane as a special category of inmates or patients. Then separate units within prisons, alms houses, and hospitals were created to confine and treat this category of people. Then separate wings and annexes were built. Then special hospitals were created for the sole purpose of confining and treating the insane. Then, much later, these hospitals turned into modern psychiatric hospitals. We therefore do not claim to have identified *the* first institution in each country, only that the institutions in the list were among the earliest (and are commonly identified as such in the country-specific literature).

Nevertheless, we learn at least two important things from Table 7.1. First of all, whereas there was a great deal of variation among countries – there are good reasons to think that the world's first asylum opened in Spain already in the fifteenth century – in most countries, the first dedicated mental institution opened between the middle of the eighteenth and the middle of the nineteenth centuries, and toward the end of that period, the first lunacy laws were adopted in Europe. Second, whereas early modern mental hospitals were often religious institutions, operated by religious orders, the mental hospitals that opened from the late eighteenth century onward were typically public institutions that were operated by secular authorities, not by the church.

7.3 CENTRALIZING MENTAL INSTITUTIONS

Table 7.2 describes how mental institutions were governed in each of the countries in our study. Figures 7.2 and 7.3, summarize the information in the table by describing the main trends in the period 1800–1939 (Figure 7.2 describes the level of centralization, whereas Figure 7.3 describes the proportion of all countries in which ecclesiastical institutions were involved in running public institutions and in which private mental institutions received public funding).[5] We begin by discussing the variation in centralization among countries and over time.

In the first four decades of the nineteenth century, local authorities were responsible for mentally institutions in almost all countries: most

---

[5] Among the many sources that we have consulted for our survey of these institutions, we would especially like to mention Henry C. Burdett's five-volume study *Hospitals and Asylums of the World* (1891) and the 1885 reports to the House of Commons on the 'lunacy laws' of various countries from British ambassadors around the world (House of Commons 1885).

TABLE 7.2 *How mental institutions were governed*

	Public only	Mix public–church–private
National	Austria (from 1934), Denmark (from 1846), Finland, Germany (from 1933), New Zealand (from 1876), Norway, Sweden.	Austria (before 1864), France (from 1838), Ireland, Italy (from 1928), Japan (from 1919).
Local or regional	Australia, Denmark (before 1846), Japan (before 1900), New Zealand (before 1876), Switzerland (before 1869), the United States (from 1870s)	Austria (1864–1933), Belgium, Canada, France (before 1838), Germany (before 1933), Italy (before 1928), Japan (1900–1918), Netherlands, Spain, Switzerland (from 1869), the United Kingdom, and the United States (before 1870s).

Notes: In 'national' systems, mental institutions were administered by the national government, as opposed to regional or local authorities. In systems with a mix of fully public, church-run, and privately provided services, at least some private insane asylums or psychiatric hospitals received public funding; in some cases, religious authorities were also involved in running public institutions.
Sources: Own categorization based on literature cited in the text

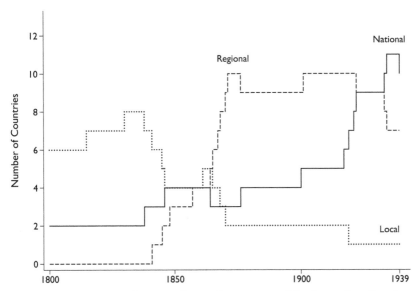

FIGURE 7.2 The centralization of mental institutions. The figure describes the number of countries in the sample that administered mental institutions at the local, regional, and national levels.

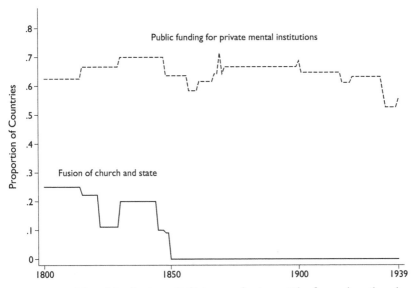

FIGURE 7.3 Mental institutions: Religious and private. The figure describes the proportion of countries in the sample in which mental institutions were governed, at least in part, by church authorities and the proportion of countries in which private mental institutions received public funding.

of the mentally ill were not confined to – or treated in – dedicated institutions; they instead lived in ordinary workhouses, poorhouses, and jails. In two absolute monarchies, however, the central state had begun to assume greater responsibility for mental institutions already in the eighteenth century. One was Austria, where the first dedicated mental hospital, the Fool's Tower (*Narrenturm*), was constructed in the 1780s. The Fool's Tower emerged as a unit within Vienna's great General Hospital (*Allgemeines Krankenhaus*), which, like its Paris equivalent, the *Hôpital général*, was an early modern institution that was very different from today's hospitals; it housed an undifferentiated crowd of the poor, the sick, and the old and indigent. Earle (1854), a nineteenth-century asylum reformer, observed during his journeys in Europe that central-government authorities in Austria were directly involved in the governance of the asylums, issuing decrees about such practical matters as transfers of patients between asylums and appointments of medical staff. Central government authorities also became predominant in Sweden, where the insane asylums were managed by the Order of the Seraphim Guild, a national administrative institution created in 1787 by king Gustav III during Sweden's brief period of absolutism (Schlaug 1989, 27), although steps toward the centralization of mental institutions were taken already during Sweden's proto-democratic Age of Liberty, before Gustav III's coup in 1772 (Eriksson 1989, 221–227). This centralized model persisted in Sweden until the second half of the twentieth century.[6]

As Figure 7.2 shows, the period between the late 1830s and the early 1870s was a particularly intense period in the political history of mental institutions. In this relatively brief period, most of the countries in our sample adopted new laws that centralized the administration of mental institutions either to the regional or to the national level.

The first country that created a national system of mental institutions during this period was France, which is typically credited with adopting

---

[6] Mental hospitals in Sweden were thus governed differently than regular hospitals, which became the responsibility of the county councils (*landsting*) after the 1862 local-government reform. The administration of mental health care was not transferred to the county councils until the second half of the twentieth century (Axelsson 2000, 48). Qvarsell (1982, 49) notes that although the *financial* burden of providing for indigent patients rested on the parishes in the nineteenth century, the parishes did not control the *administration* of the mental hospitals. On the role of local decision makers in initial decisions to commit individuals to mental hospitals in nineteenth-century Sweden, see Riving (2008).

the world's first national lunacy law. There had been repeated attempts to centralize France's asylum system already during the Napoleonic regime of the early 1800s (Castel 1988, 173), but it was the landmark *Loi sur les aliénés*, adopted in 1838, that made the prefect of each French *département* responsible for providing asylums for the mentally ill according to national regulations and standards. As Goldstein (1987, 276) observes, the new law, adopted during the liberal July Monarchy,

> mandated the creation of a nationwide network of asylums staffed by full-time medical doctors and brought into existence a race of psychiatric functionaries appointed by the minister of the interior, removable by him, and paid salaries in accordance with a scale determined by him.

In Denmark, still an absolute monarchy in the middle of the 1840s, the care for the mentally ill became the responsibility of the national government a few years later, in 1846 (as in neighboring Sweden, the care for Denmark's mentally ill was only decentralized in the second half of the twentieth century). The exception to this rule was the hospital of Sankt Hans, in Roskilde near Copenhagen, which was Denmark's first insane asylum and which remained under the control of the City of Copenhagen even as responsibility for mental institutions was transferred to the central government in the rest of the country (Bjerrum 2005; see also Møllerhøj 2008).

In most other countries, asylums were controlled by regional governments, not national authorities, from the 1830s or 1840s onward. In Switzerland, for example, mental institutions have been governed by the cantons from the late 1830s onward (Geneva's Les Vernets, the first cantonal asylum, opened in 1838) (Gasser 2003), and in the Netherlands, provincial governments became financially and administratively responsible for building and running asylums under national legislation adopted in 1841 (Boschma 2003, 33–35). In England and Wales, meanwhile, Wynn's Act 1808 authorized but did not require county justices to build and supervise public asylums (Smith 1999b, 22–23), but it was the Lunacy Act 1845 that shifted the responsibility for asylums entirely from the parishes to county boards, each of which was required to fund at least one public asylum according to the County Asylum Act, which was also adopted in 1845 (see, for example, Jones 1955; Howells and Osborn 1975, 194; Forsythe, Melling, and Adair 1999; and Smith 1999a). The legislation from 1845 created a new, national supervisory body – the Commissioners in Lunacy – but the counties effectively controlled mental institutions until the Second World War (after the war, the mental

institutions were absorbed by the new National Health Service, leading
to a centralized system; see Jones 1972, Chapter 10).[7]

In the United States, the insane asylums were gradually centralized to
the states from the 1820s onward (see Rothman 1990 [1971], Chapter
6, and Grob 1994, 18–29, 172–175). Dowdall (1996, 34) shows that a
large number of state mental hospitals opened around 1890, but quite a
few opened in the 1830s and 1840s, and the rate picked up noticeably in
the 1850s. Since the transition from town-, city-, and county-level care
to state-level care was so gradual and varied so much among the states
(Hurd et al. 1916, Volume I, Chapter IV), it is difficult to determine
exactly when the system changed from predominantly local to predominantly state-based, but by the last decades of the nineteenth century, the
states were clearly dominant. In 1895, the New York state legislature
adopted a law establishing state care for all the insane in that state – a
fully state-based model which then spread with 'comparative rapidity' to
other states (Hurd et al. 1916, Volume I, 167).

There have been two federal mental institutions in the United States.
One was the Government Hospital for the Insane in Washington, DC
(founded in 1855 and renamed St. Elizabeth's Hospital in the 1960s),
which was controlled by the federal government until the 1980s (parts
of the hospital, now managed by the District of Columbia, are still
operational). The other was the Canton Indian Insane Asylum in South
Dakota (1903–1934), which was set up under federal legislation adopted
in 1898. In Chapter 3, we noted that colonial powers have often set
up more centralized public services for the indigenous population than
for settlers; the federal insane asylum for Native Americans in the early
1900s is another example.

The shift in the authority over mental institutions to national and
regional governments in the middle of the nineteenth century is an important event in the history of public services. At the time, most other
services were not as centralized. One plausible explanation is economies
of scale: confining the mentally ill to large establishments turned out to be
a relatively cheap solution to the problem of the rising demand for mental
health care. Local governments were quite simply too small for this task,
paving the way for a shift in authority from the local to the regional or
even the national level. Another explanation is that the commitment of

---

[7] Bartlett (1999, Chapter 6) refers to the Commissioners in Lunacy as a 'soft center' of
reform, noting that they were 'in a position of administrative and political weakness'
(197).

individuals to custodial institutions was a sensitive decision that involved civic rights – an important concern to political leaders in the nineteenth century's constitutional monarchies and emerging democracies.

In Spain, care for the mentally ill remained a local affair slightly longer – the Provinces became responsible in 1868 (Aparicio Basauri 1997) – and in Belgium, local institutions remained important since Belgium's lunacy law from 1850 increased central control but left a great deal of effective authority with municipal governments, who typically contracted with religious hospitals to provide mental health care (Roekens and Majerus 2017).[8] But it was rare for local authorities to remain responsible for mental institutions after the middle of the nineteenth century.

Most of the countries that formed or became independent after the middle of the nineteenth century had already adopted legislation that made mental institutions the responsibility of either regional or national governments. In Canada (Moran 2001) and Italy (Donnelly 1992), mental health care was the responsibility of the provinces. In the German Empire, centralization varied from state to state, which meant that there were three classes of public establishments: state-level ('crown') asylums, provincial and district asylums, and municipal asylums (Burdett 1891, 406). When Australia became an independent, federal country in 1901, finally, the constituent states became responsible for mental institutions (Crichton 1990, 20), as colonial authorities had been before them (Lewis 1988; Monk 2008).

In New Zealand the Constitution Act of 1852 provided that provincial governments were responsible for lunatic asylums, but when the provinces were abolished in 1876, the national government became responsible for the administration, supervision, and governance of mental institutions. The central Lunatic Asylums Department (later renamed the Mental Hospitals Departmen), which was founded in 1876, was the main force behind mental health policy making in New Zealand from then on (Brunton 2001, 143).

When Finland, Ireland, and Norway became independent in the early twentieth century, they already had laws on the books that established national insane asylums managed by the state (for overviews, see

---

[8] As in other countries, there were individual centrally controlled mental hospitals in Spain and Belgium: the model mental hospital in Leganés, founded in 1852 (Villasante 2003), and the famous city of Geel in Belgium, which became a centrally governed *Rijkskolonie* in the same year.

Retterstöl 1975; Pylkkänen 2012; Kelly 2016; and Kringlen 2007). Brennan (2014, 20) notes that already in the beginning of the nineteenth century, the English authorities that governed Ireland opted for a much more centralized model of mental health care than the county-by-county model that was introduced in England and Wales at the same time. The addition of countries with centralized institutions explains the increasing proportion of countries with national mental health programs in Figure 7.2.

The final problem that we need to consider is fascist mental-health policy in the 1920s and early 1930s. As we discussed in Chapter 2, it is sometimes ambiguous how to categorize the organization of mental health care in fascist regimes such as Germany. On the one hand, the formal organization of mental health care did not change much when the National Socialist Party rose to power, which meant that mental institutions continued to be regulated by state governments. But the National Socialist government's eugenics policies, notably the program of forced sterilization that began in the middle of the 1930s, was administered from the Interior Ministry in Berlin (Evans 2005, 507), and the euthanasia program, the outright killing of the mentally ill, was initiated in the Public Health Section of the Interior Ministry before it was transferred to a separate administrative office that later got the name T4 (Benedict, Lagerwey, and Shields 2014, 86–87).[9] This duality of National Socialist mental health policy is consistent with the following observation by Castel in his *Regulation of Madness* (1988, 172):

One can, for example, imagine that a fascist state would have no truck with the "the problem of the mentally ill," unless it were to contrive for it a kind of "final solution" as German Nazism attempted to do.

On balance, we have categorized the fascist countries as having centralized mental institutions. In Italy, the fascist regime introduced new provincial governing boards for mental institutions in 1928, which were appointed directly by the Interior Ministry in Rome.

We end by noting that Japan was a latecomer in the area of mental health (Suzuki 2003b, 193, 202–224). Legislation adopted in 1882 authorized the police and village institutions to order the confinement of disturbing or dangerous lunatics (and to fine families that failed to control mentally ill family members), and legislation from 1900 delegated

---

[9] The first killings of the mentally ill in Germany took place in 1940 (Weindling 1989, 544; see also Foth 2013).

power to police authorities to oversee the care of the ill in their homes, and in mental wards. The first law on mental hospitals, the 1919 Mental Hospitals Act, enabled the large-scale confinement of and care for the mentally ill. The responsibility now rested with the prefectures, which were directly responsible to national authorities. As in most other policy areas, Japan put in place highly centralized institutions for mental health care.

In total, we thus observe nine shifts from a model in which local or regional governments were responsible for mental institutions to a model in which the central government was: Austria and Sweden in the late eighteenth century, France in the 1830s, Denmark in the 1840s, New Zealand in the 1870s, and Japan and the fascist states in Europe in the interwar period. In this list, we find three absolutist monarchies (Austria, Denmark, and Sweden), two constitutional monarchies (France and Japan), three fascist dictatorships, and one democracy (New Zealand). There is thus a great deal of support for the idea of an authoritarian path to centralization.

As in the two public health domains we will turn to in Chapters 8 and 9, the support is less strong for the idea of a liberal-democratic path, since the 1838 law in France, while introduced by liberals (Goldstein 1987), was not adopted in a democracy, and since the centralization of mental institutions in New Zealand was a consequence of the abolition of the provinces and not a reform that a liberal government pursued to improve mental health care per se. Nevertheless, the July Monarchy in France was an early constitutional regime and an open political system for its time, and in his discussion of the 1838 law, Castel (1988, 179) emphasizes the interest of the bourgeois class that rose to prominence after 1830 in 'if not breaking, at least in controlling the symbiosis of the traditional family and religion, which sustained the power of the most conservative Notables.' There were conflicts over the extent of the central government's authority in parliament, but as Castel (1988, 184) shows, the compromise that resulted from that conflict was one that permitted public funding for private mental institutions, not a break with centralism.

It is also worth noting, however, that in comparison with the intense political struggles over services such as schooling and vaccinations, there do not appear to have been intense conflicts over how to govern insane asylums. When the lunacy law of 1838 came up for a vote in the French legislature, all members of the upper house, the *Chambre des pairs*, and all but six of the members of the lower house, the *Chambre des députés*, voted for it (Quétel 2012, 183). When the English Lunacy Act 1845 was adopted, there was a similarly high level of support for the new legislation in the House of Commons (Jones 1955).

7.4 RELIGIOUS AND PRIVATE ASYLUMS

We now turn to the second part of our analysis, which is concerned with the role of the church in the governance of asylums and the role of private mental institutions in national systems of mental health care.

As Figure 7.3 shows, religious authorities were rarely involved in the administration of public mental institutions after the first decades of the twentieth century, which sets mental institutions apart from many of the other services we cover in this book, but which is consistent with our expectation that the fusion of church and state ended earlier and with less controversy in the domain of public and mental health than in schooling. We only find three countries where churches were involved in the administration of public mental institutions, and all of those countries opted for more secular institutions when they introduced their lunacy laws in the first half of the nineteenth century. In Spain, the Beneficence Act of 1822 led to a clearer demarcation between secular authorities and religious groups in public health and health care (Aparicio Basauri 1997, 74). In England, the central role played by the parishes before the New Poor Law and the adoption of the Lunacy Act meant that the national church had a formal role in the governance of mental institutions in the early nineteenth century (Jones 1955, 11–15). In Belgium, finally, there was no clear distinction between church and state in the first half of the nineteenth century, and after that time, religious asylums and mental hospitals continued to play a major role, although it is one that we categorize as subsidization and not fusion. In all other countries, mental institutions were secular already in the year 1800.

Secular and religious authority were thus rarely *fused* in the area of mental health care. As we will see, private asylums did receive public funding in many countries – most countries, in fact – but the relationship between public authorities and religious providers of mental health care was contractual, not constitutional. Even in countries with established state churches, insane asylums and other mental institutions were typically placed under the control of secular authorities, such as the county councils in England and Wales after the adoption of the Lunacy Law 1845 or the Order of the Seraphim Guild in Sweden, established in the late eighteenth century. Even in a country such as Ireland, where the church was deeply embedded in the provision of many other public services, notably education and health care, 'religious organisations and administrative frameworks had only marginal involvement in the national asylum infrastructure' (Brennan 2014, 2).

One possible explanation for the absence of religious involvement is the strong relationship between centralization and secularization. One of the reasons that religious authorities mattered more in other policy domains is that the church typically had a strong presence at the local level, whereas the national government did not; once the insane asylums became regional or even national institutions, the church had less to offer in terms of the needed institutional capacity.

Private asylums and mental hospitals existed in most countries. As Figure 7.3 shows, more than half of the countries in our study provided public funding for such private institutions (in the remaining countries, they only catered to fee-paying patients from well-to-do families).

There are a few countries in which the practice of providing public funding for private mental institutions appears to have been particularly widespread. Throughout the period we consider, for example, private organizations and religious orders have received public funding to care for the mentally ill in Québec, a colony and later province had operated what was known at the time as a 'farming out'-system, granting an effective monopoly to the private hospital at Beauport for much of the nineteenth century and then entering into a contract with a Catholic sisterhood (Moran 2001, Chapter 1; see also Hurd et al. 1916, Chapter XIII, Section V). In England, the practice of 'farming out' began even earlier. As William Parry-Jones documented in his study *The Trade in Lunacy* (1972), the indigent mentally ill were often boarded out to private providers already in the eighteenth century. By 1900, which is the last year that we have data for, there were still a few private institutions in England that received pauper lunatics (Murphy 2003, 341 notes that '[p]rivate licensed houses played an important and respected part in the grand scheme until the last years of the nineteenth century'). In Belgium and the Netherlands, private asylums and mental hospitals – typically run by religious organizations – have long received public funding from local and provincial authorities; indeed, as Goodwin (1997, 20–21) notes, 'asylums were largely developed by charitable groups, particularly religious organizations' (see also Gijswijt-Hofstra 2005, 40, who notes an 'important shift from the public to the voluntary sector' in the late nineteenth century). In France, the 1838 law on asylums provided funding not only for public asylums but also for private ones (*des asiles privés faisant fonction d'asiles publics*). Even before 1838, officials in some parts of France paid religious orders to provide care for the mentally ill rather than establishing new public asylums (Goldstein 1987, Chapter 6). In Italy and Spain, finally, public authorities have long provided public funding for private providers of mental health care (Donnelly 1992, 29; Goodwin 1997, 17; Lopez Ibor 1975).

In other countries, the provision of public funding for private mental institutions was not an integral part of the national system of mental health care, but a more marginal phenomenon – a recourse for local, regional, and national governments that could not otherwise meet the high level of demand for mental health care. In all the German-speaking countries in Europe, for instance, governments sometimes paid private hospitals to provide care for the mentally ill (Dowbiggin 2011, 42–43), but not on a large scale. Although most asylum patients in the German Empire were in public asylums, to take one example, the demand for mental health care was so high that patients were sometimes placed in private asylums at public expense (Engstrom 2003, 16–19, 85). In neighboring Switzerland, most private institutions catered exclusively to fee-paying patients (Shorter 1990), but in smaller, rural cantons without their own public asylums, public authorities sometimes subsidized private asylums (they also had the option of transferring patients to public institutions elsewhere).[10] In the United States, Hurd et al. (1916, Volume I, Chapter VIII) notes that many nineteenth-century hospitals for the insane were public–private hybrids, but that this practice ceased when public institutions were established in states where public authorities had until then sent patients to private institutions.

One interesting feature of mental health care is that public authorities sometimes subsidized the treatment of mentally ill individuals in private homes. This practice, *privatpleien*, had a long history in Norway, particularly in the more remote areas of the country (Kringlen 2007, 97–98). Subsidized care for the mentally ill in individual homes was also

---

[10] In Ireland, there were relatively few private providers, but as a result of high demand for mental health care after the First World War, it was not uncommon for public authorities to board out patients to private institutions (Walsh and Daly 2004). In the nineteenth century, Brennan (2014, 2) notes, there was 'minimal private enterprise in the provision of asylum accommodation.' In Japan, private mental hospitals were first established for paying patients in the 1870s; after the adoption of the Mental Patients Custody Act in 1900, patients paid for with public funding were sometimes cared for in private hospitals, leading to a private-public hybrid system that remained after the adoption of national legislation in 1919 since the government needed the infrastructure of already built private asylums for the public asylum project (Veith 1975).

an important element of mental health care in Italy in the nineteenth and early twentieth centuries (Guarnieri 2005). In these countries, the treatment of the mentally ill thus had a lot in common with the treatment of and care for orphans and other groups that could not support themselves easily.

In countries where a mixed economy of mental health care existed, the main explanation seems to be convenience, not the idea that public support for private mental institutions might offer a solution to religious conflict. States quite simply lacked the infrastructural and administrative capacity to meet the great demand for mental health care in the nineteenth-century world, and unwilling to make great investment in new institutions, they turned to the existing private sector. In most cases, public-funding-for-private-provision policies involved public authorities paying for indigent mentally ill patients who were placed in private asylums and hospitals because of overflow from the public system. The private organization that was best equipped to provide this service was often the Catholic church. Consequently, almost all of the countries in our sample that provided public funding for private mental institutions were Catholic or religiously mixed countries; in the Lutheran countries in Northern Europe, mental institutions were almost exclusively public. Over time, the subsidization of private mental institutions in countries such as Belgium and the Netherlands fit well into the 'consociational' political structures that emerged in those countries (Lijphart 1968); but such political considerations do not appear to explain the initial choices that nineteenth-century governments made to rely on private organizations.

In countries that formed or became independent toward the late nineteenth and in the early twentieth century, the subsidization of private mental institutions has been more rare. In New Zealand, as Brunton (2001, 33) puts it, 'mental health became a public policy issue and ... specialized services were provided predominantly by the state rather than by private or voluntary agencies.' In neighboring Australia, health care and social welfare were often provided by private organizations, but mental health care was not. Australia's first-ever statistical yearbook noted that whereas the 'large metropolitan hospitals' were 'partially subsidized by the State or State-endowed, but receiving also private aid,' the 'lunatic asylums in the various States' belonged to a category of institutions that were 'wholly provided by the state, *qua* State' (Commonwealth Bureau of Census and Statistics 1907, 774). According to the Statistical Yearbook from 1937 (page 238) there were only four 'licensed private houses' by 1935, with a total of 80 patients, and all were in the state

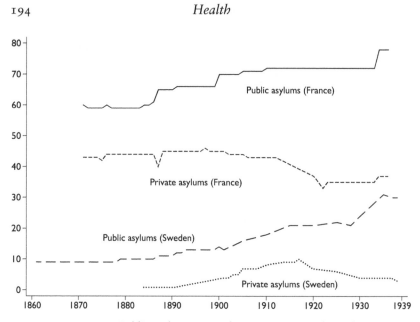

FIGURE 7.4 Public and private asylums in France and Sweden.
Sources: Ministère de l'Agriculture et du Commerce (Various years) (France) and
Statistiska centralbyrån (Various years) (Sweden)

of Victoria. In Finland, as far as we have been able to tell, private institutions also did not receive public funding. According to Burdett (1891,
503), there was, in the late nineteenth century, a home for 'idiots' in Finland that was legally private but publicly funded. To the extent that this
home was a part of the mental health system, however, it was a very small
part of that system.

In many countries, private asylums appears to have been the most
prevalent in the beginning of the twentieth century. Consider, for example, the evidence in Figure 7.4, which describes the number of private
mental institutions in France (which provided public funding for private
establishments) and Sweden (which did not), on the basis of the official
statistics of the era. As the figure shows, many private mental institutions
closed in the interwar period.

7.5 CONCLUSIONS

The expansion of mental institutions in the nineteenth and early twentieth centuries was a crucial event in the emergence of the modern state. In
some countries, such as Ireland, the establishment of a national system of

mental hospitals was the first major intervention of governments in social life in the modern era, and in all countries in our sample, the asylum population grew markedly in the nineteenth century. By the early twentieth century, it was not uncommon, among the rich countries, for half a percent of the adult population, or more, to be committed to mental institutions.

Mental institutions were much more likely to be centralized than other public services. Whereas services such as education, libraries, and midwifery were normally provided locally or in some cases regionally, most countries chose to establish large mental hospitals that were controlled by regional governments or, often, by the national government. The differences among countries and over time can be explained, as in most of the other chapters in this book, by a combination of institutional and party-political factors. Centralization was especially common in absolute monarchies (early nineteenth century) and authoritarian states (early twentieth century), but there have also been examples of liberal-democratic regimes where governments have centralized mental health services. After the Second World War, the creation of the National Health Service out of Britain's old county-by-county system of mental health care is another example of this path to centralization.

In comparison with other public services – including public-health services such as midwifery and vaccinations – mental institutions were secularized early, as power and responsibility were transferred from parishes and ecclesiastical institutions to medical, political, and legal authorities. The provision of public funding for private mental institutions, finally, was widespread, but it seems to have had relatively little to do with solving religious conflict; it seems to have had more to do with the inability of public authorities to keep up with the rising demand for mental health care during the 100-year-long age of the asylum in the nineteenth and early twentieth centuries and the availability of a private or parochial sector in many countries that could absorb new patients.

8

Vaccinations

[T]he small pox was always present, filling the churchyards with
corpses, tormenting with constant fears all whom it had not yet
stricken, leaving on those whose lives it spared the hideous traces
of its power, turning the babe into a changeling at which the mother
shuddered, and making the eyes and cheeks of the betrothed maiden
objects of horror to the lover.

Thomas Macaulay, *The History of England* (1848)

At the turn of the nineteenth century, smallpox was endemic in Western
Europe, North America, and Japan. As recently as the 1870s, hundreds
of thousands of Europeans were killed in the smallpox epidemic that
broke out during the 1870–1871 war between France and Prussia (Rolleston 1933). By the 1930s, however, smallpox was effectively eradicated
in the world's rich countries. In the second half of the 1930s, no one
died from smallpox in Austria, Belgium, Denmark, Germany, Ireland,
Norway, Sweden, or Switzerland, and only a handful died in Australia,
Finland, Italy, the Netherlands, and the United Kingdom. There were
twelve recorded deaths in Canada, twenty-five in France, and forty-two
in Japan. Among the countries in our study, smallpox claimed more than
a hundred lives in only two – one was the United States, with 183 deaths;
the other was Civil War Spain, with 626.[1]

---

[1] The death counts are from Dixon (1962, Appendix II). On the smallpox outbreak in
Civil War Spain, see, for instance, Hopkins (2002, 98). Dixon provides no data for New
Zealand, but smallpox was always rare in New Zealand due to the country's remoteness
from everywhere else; see Maclean (1964, Chapter XI), who notes that there were only
nine recorded deaths between 1872 and 1900, and Dow (1995, 12).

One of the main causes of the decline of smallpox in Western Europe, North America, and Japan was the discovery of the world's first vaccine in the late 1790s and the ensuing efforts by governments, professional societies, and others to encourage or enforce vaccination.[2] The introduction of national vaccination programs is an early example of how the nineteenth century's revolution in government changed the state's role in society. When the English physician Edward Jenner published his findings on the smallpox vaccine in 1798, states provided few broad-based public services, yet most governments in Western Europe put in place some form of vaccination policy within a few decades of Jenner's discovery. The smallpox programs are also an early example of how the nineteenth century's revolution in government changed *politics*, for anti-vaccinationism was a powerful political movement in the nineteenth and early twentieth centuries, as it is today.[3]

The delivery of the smallpox vaccine was different from other public services such as policing (Chapter 3), schooling (Chapter 5), and psychiatric care (Chapter 7) in at least two important respects, which complicates the analysis of the role played by national, regional, and local authorities, churches, and private organizations and individuals. First of all, as Chapter 1's tours of Gothenburg and Montreal suggested, vaccinations were not provided in designated buildings. Second, vaccine delivery was not the province of one particular profession. In today's world, vaccines are almost always provided by medical professionals such as doctors and nurses, but in the nineteenth century, governments relied on a wide array of officials and volunteers, including teachers, priests, midwives, general practitioners, and district physicians, to deliver the new smallpox vaccine.

---

[2] Even McKeown (1979, 30), who famously argued that the nineteenth century's decline in mortality was a result of broad public health measures such as improved sanitation, and not of medical advances, agrees that the smallpox vaccine contributed to the decline in the death rate in Europe before 1900.

[3] The most comprehensive study of the relationship between public health and the state in the nineteenth and early twentieth centuries is Peter Baldwin's *Contagion and the State* (1999), which analyzes government responses to cholera, smallpox, and syphilis in England, France, Germany, and Sweden between 1830 and 1930. With the exception of Baldwin's book and a few other important studies that are mainly concerned with anti-vaccinationism, most available studies of smallpox and the smallpox vaccine are written by public health specialists, who deal mainly with problems such as the effectiveness of vaccines and the costs and benefits of making vaccinations compulsory, not with the broader political and administrative problems that concern us here.

We identify a few countries that achieved a particularly high level of centralization of their national vaccination programs, and most of those countries were nineteenth-century monarchies, although one, New Zealand, was a liberal democracy. The findings in this chapter are thus consistent with this book's general argument about two paths to centralization, one authoritarian and one liberal-democratic. But we also note that most of the major administrative reforms regarding vaccine delivery occurred in the nineteenth century, and especially in the aftermath of the Franco-Prussian War in the 1870s; after that period, the prevalence of smallpox declined, and the salience of vaccination policy declined with it. Except for a few reforms that were occasioned by resistance to compulsory vaccination, the early twentieth-century history of smallpox vaccination is largely a matter of the incorporation of vaccinations in each country's growing health care system. Interestingly, the National-Socialist government in Germany after 1933, which centralized so many other public services, does not seem to have pushed for the centralization of Germany's vaccination program; indeed, at least initially, the Nazi government continued a policy of liberalization that had begun in the Weimar Republic (Thießen 2013, 46–56).

When it comes to the role of churches and private service providers, we find that many governments relied on the clergy and on doctors in private practice, but they typically did so for pragmatic and not for political reasons. The clergy played an important administrative role in some European countries since public authorities sometimes relied on priests and church wardens to deliver the vaccine, notably in Lutheran states such as Sweden (Sköld 1996b). Moreover, and perhaps more importantly, church officials were sometimes tasked with keeping track of each individual's vaccination status in civil registries and other public records. The influence of the church waned without much controversy, however, once medical authorities enhanced their administrative capabilities toward the end of the nineteenth century. When it comes to the role of private vaccinators, we find a mixed economy of vaccine delivery in most of continental Europe and on the British Isles.

In addition to answering our main research questions about when and where vaccination programs emerged and how they were governed, this chapter highlights a few topics that set vaccinations apart from other public services, notably the emergence of antivaccinationism as a significant political movement in the nineteenth century.

8.1 DISEASE BEFORE THE NINETEENTH CENTURY

The titles of two recent popular histories of smallpox, *The Greatest Killer* (Hopkins 2002) and *The Angel of Death* (Williams 2010), speak for themselves: smallpox was a lethal and frightening disease. In fact, going by the total number of fatalities, smallpox was the deadliest infectious disease in human history. It was caused by two different viruses: *Variola major*, which caused the more common and more deadly form of the disease, and *Variola minor*, which caused a less common and less deadly form. *Variola major* killed approximately 30 percent of its victims and left survivors horribly scarred (Bliss 1991, 40 notes that mirrors were not allowed in smallpox hospitals). Smallpox was endemic in human populations for at least 3,000 years, probably much longer, until its eradication in the late 1970s through a worldwide program run by the World Health Organization (Fenner et al. 1988).[4]

The story of the discovery of the smallpox vaccine is well known. After observing that milkmaids rarely contracted smallpox, the English physician Edward Jenner conjectured in the 1790s that exposure to cowpox, a disease that is similar to smallpox and transferable from cows to humans, rendered milkmaids immune. To test this hypothesis, Jenner infected a young boy with cowpox and later exposed him to the smallpox virus. When the boy showed no signs of smallpox infection, Jenner wrote up his results in a paper that was published in 1798. The most important implication of Jenner's finding was that exposure to cowpox, which is not dangerous for humans, gave immunity to smallpox, which is very dangerous indeed.

The term vaccine – derived from the Latin word for 'cow,' *vacca* – serves as a reminder that a cow-borne disease was used to produce the world's first vaccine. For almost a century after Jenner's discovery, the smallpox vaccine was the only vaccine in use (the cholera vaccine was invented in the 1880s). The first documented use of the term vaccination in a more general sense – referring to immunization against diseases other than smallpox – is typically attributed to the French biologist Louis Pasteur in 1881.

---

[4] Smallpox is the only infectious disease affecting humans that has ever been eradicated. Today, the world's only known stocks of the smallpox virus are held in two laboratories in Russia and the United States. On July 1, 2014, around lunchtime, six vials containing *Variola major* were found in a cardboard box in a cold-storage room in Maryland (Reardon 2014). Those vials were destroyed in 2015.

Early modern states did not stand idly by when infectious diseases spread. In early modern England, for example, the state sought to prevent the spread of plague by quarantining the sick, discouraging public gatherings, and forcing those who had been exposed to infection to carry identifying marks (see Slack 1985, especially Part III). In early modern German states, governments appointed officials at all levels of public administration who were responsible for the supervision of public health and health care (Hennock 1998, 50); the German term *Medizinpolicey*, 'medical police,' stems from this period (Heidenheimer 1986, 4, see also Chapter 3 in this book).[5]

Quarantines, *cordons sanitaires*, and other policies at the more coercive end of the spectrum remained important instruments of disease control in the nineteenth century and beyond (as discussed extensively in Baldwin 1999). But vaccination was a different sort of policy, which heralded a new era in the governance of public health. It was an individualized approach to the prevention of disease, not a collective one. It was also a service that was provided to the population as a whole, not in particular areas, as Victorian sanitation policies were, and it involved everyone, not only particular groups in which disease was spreading, as quarantines were. Consequently, vaccination was a broad-based 'human' service, as defined in Chapter 2.

Vaccination was also qualitatively different from an earlier method that was sometimes used to render individuals immune to smallpox in the eighteenth and even the early nineteenth centuries: 'variolation,' which was the practice of blowing dried smallpox scabs into the nose or rubbing infected pus into small cuts in the skin. From a medical point of view, the advantage of vaccination over variolation was that it did not risk causing a full-blown smallpox infection, as variolation did. As James Scott (1998, 325–327) notes in *Seeing Like a State*, vaccination was also qualitatively different from variolation in another sense: the adoption of vaccination instead of variolation is a paradigmatic example of how social problems become amenable to state action and the creation of uniform, comprehensive public programs. In Scott's terms, vaccination was a scientific approach that enabled political authorities to 'see' disease 'like a state,' whereas variolation was, by its very nature, more difficult for states to implement uniformly. There are several examples among the countries

---

[5] In the nineteenth century, the distinctively German tradition of medical police was an important part of the explanation for the early adoption of compulsory vaccination in some preunification German states (Hennock 1998, 50–52).

we have studied of political leaders that sought to promote and encourage variolation in the eighteenth century – consider, for example, future US president George Washington's decision to order the variolation of the Continental Army during the Revolutionary War – but there was nothing as broad based as the vaccination programs of the nineteenth and twentieth centuries.

With the dissemination of the smallpox vaccine, it became possible, for the first time ever, to establish a uniform, national public health program that targeted a particular disease and that reached, at least potentially, the entire population. Smallpox was but one of many widely feared infections in the nineteenth-century world, and other communicable diseases – such as cholera, diphtheria, dysentery, tuberculosis, and typhus – were often more deadly.[6] But because of the discovery of the smallpox vaccine the policies that states adopted to prevent the spread of smallpox were different. This point has not gone unnoticed by historians of health care and public health. For example, Lambert (1962) treats the English mid-nineteenth-century vaccination program as a precursor of the postwar National Health Service, and Huerkamp (1985) regards the spread of smallpox vaccination in Germany as an important first step in the 'medicalization' of the general public.

8.2 GOVERNMENTS AND THE SMALLPOX VACCINE

News of Edward Jenner's discovery of the smallpox vaccine spread quickly across Europe at the turn of the nineteenth century (on the 'remarkable speed of dissemination of Jennerian vaccination,' see, for example, Bazin 2011, 76–87; see also Jannetta 2007, Chapter 2). By 1803, Jenner's 1798 paper had been translated into all major Western European languages. The first vaccinations were typically carried out by individual physicians who had received samples of the vaccine through professional networks, often under the auspices of learned societies (in France, interestingly, the first vaccination, in 1800, was performed by Philippe Pinel, the psychiatric reformer at the Paris hospitals of Bicêtre and La Salpêtrière whom we encountered in Chapter 7). Within a few years, the smallpox vaccine spread to continents other than Europe; it

---

[6] In Sweden in 1865, to take just one example, there were 661 deaths from smallpox, a normal number for the 1860s; in the same year, there were 2,250 deaths from scarlet fever and 929 from 'typhoid fevers' (Statistiska centralbyrån 1880).

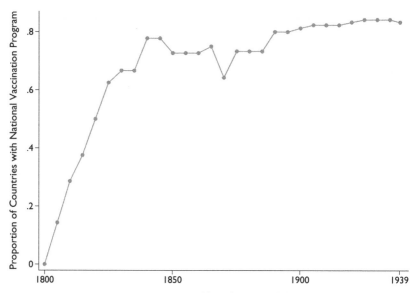

FIGURE 8.1 Vaccination: National legislation and directives. The figure
describes the proportion of countries in the sample in which governments had
put in place some form of vaccination program, understood as a piece of
legislation or government directive promoting or requiring vaccination within
the country's territory.
Sources: Andersen (1973), Bazin (2000), Cardona (2005), Cumpston (1925), Darmon
(1986), Dow (1995), Flamm and Vutuc (2010), Hennock (1998), Hopkins (2002), Irwin
(1910), Jackson (1969), Jannetta (2007), Lambert (1962), Larsen (2012), Pitkänen,
Mielke, and Jorde (1989), Porter (1999), Ritzmann (2015), Rutten (1997), Sköld (1996a),
SOU (1937:28)

reached the United States in 1800 and South America and Asia in 1803–
1806. Since no method of storing the vaccine in bottles or vials had yet
been invented, the early nineteenth century's intercontinental expeditions
brought along orphans from European orphanages, who were vaccinated
from arm to arm during the long sea voyages, storing the live cowpox
virus within their bodies (Smith 1974).

Governments became involved in the provision of vaccinations within
their territories remarkably quickly, when one considers how few public services governments provided otherwise at the turn of the nineteenth
century. Figure 8.1 describes the proportion of countries in our sample
that had adopted some form of legislation or issued some authoritative
government directive concerning vaccination over the period between
1800 and 1939. It only took twenty years for more than half of the countries in our study to adopt such a policy. Toward the end of the period, the

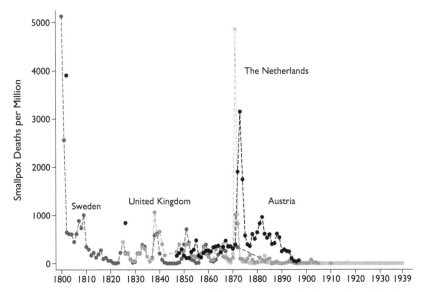

FIGURE 8.2 Deaths from smallpox in four countries. The figure describes the number of smallpox deaths per million living in Austria, the Netherlands, Sweden, and the United Kingdom.

Sources: Edwardes (1902), Hennock (1998), Pitkänen, Mielke, and Jorde (1989), Rutten (1997), Simon (1857), and Sköld (1996b)

only countries in our study that had not put in place a national vaccination policy were the three large, federal states of Australia, Canada, and the United States (each of which had state-level legislation on the books).

Figure 8.2 describes the number of smallpox deaths per million per year in four countries: Austria, the Netherlands, Sweden, and the United Kingdom. The high death tolls in the beginning of the period are clearly visible in the Swedish data (which go back the longest). So is the large drop in infections once the vaccine was introduced, and so is a cyclical pattern of infection and death during the nineteenth century. So are the high death rates in the wake of the Franco-Prussian War – particularly in Austria and the Netherlands, as one would expect, given their proximity to the main theater of the war. The many deaths from smallpox in the early 1870s had a powerful effect on the politics of vaccinations, as it led to a flurry of legislative activity in many countries.

The most contentious issue in political debates over vaccination in the nineteenth and early twentieth centuries was whether vaccination should be made compulsory (and, if so, whether it should be compulsory for the general population or only for infants and school-age children).

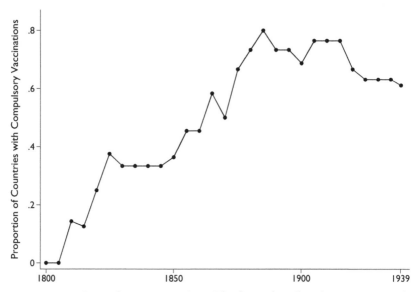

FIGURE 8.3 Compulsory vaccinations. The figure describes the proportion of
countries in the sample in which vaccinations were compulsory, either for
children or for the general population.

Sources: Baldwin (1999), Cardona (2005), Cumpston (1914, 1925), Darmon (1986),
Dixon (1962), Dow (1995), Edwardes (1902), Fenner et al. (1988), Hennock (1998),
Hopkins (2002), Irwin (1910), Jackson (1969), Jannetta (2007), Kohn (2007), Laurent
(2012), Maclean (1964), Porter (1999), Rolleston (1933), Rutten (1997), SOU (1937:28),
Tortella (2000), Williams (2010)

Already in the 1800s and 1810s, several states in Continental and Northern Europe, including Bavaria, Bohemia, Denmark, and Sweden, made
smallpox vaccination compulsory for children. Many other states followed. In some countries, compulsion was direct: there were immediate
penalties for those who refused to vaccinate their sons and daughters.
In other countries, compulsion was more indirect: unvaccinated children
were not allowed to enroll in schools, or unvaccinated men and women
could not get a marriage certificate.

As Figure 8.3 shows, the proportion of countries in our sample in
which smallpox vaccination was compulsory increased from approximately 20 to approximately 70 percent between the early 1850s and the
1880s. During the nineteenth century, it was found that a single smallpox vaccination was insufficient to produce lifelong immunity; beginning
in the middle third of the nineteenth century, public health authorities
in many countries therefore began to encourage – or even require –
revaccination.

Since the smallpox vaccine contributed to the decline of one of history's most dreaded diseases, one might have expected vaccinators to be universally welcomed, but they were not. As Schumpeter (1942, 252) noted long ago, "'Health' might be desired by all, yet people would still disagree on vaccination and vasectomy,' and in many of the countries in our study, there were influential antivaccinationist movements. In a few countries, those movements were politically successful.

England is a particularly interesting, and well-known, example (see especially Williamson 2007). Compulsory vaccination was introduced in England 1853, but in 1898, the law on vaccination was changed, allowing parents who were 'conscientious objectors' to refuse vaccination for their children (a subsequent change in the law in 1907 reinforced this new and more liberal policy). Section ii, Subsection (i) of the Vaccination Act of 1898 reads,

No parent or other person shall be liable to any penalty ...if within four months from the birth of the child he satisfies two justices or a stipendiary or metropolitan police magistrate in petty sessions that he conscientiously believes that vaccination would be prejudicial to the health of the child, and within seven days thereafter delivers to the vaccination officer for the district a certificate by such justices or magistrate of such conscientious objection. (British Medical Journal 1898)

This was the first time ever that 'conscientious objection' appeared in any piece of legislation.[7]

In other countries, antivaccinationist groups organized large-scale protests, and even riots. The social unrest during the smallpox epidemic in Montreal in 1885 is one example (Bliss 1991; see also Chapter 1). Two other examples are the vaccination riots in Milwaukee in the mid-1890s (Leavitt 1976) and those in Rio de Janeiro in 1904 (Needell 1987).

In today's world, antivaccinationism is primarily directed against the childhood vaccine against measles, mumps, and rubella, following fraudulent reports in the 1990s of a link between the MMR vaccine and autism. But antivaccinationism is as old as vaccinations: the very first vaccine provoked similar opposition.

The antivaccinationist movements of the nineteenth and early twentieth centuries were composed of different religious, ethnic, and social groups, and there is no obvious connection between antivaccinationism

---

[7] In Germany in 1874, the compulsory vaccination bill that the government introduced after the Franco-Prussian War was opposed by many members of the Catholic and Social Democratic Parties (the bill passed with 183 votes in favor and 119 against) (Huerkamp 1985, 627).

and any particular creeds or social classes. For example, in Montreal in the 1880s, conservative Catholics were staunch opponents of vaccinations (Bliss 1991), but in majority-Catholic France and Italy, Catholic priests were among the most important advocates of vaccination (Bercé 1983). In the United States at the turn of the twentieth century, African Americans and recent immigrants were more likely to be opposed to vaccinations than whites, although most of the activists in the anti-vaccinationist organizations were middle-class Americans of European descent (Willrich 2011); in England, on the other hand, antivaccination-ist organizations had a working-class base. Looking for the causes of antivaccinationism in the doctrines of any particular religious denomina-tion, or in the specific interests of any particular ethnic group or social class, therefore seems unpromising. More likely, antivaccinationism was a result of more general antiestablishment sentiments and a sense of political exclusion and distrust among different groups.

8.3 CENTRALIZING VACCINATIONS

Vaccination programs varied in both of the two main dimensions we examine in this book: the vertical and the horizontal. Table 8.1 sum-marizes our categorization of how national vaccination programs were governed in the nineteen countries in our study between 1800 and 1939. In some countries, vaccination programs were highly centralized; in oth-ers local and regional authorities were mainly responsible for vaccine delivery and enforcement. In some countries, but not others, the church played an important role in the administration of vaccinations in the nineteenth century. Finally, in some countries, local, regional, or national governments channelled public funding to private vaccinators; in other countries, governments relied exclusively on some combination of public initiatives and voluntary and philanthropic efforts.

As we discussed in the introduction to this chapter, smallpox vacci-nations were different from other public services in important respects, since vaccinations were performed by many different sorts of officials, organizations, and individuals, not by a single profession, and since they were not provided in designated buildings. Local, regional, and national governments played a different role when it came to vaccinations than they did for other public services; especially in the first decades after the invention of the smallpox vaccine, the role of public authorities was often to encourage and coordinate wider efforts to deliver the smallpox

TABLE 8.1 *How vaccinations were governed*

	Public only	Mix public–church–private
National	Denmark (from the 1870s), Japan (from 1872), New Zealand (from 1872), Norway, Sweden (from 1873)	*Church involved*: Denmark (1810s to 1870s); *funding for private vaccinators*: Netherlands (from 1872)
Local or regional	Australia, Austria (from 1836), Belgium, Canada, Finland, Japan (1869–1871), the Netherlands (before 1872), New Zealand (before 1872), Spain (from 1820s), Sweden (1850s to 1872), United Kingdom (before 1867), United States	*Church involved*: Austria (before 1836), Denmark (before 1810), Spain (before 1820s), Sweden (before 1850s); *subsidies for private vaccinators*: France, Germany, Ireland, Italy, Japan (before 1869), Switzerland, United Kingdom (from 1867)

Notes: In 'national' systems, the national government played a particularly important role in the direction and coordination of national vaccination programs. In systems that are categorized as having a mix of public, church, and private, either religious authorities were directly involved in the administration or governance of vaccinations that were carried out by public authorities, or public authorities paid private vaccinators to provide vaccinations (typically for the poor), or both.
Sources: Own categorization based on literature cited in the text

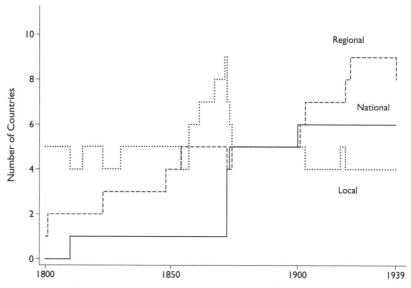

FIGURE 8.4 Vaccinations: Local, regional, and central. The figure describes the number of countries in the sample that administered public vaccination programs primarily at the local, regional, and national levels.

vaccine, not to provide it directly. Our standard approach to the problem of centralization – which is to begin the analysis with how public officials were appointed, monitored, and promoted – is complicated by these characteristics of vaccination programs.

What we have tried to do, therefore, is to identify countries in which some central government authority was responsible for directing and coordinating efforts to increase vaccination coverage, and where there were administrative mechanisms – such as a network of centrally appointed district physicians or other agents of the national government – that assisted central authorities in implementing their policies.

As Figure 8.4 shows, local authorities were primarily responsible for carrying out vaccinations in most countries until the beginning of the 1870s. By the last third of the nineteenth century, however, after the smallpox epidemic in the 1870s, it was just as common for provincial and national authorities to administer vaccinations, and in the first decades of the twentieth century, the most common arrangement was for regional authorities to be in control. The information summarized in Table 8.1 and Figure 8.4 suggests once more that the epidemic during and after the Franco-Prussian War of 1870–1871 was a watershed in the development of national vaccination programs – what proved to be the last major smallpox epidemic in Western Europe also proved to be a formative moment in the development of public health policy.

Judging from the literature we have consulted on national vaccination efforts, all of the states that centralized their vaccination programs were nineteenth-century monarchies – Denmark, Japan, the Netherlands, and Sweden – with the exception of one nineteenth-century liberal democracy, New Zealand. These findings are largely consistent with the principal argument about centralization in this book, which is that there were two paths to centralization, one authoritarian and one liberal-democratic.

In the Danish case, we base our conclusions on the early establishment of a Royal Commission on vaccination (General Board of Health 1857, 174), which was active between 1801 and 1825 (when its function was taken over by the national Board of Health); the early adoption of compulsory vaccination in 1810 (although direct penalties were only introduced in the 1870s, as discussed in Bonderup 2001); and, importantly, the decision, also in 1810 (Sköld 1996b, 385), to involve district physicians appointed by the national government in the implementation of national vaccination policies in Denmark's health districts (on the policy changes in 1810, see also Vallgårda 2004, 94). Bonderup (2001, Chapters III–IV) offers a nuanced picture of early vaccinations in Denmark, emphasizing the interaction between public authorities and private initiatives, but notes several early initiatives at the central political and administrative levels.

In Denmark's neighbor Sweden, a much larger country, the local level was predominant during much of the nineteenth century, even if Sweden also has a long history of centralization of medical authority and central state authorities advocated vaccination early on, with compulsory vaccination being introduced as early as 1816. As Sköld has shown (1996b, see especially Sections V:4 and V:5), the high vaccination coverage in Sweden in the first half of the nineteenth century can be explained, at least in part, by the state's reliance on officials at the local level, especially the clergy, church wardens, and midwives (whose early professionalization in Sweden we describe in Chapter 9). By the early 1870s, however, a revision of the national vaccination guidelines placed so much authority with national authorities that Sweden's vaccination program is best seen as centralized; as Hollingsworth (1990, 119) notes, 'after 1873, the central government was deeply involved in the entire vaccination program.'

Around the same time, on the other side of the world, the government of New Zealand changed that country's vaccination laws, giving a more prominent role to central state authorities (see especially Maclean 1964,

Chapter 9; cf. Dow 1995, 29). After the abolition of New Zealand's regional layer of government, the provinces, in 1876, most health policies were in fact centralized to the national level (Bassett 1998, Chapter 3). Interestingly, the provision of vaccines to New Zealand's indigenous Maori population had been governed centrally for much longer (Dow 1995, 30–31). As we noted when we discussed the provision of mental health care to Native Americans in the United States in Chapter 7, states have often chosen more centralized administrative solutions when providing services to indigenous and colonized populations.

Japan is an especially interesting case in the history of smallpox vaccinations, since it was closed off from Western influence for much of the nineteenth century, which meant – as Jannetta (2007) shows in her study of early vaccinations in Japan – that the smallpox vaccine did not reach Japan until the late 1840s. Vaccinations were administered locally until the Meiji government began to centralize the administration of the smallpox vaccine in 1872, although it took some time for this new, more centralized policy to be implemented. Jannetta (2007, 177) notes that during the Meiji period, vaccination became 'state policy'; indeed, the development of a national vaccination program was one of first major public health initiatives of the new government (Jannetta 2009), and 'the cornerstone of public health policy from the outset' (Jannetta 2007, 176).

The reform of the vaccination program in the Netherlands in 1872 arguably also qualifies as an instance of centralization. Local governments remained responsible for carrying out vaccinations, but the central government issued detailed instructions on when vaccinations were to be carried out (every two months) and at what cost (free of charge) (Rutten 1997, 279). Both state health inspectors and state school inspectors monitored the implementation of the vaccination laws. As Rutten shows (1997, 410), the policies that were put in place in 1872, during the great smallpox epidemic of the early 1870s, put considerable pressure on local governments to improve vaccination coverage and greatly reduced disparities among different parts of the Netherlands.

Another borderline case is England, where the central government also took on a greater role concerning vaccinations in the middle of the nineteenth century. From 1855, vaccinators were trained in provincial centers, and in 1871, a government department called the Local Government Board was established, which – in spite of its name – was a department of the central government that 'assumed oversight over the vaccination service' (Hennock 1998, 56). Because of these changes, the English vaccination program that was put in place in the middle of the nineteenth century is often described as a centralized program – even as a precursor of the postwar National Health Service (Lambert 1962). However, as Brunton (2008, Chapter 5) shows, the national government's role was chiefly a supervisory one, and the policy of centralization was not effectively implemented.[8]

In many other policy areas, as we have seen, Europe's fascist governments in the 1920s and 1930s centralized public services. For example, they took steps to centralize both mental institutions and midwifery, two other domains of public health that we examine in this book (Chapters 7 and 9). It is interesting to note, therefore, that fascist governments appear to have done little to centralize their vaccination programs. One explanation is most likely that by the time the Fascists rose to power in the 1920s and 1930s, the smallpox death rate was already very low in Europe. In the German case, there is also evidence that the national socialist government was reluctant to promote vaccinations for ideological reasons (Thießen 2013, 46–56).

In some of the countries in our study, local governments remained effectively responsible for vaccinations well into the twentieth century (in a few, such as Belgium, Italy, and Spain, regional governments were, or became, responsible *de jure*, but typically delegated the authority over vaccinations to municipalities).[9] In most other countries, however, the responsibility for vaccinations shifted to the regional level in the course of the nineteenth century or in the beginning of the twentieth. As Figure 8.4 shows, by the 1920s and 1930s, leaving vaccinations to regional governments was the most common arrangement, which makes vaccinations unique among the services we study. In the United States, vaccination policies were administered locally, city by city, in the beginning of the nineteenth century, then state governments became more involved (Willrich 2011).[10] In Austria, the provinces became responsible for vaccinations when the government issued general guidelines for smallpox vaccination in 1836 (Flamm and Vutuc 2010). In France, there were strong centralizing tendencies early on, with the prefects being asked

[8] On the history of English vaccination legislation and administration, see also Dixon (1962, 278–281) and Baldwin (1999, 344–350).
[9] See, for example, Zocchi (2006) on Italy and Porras Gallo (2004) on Spain.
[10] The states made different choices about how to govern vaccinations early on (Green 2014). States such as Massachusetts were among the first jurisdictions in the world to make vaccination compulsory, and it was a Massachusetts law that was contested in the famous Supreme Court case on the constitutionality of compulsory vaccination in 1916, 197 US 11 (1905).

already in 1804 to promote vaccinations and submit reports on their success (Darmon 1986, 201), but there appears to have been relatively little direct control from Paris, and vaccinations were governed by departmental committees that were chaired by the prefect but otherwise made up of local and departmental officials and physicians (Darmon 1986, especially Chapters 10 and 11). Even after the introduction of a strict vaccination law in the Third Republic, in 1902, Baldwin (1999, 266) notes, 'the machinery of vaccination remained rudimentary in many departments, with some large communes undertaking none at all.' In neighboring Germany, the responsibility for vaccinations shifted to the state level with the adoption of new, comprehensive legislation on vaccinations in the German Empire after the early-1870s epidemic, although until the 1880s and 1890s, localities remained relatively autonomous (Huerkamp 1985, 629). In Canada, state authorities assumed greater responsibility for vaccinations in the early nineteenth century.[11] In two other federal states, Switzerland (Ritzmann 2015) and Australia (Cumpston 1914, 1925), canton and state governments were responsible for vaccinations from the adoption of the 1848 Swiss constitution and the federation of Australia in 1901.

With the exception of New Zealand, which is an early example of what we call liberal-democratic centralization, the creation of centrally governed vaccination programs occurred mainly in nineteenth-century monarchies – in one absolute (Denmark) and in a group of late nineteenth-century constitutional monarchies (Japan, the Netherlands, Sweden, with centralizing tendencies also in England). Among the more democratic countries in our sample – whether in the same period or in other periods – we find no examples of such centralizing reforms.[12] In other words, the idea of two paths to centralization holds for vaccinations, but with two important nuances: there is only one single example of a liberal-democratic centralizing reform, New Zealand, and twentieth-century authoritarian regimes were not as prone to centralize vaccinations as they were to centralize other services.

---

[11] On the history of the smallpox vaccine in Canada, see Barreto and Rutty (2002); see also the discussion of the relationship between local and state authorities in the 1885 smallpox epidemic in Bliss (1991).

[12] Since the centralization of national vaccination programs was typically associated with the enforcement of compulsory vaccinations, these nineteenth-century findings are consistent with findings from research on today's world. Ahlskog (2017) finds, for instance, that vaccine uptake is higher in authoritarian regimes, which he interprets as a result of the reluctance of democracies to adopt and enforce more coercive policies.

8.4 CHURCHES AND PRIVATE VACCINATORS

There were churches and religious communities that opposed vaccination in the nineteenth century – the conservative Catholic hierarchy in Montreal is one example (Chapter 1) and the strict Calvinist community in the Netherlands is another (Rutten 1997). Majority churches and state churches, however, were typically in favor of vaccination and actively promoted it among churchgoers, both in Protestant countries such as Denmark and Sweden (Larsen 2012, 32–33; Sköld 1996b) and in Catholic countries such as France and Italy (Bercé 1983; Phillips 2016). In a papal bull issued on March 10, 1822, Pope Pius VII encouraged the Catholic faithful to have their children vaccinated. What concerns us here, however, is the role that priests and other church officials sometimes played in the provision and administration of smallpox vaccinations. Figure 8.5 describes the results of our comparative analysis of the role the church played (the solid line) as well as the provision of public funding for private vaccinators (the dashed line). In approximately half of the countries that existed as independent states in the early nineteenth century, the clergy played some role in early attempts by governments to disseminate the smallpox vaccine. The proportion decreased greatly in the early to mid-nineteenth century – in part because governments transferred these authorities to health boards and equivalent institutions and in part because most countries that were formed or became independent in the nineteenth and twentieth centuries had secular institutions. By the late 1880s, the clergy played no major role in any national vaccination program.

On the one hand, the role that the church played in the early to mid-nineteenth century was administrative: local priests were involved in recording and reporting vaccinations (see, for example, Sköld 1996b, 390 on the Swedish case). This practice was especially common in countries with Protestant state churches, such as Denmark, Sweden, and a few preunification German states, where compulsory vaccinations were introduced early on, but also in early nineteenth-century Austria, with its close connection between church and state (Flamm and Vutuc 2010). Where church and state were closely connected, the clergy was often responsible for the local maintenance of population statistics and civil registries (Brambor et al. 2019, 9).

On the other hand, priests and other church officials were sometimes involved in actually carrying out vaccinations, especially in the beginning of the nineteenth century, when governments had not yet organized

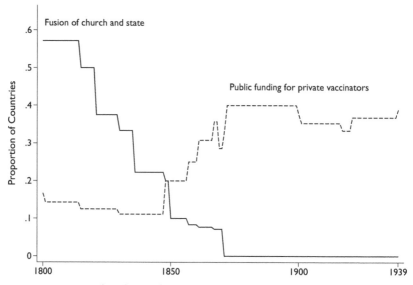

FIGURE 8.5 Churches and private vaccinators. The figure describes the
proportion of countries in the sample in which vaccination programs were
governed, at least in part, by church authorities and the proportion of countries
in which private vaccinators received public funding.

their own public health bureaucracies and therefore relied on cooperation with the clergy. Again, Sweden stands out as a country where priests
and church wardens played a particularly prominent role (Sköld 1996b,
390), but there are also documented examples in Denmark (Bonderup
2001), Spain (Olagüe de Ros and Astrain Gallart 2004), and in some
preunification German states.[13]

All the countries in which the church played some role were either
Protestant countries with state churches or majority-Catholic countries.
In other words, the clergy only participated in national vaccination
programs where there was one single church that could take on the
responsibility for recording, reporting, and occasionally performing
vaccinations.

The best explanation for the involvement of the clergy in early
nineteenth-century efforts to provide vaccinations is that the state and

---

[13] Interestingly, the Church of England does not appear to have played a significant
role when it comes to the provision of smallpox vaccinations in England. The local-
government institutions responsible for vaccinations under the 1840 vaccination law
were the local Boards of Guardians that had been created under the 1834 Poor Law, not
the parishes.

local governments, if they even existed, lacked the organizational capacity to deliver the smallpox vaccine to an entire country. By mobilizing the resources of the church, it was possible to provide vaccinations on a larger scale, and more quickly, than what would otherwise have been possible. Once states and local governments had created secular public health and health care authorities that were ready to take over, the church withdrew without much controversy, which again suggests that capacity, not state–church conflict or any desire of the church to involve itself in vaccinations, explains the involvement and later noninvolvement of the clergy in vaccinations. Secularization sometimes happened under relatively liberal governments – such as in Spain during the so-called *Trienio Liberal* of the 1820s – but no state–church conflict over public health was ever comparable to the state–church conflicts over education we discussed in Chapter 5.

As Figure 8.5 shows, from the middle of the nineteenth century onward, there were several countries in which either the national government or local or regional governments sought to promote vaccinations by providing financial compensation to doctors in private practice who carried out vaccinations.

The countries in which we have found some evidence that private vaccinators received funding are all European – England, France, Germany, Ireland, Italy, the Netherlands, and Switzerland. It is noteworthy that these countries were all religiously mixed, for in most of the policy areas we study in this book, the subsidization of privately provided services was most common in countries where Catholics and Protestants live side by side. But there is little evidence that subsidies for vaccinators was treated as a solution to religious conflict, as subsidies for private schools were (Chapter 5). It is more likely that a lack of administrative capacity, in the form of district physicians or other publicly employed medical professionals, explains why governments sought cooperation with private practitioners. We have found no evidence that governments contracted with civil-society organizations or religious orders to spread the smallpox vaccine: subsidization, in this context, meant paying doctors in private practice to perform vaccinations on behalf of public authorities.

The discussion so far – and the evidence in Figure 8.5 – is concerned with the provision of public funding for private *vaccinators*. In some countries, there was also a form of public–private partnership when it came to the production and distribution of the vaccine *itself*. In Austria, to take one example, the production of vaccine lymph in the late nineteenth century was carried out by publicly subsidized private institutes (Flamm and Vutuc 2010).

We end by noting one peculiarity of vaccination programs when it comes to compensating private service providers for their efforts: in several countries, particularly in the beginning of the nineteenth century, there were no financial subsidies for private vaccinators, but governments offered various forms of prizes and awards for vaccinators, public or private, who helped to spread the smallpox vaccine. In Belgium, for instance, the best-performing vaccinators in some regions received valuable gold medals in recognition of their work (Van Den Abeele 2006).[14] We have found no other examples of prizes and awards being used to encourage voluntary efforts to provide public services, which again suggests that vaccinations were different, in important ways, from other services.

8.5 CONCLUSIONS

The vaccine against smallpox was the world's first vaccine, and the widespread provision of the smallpox vaccine in many countries in the nineteenth century was typically one of the first large-scale public health programs in the countries in our sample, if not the first. Within a few years of Edward Jenner's invention of the smallpox vaccine in the late 1790s, most countries in Western Europe had created some form of national smallpox vaccination program, either through legislation or through government decrees.

The speedy diffusion of the smallpox vaccine and the early involvement of governments reveals how the role of national governments – and of political authorities more generally – was changing in the domain of health. Early modern governments made efforts to prevent the spread of infectious diseases, but not through broad, preventative public health programs such as vaccinations. The promotion of Jennerian vaccinations was thus a recognizably modern program, and a harbinger of things to come. As scholars such as Lambert (1962) have suggested, the nineteenth century's efforts to eradicate smallpox anticipated the postwar period's expansion of publicly funded public-health programs and medical care.

Perhaps because they were introduced so early, the governance of vaccination programs was in some ways different than the governance of

---

[14] In early nineteenth-century Denmark, vaccinators were mentioned in the newspaper *Collegial-Tidende* (Bonderup 2001, 87).

the other public services that we study in this book. This is especially clear when it comes to centralization. From the late 1800s onward, most vaccination programs were run by regional governments, which sets vaccinations apart from other services – policing, prisons, and mental institutions have more often been run by central governments, whereas schools, libraries, and midwifery have more often been run by local governments. But the cases of outright centralization that we do find are clear examples of either the authoritarian path to centralization we discuss throughout this book (nineteenth-century monarchies in Europe and Japan) or, in one case, the alternative liberal-democratic path (New Zealand). By the time twentieth-century fascist parties came to power, however, smallpox vaccination was no longer a salient policy area: by the early twentieth century, very few people contracted smallpox in Western Europe, North America, or Japan (in Australia and New Zealand, the disease was always rare).

In several countries in Europe, we found that the church was involved in the administration or provision of vaccinations in the nineteenth century. The main reason was that churches were often responsible, at least in part, for civil registration and population statistics, and taking on the additional task of recording and reporting vaccinations was a natural extension of that responsibility. In the course of the nineteenth century, medical authorities took over from ecclesiastical authorities, however, and typically without much controversy, suggesting that the infrastructural capacity of the church, not religious conflict, led to the early involvement of churches in national vaccination programs. Finally, in a number of countries, private vaccinators received public funding, but again, the reason was most likely that public authorities lacked sufficient organizational capacity to rely on public officials such as district physicians.

Among nineteenth-century intellectuals and political leaders, the smallpox vaccine was regarded in many quarters as a triumph of civilization. In the 1830s, for example, the Swedish poet-bishop Esaias Tegnér famously wrote that Sweden's growing population was a result of 'the peace, the vaccine, and the "taters"' (1922 [1832], 133). Meanwhile, however, there were powerful antivaccinationist movements in both Europe and America in the late nineteenth and early twentieth centuries, which were motivated by distinctly modern antiestablishment sentiments. In that sense, too, the politics of vaccination in the nineteenth century was a harbinger of things to come.

9

Midwifery

In our days, everything seems pregnant with its contrary.
Karl Marx, Speech at the anniversary of the *People's Paper* (1856)

In the beginning of life, there is death: childbirth is inherently dangerous
for mothers and children. Throughout history, mothers have therefore
sought the help of others when giving birth. This sets humans apart
from other species, for even the nonhuman primates, our closest rela-
tives among the animals, give birth alone.[1] Until quite recently, expectant
mothers who sought the help of someone outside their own family almost
always called for a midwife – a woman skilled at assisting other women in
childbirth. When nineteenth- and early twentieth-century states began to
develop new public health programs to address pressing problems such
as high maternal and infant mortality, the role and status of midwives
therefore became a pressing political issue.[2]

Nineteenth- and early twentieth-century debates about midwifery concerned two related policy questions: whether governments should do
more to assist pregnant women, and whether they should do so by
improving the practice of midwifery or by instead privileging medical
care provided by (male) doctors and obstetricians. These debates played
out differently in different countries. By the 1930s, at the end of the

---

[1] Among the nonhuman primates, 'Other animals may observe the birth process from a
distance, but do not assist the mother or infant. ...Labouring mothers typically seek
seclusion, often among trees' (Rosenberg and Trevathan 2002, 1199–1200).
[2] In this chapter, we only discuss female midwives, although there are historical examples
of male midwives, often known by their French name, *accoucheurs*.

long period we study in this book, the role and status of midwives therefore varied greatly. In a few states in Europe, where governments had long regulated midwifery and required local authorities to employ or pay for trained midwives to assist local women, midwives continued to play an important role even if women increasingly gave birth in hospital wards, not in their homes. In the English-speaking former colonies of North America and Oceania, by contrast, significant public funding for midwifery was only introduced in the twentieth century, if at all, and midwives were quickly losing ground to doctors and obstetricians. These differences remain. By the middle of the 2000s, there were more than 8,000 licensed midwives of working age in Sweden, approximately 900 per 1 million inhabitants, and almost all normal births were attended by midwives. Meanwhile in Canada, there were only 500 registered midwives, or 16 per 1 million inhabitants.[3]

After discussing the history of midwifery legislation and the history of professional conflicts between midwives and doctors, we begin our analysis of the distribution of power over midwifery among local, regional, and central political authorities. Midwifery services have been provided locally in most parts of the world. There are countries where central governments have been involved in training and licensing midwives for centuries, but midwives have nevertheless been employed locally (or, in a few cases, compensated by local authorities for attending births among the poor). We have only found three examples of centralization, all in the twentieth century: the creation of a national system of maternity hospitals in liberal New Zealand in 1904 and the creation of national midwifery organizations and adoption of national midwifery policies in fascist Italy and Germany in the interwar period. Our idea of two paths to centralization, one authoritarian and one liberal-democratic, thus contributes to explaining the development of midwifery, but there are only one or two examples of either path, since, like public libraries (Chapter 6), midwifery has been provided locally in most parts of the world. The centralization of midwifery in fascist Italy and Nazi Germany is noteworthy since these two authoritarian twentieth-century regimes elevated the status of midwifery as a profession but also used midwives to achieve their own political ends.

We then turn to the relationship between governments, churches, and the private and voluntary sectors. We show that churches were involved

---

[3] The Swedish data for 2006 are from Socialstyrelsen (2011); the Canadian data for 2005 are from the Canadian Association of Midwives. The number of midwives has increased in Canada since 2005; at the time of writing, in 2020, there were some 1,500.

in the regulation of midwifery early on, especially in countries with state churches, but they lost their historical influence during the nineteenth century, just as they did in the cases of mental institutions and vaccinations. We also show that local and, later, national governments subsidized midwives in private practice in a few countries in the nineteenth and early twentieth centuries. This occurred where governments were unable or unwilling to expand publicly provided midwifery services, but nevertheless saw a pressing need to provide for birth attendance among the poor.

Most scholars of the history of midwifery have not been concerned with these administrative and political matters, but with two other important problems. One is a public health problem: the relationship between the professionalization of midwifery and the decline of maternal mortality and infant mortality over time (see especially Loudon 1992). The other is a problem of feminist scholarship, professional sociology, and social and medical history: the development of professional conflicts between midwives and doctors (for a few examples, see Donnison 1977 on England, Mein Smith 1986 on New Zealand, Kjærheim 1987 on Norway, Öberg 1996 and Romlid 1998 on Sweden, and Ehrenreich and English 1973, Leavitt 1986, and Borst 1995 on the United States). We analyze the political perspective of these important events and put midwifery in perspective by comparing it with the many other public services that emerged and expanded in the nineteenth century.

9.1 CHILDBIRTH BEFORE THE NINETEENTH CENTURY

Midwifery is as old as civilization. 'I am the son of a midwife, brave and burly, whose name was Phaenarete' Socrates says in *Theaetetus* (1892 [369 BC]). For most of history, however, practicing midwives had little formal training; they learned from experience and practice, and were typically expected to have children of their own before assisting other women in childbirth. Socrates, for one, took for granted that all midwives must be past child-bearing age. 'No woman, as you are probably aware, who is still able to conceive and bear, attends other women, but only those who are past bearing,' he says to Theaetetus, for 'human nature cannot know the mystery of an art without experience; and therefore she assigned this office to those who are too old to bear.'[4] In some countries,

---

[4] In the same dialogue, Socrates famously compares his own role as a philosopher to that of a midwife; the word that is used to describe Socrates' teaching style, *maieutics*, comes from the Greek *maieutikós*, 'midwifery.'

these sorts of ideas and customs prevailed well into the early modern period, and beyond.

Beginning in the early modern period, however, midwifery developed into a profession that required specific training and skills. As a result of this process of professionalization, both churches and local, provincial, and national governments have sought to regulate the education, training, and licensing of midwives. Shorter (1991 [1982], 36–41) distinguishes among three phases in the history of early modern midwifery regulation (on early modern midwifery, see also Marland 1993). In the fifteenth and sixteenth centuries, church laws and municipal regulations detailed the moral and religious requirements for practicing midwives. In the seventeenth century, doctors became responsible for examinations and supervision. Then, in the eighteenth century, the first formal training schools for midwives were introduced.

But there were big differences among countries. By the year 1800, Shorter notes, there were medically trained midwives all over continental Europe, but there was no formal midwife training available in the Anglo-Saxon world. Shorter's periodization of early modern midwifery regulation is therefore only a rough approximation. There were other differences among countries as well; in some countries, for example, the clergy continued to supervise local midwives long after the seventeenth century.

The first country that turned midwifery into a public service that was provided and paid for by governments and political authorities was Sweden in the eighteenth century. As one might have expected on the basis of Shorter's periodization, Swedish midwifery was regulated in church law in the sixteenth century, but in 1663, a new, secular medical institution, the Collegium Medicum, became responsible for the registration of midwives nationally (Rehn and Boström 2011, 56). The 1688 Medical Regulations, adopted a few years later, provided that only trained and licensed midwives were allowed to practice (Romlid 1998, 51–52). In the early eighteenth century, even stricter regulations were introduced in Sweden's capital, Stockholm: in 1711, the Collegium Medicum required an apprenticeship with an experienced midwife for two years followed by an examination at the Collegium for all midwives.

On this basis, a national midwifery program was introduced in Sweden in 1757. All parishes were now encouraged to hire a midwife and to help pay for her education in the capital (Högberg 2004; Romlid 1998, 105). It took some time before all parishes followed these directives, but from 1819, they were compelled to do so. In other words, already in the

eighteenth century, the Swedish government went beyond merely training and licensing midwives and turned midwifery into a publicly provided
service throughout its territory. Two hundred years after the adoption of
these laws and regulations, midwives continue to provide most maternal
and infant care in Sweden.[5]

9.2 MIDWIVES, DOCTORS, AND GOVERNMENTS

The employment conditions and the social and economic status of midwives varied greatly among the countries in our study throughout the
nineteenth and early twentieth centuries. In most other policy areas,
Oceania, Japan, and the countries in Western Europe and North America converged during the period covered in this book: all countries had
civilian police forces, education systems, and mental institutions by the
early twentieth century. When it comes to midwifery, however, countries
did not converge; they diverged.

Already in the beginning of the nineteenth century, all of the Nordic
countries had introduced, or were introducing, legislation similar to Sweden's, which meant that midwifery was a publicly recognized profession
and midwives were in the process of becoming public employees. In
Denmark and Norway, the 1810 Midwifery Regulations required each
locality to appoint a midwife and to pay for her education at a central midwifery school, her salary, and housing. Poor women were treated
free of charge; others were charged according to their income (Blom
1988, 33; Cliff 1992, 17; Kjærheim 1987, 31, 88–89; Løkke 1997, 106;
see also Løkke 1998). Finland had been a part of Sweden when its
eighteenth-century regulations were introduced, and local governments
in Finland were required to retain a midwife from then on (Wrede 2001).

---

[5] One particularly interesting feature of midwifery regulations in Sweden is that the midwives were authorized to use surgical instruments, unlike in almost all other countries: in
1829, midwives who had undergone extended training were authorized to use forceps,
hooks, and perforators and to perform manual removal of the placenta as well as extraction after breech presentation (Högberg 2004), and already in 1777, midwives had been
authorized to use instruments when the nearest doctor was too far away (Romlid 1998,
59). Entrusting midwives with surgical instruments was rare, in comparative perspective,
although similar but less far-reaching provisions existed in Norway (Kjærheim 1987,
94–101). *Forceps* are a surgical instrument that is used to deliver babies. The use of
forceps to assist deliveries had a distinct advantage over the surgical procedures that had
been used before then: whereas earlier instruments could only be used to save the life of
the mother, forceps allowed those assisting childbirth to avoid – in some circumstances –
both maternal death and fetal demise (Sheikh, Ganesaratnam, and Jan 2013).

In most of continental Europe, by contrast, midwifery was a private profession. To the extent that governments paid midwives to attend births, the arrangement was often that parishes or local governments subsidized privately practicing midwives who provided services for the indigent poor. In some German states, for instance, parishes paid midwives a fixed or variable sum in return for attending all poor women who could not afford these services themselves. In most of continental Europe, midwives only became public employees, if at all, when childbirth moved into maternity wards and hospitals in the twentieth century – as, for example, in Belgium (Gijbels and Wils, forthcoming).

There were exceptions to this rule. In France, for example, a significant number of midwives became public employees early on, due to Revolutionary-era legislation providing that indigent women had a right to assistance during childbirth (Sage-Pranchère 2014, 193). In the nineteenth century, this service was provided in local-level *bureaux de bienfaisance*, or 'welfare offices.' There were also some German lands in which midwives were public employees even in the nineteenth century (Fallwell 2013, 52). In fact, in interwar German debates over midwifery, there were two contrasting models, the 'Freital System,' which meant public employment, and the 'Prussian System,' which meant private practice, perhaps supported by a guaranteed minimum income (Lisner 2006, 83).[6] In the Netherlands, some women were employed by town councils to assist poor women (Van Lieburg and Marland 1989, 299). Yet, unlike in the Nordic countries, most midwives in Continental Europe were in private employment, even in a country such as France (Fuchs and Knepper 1989); to the extent that public authorities were involved in the provision of midwifery services, those efforts were directed at poorer women.

In the English-speaking countries, midwives had a comparatively weak position in nineteenth- and twentieth-century society, particularly in the settler countries in North America and Oceania, where there was little or no history of formal training for midwives. England – in which new legislation on midwifery was adopted through the Midwives Act 1902 – is a partial exception (before that legislation, the variation within England was so large, Loudon 1986, 10 notes, that 'it is extremely difficult to reconstruct a picture of midwifery for England and Wales as a

---

[6] Scheuermann (1995, 438) notes that midwifery 'was formalized as a public position in the 16th and 17th century,' but it then became, in most of Germany, a 'traditional, independent profession in the 18th and 19th century.'

whole in the nineteenth century'), as is Ireland, where midwifery services were offered within the dispensary system (Breathnach 2016). Midwives in Australia, Canada, New Zealand, and the United States therefore found it especially difficult to resist attacks from the medical profession in the late nineteenth and early twentieth centuries, and midwives were displaced by other health care professionals such as physicians and obstetricians. Canada stands out among the countries in our study since midwifery was not recognized as a profession until the 1990s. Although most births in Canada were attended by midwives in the nineteenth century, midwifery 'remained a traditional craft across most jurisdictions of the country' (Benoit, Wrede, and Sandall 2001, 41).

In several of the English-speaking settler countries, there were important public health initiatives in the early twentieth century that aimed to improve and expand midwifery services, but those initiatives were typically short-lived.

The most well-known example is the Sheppard–Towner Act in the United States, which was adopted in 1921. The Sheppard–Towner Act allocated money is to maternal care and infant care, administered through the Children's Bureau. Under to the provisions of the act, states were encouraged to employ public-health nurses to instruct untrained midwives (Varney 1997, 8–9); thirty-one states did so, and many health clinics were established (Ladd-Taylor 1992, 126). Yet, the act expired in 1929. After that, many states cut back on midwifery once more (Barrett Litoff 1982, 9).[7] One part of the explanation for this reversal was that there was a rapid decline in midwife-attended births in the United States in the first decades of the twentieth century. In 1910, at least 50 percent of all births were attended by midwives; in 1930, the figure was approximately 15 percent (Brouwere 2007), in 1940, it was 8.7 (Devries and Barroso 1997, 255). By the 1930s, midwifery had therefore become locally concentrated in the South – of the approximately 50,000 midwives in the United States in 1930, 80 percent practiced in Southern states (Loudon 1992, 282). It seems likely that the increasing concentration of midwifery among African Americans explains why the ambitious initiatives of the early 1920s did not result in the establishment of a permanent midwifery service.[8]

---

[7] The Social Security Act of 1935 reintroduced federal funding for maternal and infant care, but in contrast to the Sheppard–Towner Act, it did not provide for a universal program (Ladd-Taylor 1992, 122).

[8] On African American midwives in the South, see Fraser (1998).

In the first two decades of the twentieth century, the state also supported midwifery in Australia, especially because of the need for childbirth assistance in rural parts of the country (Mein Smith 1993). This policy, too, proved short-lived, and Reiger (2014) notes that Australia differs from New Zealand in that 'birth in Australia was never considered automatically deserving of public financial support.' The nineteenth and early twentieth centuries' professional struggles between midwives, who were almost always women, and medical professionals such as physicians and obstetricians, who were almost always men, are the topic of a large scholarly literature. For good reasons, scholars have long treated those struggles as a case study in the subjugation of women. Medical men mobilized their strong professional organizations, their purported claims to scientific superiority, and their political connections in claiming that untrained midwives posed a grave threat to public health. In the early twentieth-century United States, for example, midwives were increasingly blamed for the poor status of maternal and infant care, and in the 1910s, there was an intense debate on the 'midwife problem' in that country. When obstetrics emerged as a stand-alone medical specialization, many medical professionals argued that midwifery should be abolished altogether (Barrett Litoff 1978, Chapters 4–6). Much of the literature on these struggles is concerned with the English-speaking countries, but there were related political struggles in other countries as well, including a country such as Sweden, with its traditionally strong midwifery profession (Öberg 1996; Romlid 1998).[9]

One indication of the professionalization of midwifery in many countries in the late nineteenth and early twentieth centuries is the creation of national midwife organizations. By the end of the 1930s, the only countries in our study that lacked a national organization for midwives were the English-speaking former settler colonies Australia, Canada, New Zealand, and the United States (the organizations that exist in those countries today were created after the Second World War). As Figure 9.1 shows, the first national organization, Britain's Royal College of Midwives (known at the time as the Matron's Aid Trained Midwives Registration Society), was established in 1881. Other countries soon

---

[9] In reality, birth attendance by a skilled midwife is one of the most effective and cheap of all public health interventions (Loudon 1992; Pettersson-Lidbom 2014), which suggests that in countries with untrained midwives, investing in training for midwives would have been a more sensible policy from the point of view of public health than banning midwifery.

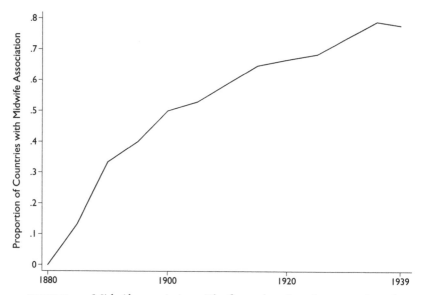

FIGURE 9.1 Midwife associations. The figure describes the proportion of countries in our study that had a national midwife association.
Sources: Conseil National des Accoucheuses (2006), Balmer-Engel (1994), Svenska Barnmorskeförbundet (1986), Barrett Litoff (1982), Drenth (1998), Fleming (1996), Halliday and Halliday (2007), Japan International Cooperation Agency (2005), Kjærheim (1987), Ó hÓgartaigh (2012), Ortiz and Padilla (2002), Osler (2002), Plummer (2000), Sage-Pranchère (2018), Reiger (2014), Scheuermann (1995), Triolo (1994), and Wrede (2001)

followed, and by the 1920s, most countries in our study had a national midwifery association. Around that time, these organizations also began to cooperate with each other: there were several international meetings for midwives in the first decades of the twentieth century and a formal organization, the International Midwives Union, was created in 1922. It was the forerunner of the International Confederation of Midwives, which exists today.

9.3 CENTRALIZING MIDWIFERY

What roles did national, regional, and local governments play in the administration and provisioning of midwifery in the nineteenth and early twentieth centuries? Answering that question is complicated by the fact that the practice of midwifery has varied so much among countries and over time. Beginning with the differences among states, we have already noted that midwives were public employees in some countries, that midwifery was an independent profession in other countries, and that in a third group of countries, it was more craft than profession since midwives had little formal training. Because of these differences, governments played different roles both among and within countries. In general, the public authorities that were responsible for licensing midwives and for regulating the practice of midwifery, the main roles of governments where midwifery was an independent profession, were often provincial or national. But the public authorities that provided midwifery services directly, employing midwives or compensating midwives in private practice who assisted poor mothers, were typically local, sometimes provincial, and only occasionally national.

When it comes to the differences over time, arguably the most important shift in the history of midwifery in the nineteenth and twentieth centuries was the hospitalization of childbirth, which was a process that began around the turn of the twentieth century and accelerated in the interwar period. Before that time, most women gave birth at home. Today, the vast majority of women in the rich industrialized countries, with one or two exceptions, give birth in hospitals. In some countries – such as New Zealand – the transition to hospital-based births was remarkably quick: in 1920, 35 percent of all mothers in New Zealand gave birth in hospitals; by 1926, 50 percent did; and ten years later, in 1936, almost 82 percent of all delivers occurred in hospitals (see Loudon 1992, 155, 476–477; and Stojanovic 2008). In England, the proportion of hospital births also increased sharply in the course of the interwar period, but not as sharply as in New Zealand (Lewis 1980, 120): in the first decade of the twentieth century, very few births were hospital births, and in the early 1920s, 6 percent were; in the late 1930s, however, the proportion of hospital births was 41 percent.[10]

The hospitalization of childbirth reduced the demand for midwives, since hospital-based births made it possible for each midwife to assist many women per day. Even in Sweden, the country in the world where the midwifery profession was the strongest, the hospitalization of birth resulted in a decline in the total number of midwives in the interwar period (Figure 9.2). This was a problem that Swedish midwives

---

[10] One interesting feature of the history of childbirth in Japan is that the hospitalization of childbirth happened late. In 1950, 95 percent of all births were still home births (Japan International Cooperation Agency 2005, 65).

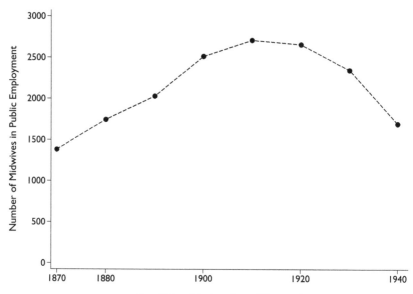

FIGURE 9.2 Swedish midwives in public employment.
Source: Carlsson (1966)

eventually solved by broadening their remit, taking on contraception advice and other public health tasks in addition to their traditional tasks of maternal and infant care (Milton 2001; Rehn and Boström 2011).

The early twentieth century's hospitalization of childbirth typically also led to administrative changes since the public authorities that were responsible for hospitals were typically different from the public authorities that were responsible for hiring, managing, and paying for midwives who provided services in people's homes. Since there were maternity hospitals long before the large-scale hospitalization of childbirth in the early twentieth century, this ambiguity in the employment conditions of midwives existed in the nineteenth century as well; it was not uncommon for most midwives to practice locally, while some midwives worked for provincial hospitals.

When compiling the evidence that is described in Table 9.1, which shows how midwifery was governed in the nineteen countries in our study, we have tried to determine which level of government was mainly responsible for hiring midwives or administering the actual provision of midwifery services (as opposed to regulating midwifery and licensing midwives). The first thing to note is that midwifery was typically governed locally (see Figure 9.3). In the previous two chapters – which

TABLE 9.1 *How midwifery was governed*

	Public only	Mixed public–church–private
National	Germany (from 1938), Italy (from 1925), New Zealand (from 1904)	
Local or regional	Australia, Austria, Belgium, Canada, Denmark, Finland, France, Ireland, Italy (before 1925), Japan, the Netherlands (before 1927), New Zealand (before 1904), Norway, Spain, Sweden (from 1860s), Switzerland, United Kingdom (1834–1917), United States	*Midwives supervised by state-church priests:* Sweden (before 1860s) and United Kingdom (before 1834); *subsidies for midwives in private practice:* Germany (before 1938), Netherlands (from 1927), United Kingdom (from 1918)

Notes: In 'national' systems, most midwives were employed by, or otherwise responsive to, national political authorities, as opposed to regional or local authorities. In countries with a mix of public, church, and private governance, either religious authorities or the clergy were directly involved in supervising midwives, or at least some midwives in private practice received public subsidies (typically when assisting poor mothers).
Sources: Own categorization based on literature cited in the text

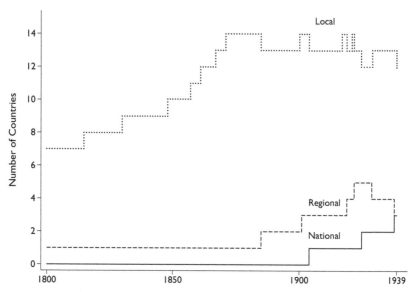

FIGURE 9.3 The centralization of midwifery. The figure describes the number of countries in the sample that administered midwifery services at the local, regional, and national levels.

dealt with other aspects of health care and public health – we found that most countries had moved away from local modes of service provision the interwar period: by the 1930s, mental institutions were typically centralized to the national level and vaccination programs were typically administered at the regional level. The governance of midwifery is more similar to the governance of elementary schooling and, especially, public libraries, which is perhaps best explained by the fact that there was sufficient local demand to justify the employment of a local midwife or teacher, and, in towns and cities, a librarian.

Midwifery has only been centralized in a handful of twentieth-century states. The two clearest and most well-known cases of centralization were interwar Italy and Germany. The fascist governments in these countries introduced new legislation on midwifery and established new, central midwifery organizations. Both regimes raised the status of midwives and improved their employment conditions – but both regimes also made midwives complicit in their nativist policies and eugenics programs.

In Italy in 1925, the fascist government created a new national institution called *Opera nazionale maternità e infanzia*, which offered maternity care and infant care to poorer women. It was a semi-governmental body with both central and peripheral agencies and offices in every province (Saraceno 1991, 206). In 1937, midwives were given the fascist title of *visitatrice domiciliare*, or 'home visitor' (Triolo 1994, 264), a word that replaced the more traditional Italian term (and the word most commonly used today), *levatrice*. Meanwhile, midwives were required to join a national union that was connected to the fascist party.[11]

These reforms, and others, were motivated by the natalist policies of Italy's fascist government. On the one hand, the government wished to control and regulate midwifery since many midwives performed, or could perform, abortions, which were anathema to the fascists. On the other hand, fascists pursued 'intrusive … policies regarding the domestic sphere' that 'thrust what had been previously considered the private intimacies of the family into the forefront of political life,' as Triolo (1994, 264) notes. Midwives were expected to carry out these policies. Triolo cites an article by the editor of the journal of the fascist midwives' union *Lucina* who described the role that midwives should have under fascism:

The midwife can easily enter the homes of the urban and rural poor to inquire about the condition of the family, to oversee the health of family members, to watch over the lives and education of the children, and to gather the most intimate confidences in order to direct, to the proper authorities, the involuntary victims of evil or vice, in order to return them, healthy, to the family and the Nation.

In Nazi Germany, the role played by midwives was even more menacing. In the German Empire and in the Weimar Republic, midwives had fought long and hard to improve their employment conditions. There was a great deal of support for midwifery reform among liberals, Catholics, and socialists, but the ministries of finance and justice resisted these efforts and the principle that medical affairs should be left to the states prevailed (Weindling 1989, 194–196). The major political breakthrough for the midwives therefore came during the Nazi period. The National Midwife Law of 1938, the *Reichshebammengesetz*, required the presence of a midwife at every birth (Lisner 2006, Section 2.3, Lisner and Peters 2014) and provided licensed midwives with a state-mandated minimum wage and access to medical insurance and a pension plan (Fallwell 2013, 68). Meanwhile, the national midwife organization *Reichsfachschaft Deutscher Hebammen*, from 1939 the *Reichshebammenschaft*, exercised control over Germany's midwives through a central-

---

[11] On the postwar legacy of fascist family policies in Italy, see especially Whitaker (2000).

ized National-Socialist power structure that was superimposed on earlier regional and national health regulations (Lisner 2006, 387).

This increased recognition came at a cost, however. Under the German national-socialist government, midwives were involved in the registration of 'hereditary diseases' and they later helped to select some 5,000 children for extermination, many of them with Downs Syndrome (Weindling 1989, 546). As Lisner (2006, 259) puts it, 'Loyalty to the Nazi state and commitment to the implementation of the state's racist population policy were prerequisites of the professionalization and upgrading of the midwifery profession during the Nazi era.' In a manner reminiscent of the example from fascist Italy that we gave above, Lisner describes Nazi midwifery policy as the 'arm of the state reaching into every apartment.'

As the Italian and German cases show, there is clear evidence of an authoritarian path to the centralization of midwifery, although centralization is a twentieth-century phenomenon in this particular policy area, unlike, for instance, the areas of prisons and mental institutions. The fascist governments in Benito Mussolini's Italy and Adolf Hitler's Germany recognized that midwives were uniquely well positioned to promote and enforce the family policies and population policies these governments sought to implement. They therefore adopted new laws on midwifery and created national midwifery organizations that were incorporated in the ruling parties through methods that were distinctive to fascist regimes.

The third example of centralization that we have found in our data is an example of the liberal-democratic path to centralization. New Zealand's first national legislation on midwifery, the Midwives Act, was adopted in 1904 and introduced by Richard Seddon's liberal government. Under the provisions of the Midwives Act, all midwives had to be registered with the government and unlicensed midwives were prohibited from practicing (Stojanovic 2008). By March 1908, 1004 midwives were registered under this legislation (Census and Statistics Office of the Dominion of New Zealand 1908). At the same time, the government decided to set up a network of maternity hospitals that employed and trained midwives: the so-called St. Helens Hospitals. As in other policy areas, New Zealand chose a highly centralized approach. Midwives were registered with the national government, not local authorities, and the public maternity hospitals were administered directly by the Department of Health (Stojanovic 2008). They were free for the families of soldiers and had low rates for others. Only seven such hospitals were ever established, however, and doctors gradually gained control over child-birth in the 1920s and 1930s; most babies were now delivered in regular hospitals (Donley 1986).

In other democratic states, midwifery was occasionally centralized to the regional level in the beginning of the twentieth century since governments had determined that it was better to let midwives operate across municipal borders. In Norway, for instance, legislation introduced in 1898 left it up to provincial authorities to divide provinces into midwifery districts instead of relying on the parishes (see Peterson 2013, Chapter 1 for a discussion; cf. Peterson 2018). In neighboring Sweden, so-called district midwives were introduced in 1919, and although some midwives remained employed by the municipalities, the district midwives soon became more numerous (Lundqvist 1940, 146).[12] In 1920, the government also introduced national grants for midwife salaries (Romlid 1998, 264). These reforms were adopted under liberal or liberal-socialist governments, which stopped short of creating a national corps of midwives, as the fascists did in Italy and Germany a few years later. In this respect, too, we thus find important similarities between midwifery and public libraries: twentieth-century liberal reformers sometimes shifted the responsibility for public services to regional governments, but often refrained from creating the sorts of national programs and institutions that fascists favored.

Overall, however, midwifery is a service that has typically been provided locally. In the Nordic countries, midwives were employed by parishes and, later, municipalities or by small midwifery districts until the beginning of the twentieth century. In German-speaking continental Europe and in Italy, before the rise of fascism, midwives were also employed locally and paid by local governments to assist poor mothers. In Italy, for instance, postunification legislation required cities and towns to hire public, trained midwives to serve the poor; those midwives were supervised by the mayor and the local public health doctor (Basso 2015, 22).

The Netherlands is well known for its large decline in maternal death rates at the turn of the twentieth century; its high proportion of

---

[12] Although the midwives were trained in Stockholm and regulated nationally in the eighteenth and nineteenth centuries, local governments employed most midwives before the 1920s; the 1862 local government reform made regional governments, or county councils, responsible for the health care system, but that reform only affected midwives who were employed in hospitals, so most midwives remained employed locally until the twentieth century.

home births, even today; and its strong midwifery profession. In the Netherlands, public midwife training and the licensing of midwives were introduced early on (Van Lieburg and Marland 1989). The first national legislation on midwifery was adopted in 1818, but by then, municipal training courses had already been provided for more than a hundred years in some parts of the country. Under the Medical Act of 1818, it was compulsory for town councils to employ midwives to serve the poor. With the exception of these publicly employed midwives, however, most of the midwives in Netherlands were in private practice.

In England and Wales, local governments were also responsible for midwifery. In the beginning of the twentieth century, the British government increased funding for midwives employed by local governments through the Maternity and Child Welfare Act 1918. Local governments were also authorized to establish Maternity and Child Welfare Committees, which provided among other things, for maternity hospitals (Thane 1991, 105–106). In 1922, midwives attended approximately 54 percent of all births in England and Wales; by 1938, the proportion was 76 percent (Loudon 1992, 231, 314). In Ireland, maternity services at the turn of the century were based on the dispensary system: the more than 700 dispensary districts were encouraged to employ midwives, although the decision was up to local boards of guardians (Barrington 1987, 8).

In France, as we have seen, revolutionary-era legislation provided that indigent women had the right to public assistance during childbirth. In the nineteenth century, this service was provided in local *bureaux de bienfaisance*, or 'welfare offices.' Under the Law of July 15, 1893, on free medical assistance, maternity service and medical assistance were provided for free of charge for two months before the delivery and two months after. Each *commune* was required to have a *bureau d'assistance*, with at least one midwife who attended deliveries in people's homes at a fixed cost, and each department was required to establish a maternity hospital for unmarried mothers (Sage-Pranchère 2014). In other words, there was a mix of local and regional services in the French case, but the local level remained predominant.

The absence of centralization of midwifery in Japan – among the most centralized countries in our study – is indicative of the essentially local character of midwifery services. According to Yanagisawa (2009, 86), birth attendance first became a profession in the Edo period. In the early Meiji period, the government launched programs that were meant to replace traditional birth attendants with formally trained professionals.

Midwifery was first regulated in the early-Meiji Comprehensive Medical Code of 1874, which introduced licensing for midwives and specified the qualifications required of a midwife (Japan International Cooperation Agency 2005, 29). But these public health and health care policies were based on the principle of central regulation and private provision (Japan International Cooperation Agency 2005, 15). Only in the 1920s did some cities and villages begin to organize their own midwifery services, which were paid for with municipal funds. These so-called circulating midwives assisted poor women in their homes (on midwifery in Meiji Japan, see especially Terazawa 2018, Chapter 4).

9.4 CHURCHES AND MIDWIVES IN PRIVATE PRACTICE

We now turn from the vertical distribution of power over midwifery to the horizontal distribution of power between secular public authorities, churches, and private providers. Figure 9.4 describes the proportion of countries in our study in which the clergy was responsible for supervising midwives and the proportion of countries in our study in which midwives in private practice received public funding.

As we discussed in the beginning of this chapter, the practice of midwifery was typically regulated in church law in the early-modern period, and parish priests often supervised midwives who practiced locally. In the countries where local governments were required to employ midwives already in the early nineteenth century, parish priests were often involved in those hiring decisions. As Figure 9.4 shows, however, by the nineteenth century, midwives only remained responsible to religious authorities in a few countries, all of which had established state churches.

One example was England and Wales. The Church of England had traditionally been responsible for the inspection of medical practitioners, including midwives (Anisef and Basson 1979), and to the extent that public authorities provided midwifery services, as opposed to merely regulating the practice, this was done through the parishes. With the 1834 Poor Law Amendments, however, as we have discussed in previous chapters, the parishes no longer administered the Poor Laws in England.

In some of the Nordic countries – where most midwives were public employees already in the nineteenth century, not private practitioners – the clergy also continued to play a role in the hiring and supervision of midwives in the parishes well into the nineteenth century. For example, as Blom (1988, 25) notes, until 1898, parish priests in Norway were

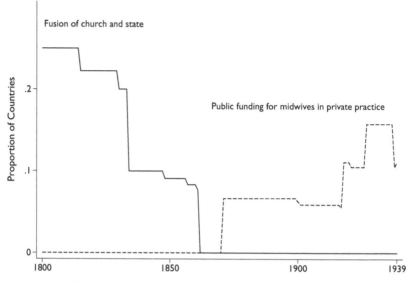

FIGURE 9.4 Church oversight and funding for midwives in private practice. The figure describes the proportion of countries in the sample in which midwives were governed, at least in part, by church authorities and the proportion of countries in which midwives in private practice received public funding.

responsible for issuing certificates about a candidate's moral character and suitability before a new midwife could be appointed. In neighboring Sweden, the parish council was responsible for the supervision of local health care, including midwifery, until the adoption of the 1862 municipal reform (Romlid 1998, 185). Similarly, parish priests and church authorities in many of the German states were involved in regulating midwifery at least until the middle of the nineteenth century, although this practice had largely ceased in Imperial Germany.

When it comes to the role of the church, the pattern we find for midwifery is thus similar to the pattern we found for mental institutions and vaccinations: there was a fusion of church and state in some countries, especially countries with established churches, but it only lasted until the middle of the nineteenth century, at most. This means that secularization happened later for mental and public health than it for the police and for prison services, which were secularized already in the early modern period. But when it did happen, it seems to have been relatively uncontroversial: the clergy lost their prior supervisory role in connection with broad administrative reforms, not as a result of state–church conflict. These findings are consistent with our main argument about church and state: outside the domain of education, the fusion of church and state was largely a matter of convenience and administrative capacity, and when medical authorities and secular bureaucracies were ready to take over the old functions of the church, they did.

As 9.4 also shows, it was rare for midwives in private practice to receive public funding. The few countries where we have found evidence of the subsidization of midwives in private practice are all in northwestern Europe. In most German states, for instance, midwives were private practitioners after the early modern period, but they were typically paid by public authorities when they assisted poor mothers. Campbell (1917, 42–45) notes that poor-law authorities in Germany paid midwives to take care of mothers who were unable to pay themselves. In some localities and regions, midwives received a fixed sum to take care of all poor mothers in a district; in others, midwives were paid on a case-by-case basis. In 1890, an agreement on fee-for-service payments was also concluded between Germany's publicly regulated sickness insurance funds and the Germany midwifery association (Scheuermann 1995, 441).[13]

In England and the Netherlands, different forms of subsidies for midwives in private practice – via charitable organizations – were introduced later. In England, the Maternity and Child Welfare Act 1918 provided for government grants to voluntary organizations that provided midwifery services and other health services for mothers and children (Marks 1992, 50). A few years earlier, in 1911, paragraph 18 of the new National Insurance Bill had enabled married women to choose between being attended by a midwife or a doctor (Benoit, Wrede, and Sandall 2001, 30; Thane 1991, 105), covered by national insurance. In the Netherlands, the government began to introduce subsidies for infant and maternal health care centers run by the Dutch Confederation for the Protection of Infants in the 1920s (Marland 1992, 78).

It is striking that the countries in which we find the clearest evidence of subsidization are religiously mixed societies, but we have found little evidence that public subsidies for midwifery services were treated as a solution to religious conflict, as they were in the domain of education. It

---

[13] It is sometimes difficult to draw the line between public employment and subsidization in countries where most midwives were private practitioners, although some midwives were paid to assist poor women in childbirth. Van Lieburg and Marland (1989) note that although town councils employed some women as midwives to the poor in the nineteenth century, those women 'were able to supplement this with fees from private practice.' Whether such arrangements should be seen as a form of public employment or as a form of subsidization ultimately becomes a matter of definition.

seems more likely that some governments who wished to address growing concerns about maternal and infant health chose to support private providers instead of putting in place public bureaucracies. In England, however, the midwives were eventually incorporated in the National Health Service under the new health care legislation that Clement Attlee's Labour government adopted after the Second World War.

We end by noting that we have found a few local examples of public subsidies for midwives in private practice that we do not find significant enough to alter the way we categorize entire countries. One example is the midwives in Sweden's capital, Stockholm. Although most midwives in Sweden were public employees in the nineteenth century – indeed, midwives were one of the largest groups of public employees in the nineteenth century, after primary school teachers and priests – the midwives in the capital were not, largely because the Stockholm bourgeoisie could afford to pay fees to private midwives (on midwives in private practice in Sweden, see Öberg 1994). For these reasons, city authorities sometimes paid midwives to assist poor women, who could not afford the fees (Öberg 1996, 121). In Denmark's capital Copenhagen and Norway's capital Kristiania (now Oslo), pmidwives were also predominant (Cliff 1992, 79–83).[14] This is another example of how complicated the relationship between public and privately provided services was in the nineteenth-century world; indeed, it is sometimes difficult to determine where the public sector ended and the private sector began.

9.5 CONCLUSIONS

The decline of maternal mortality and infant mortality in most of the world's countries over the last two centuries is one of the great public health achievements of the current era. One of the causes of this decline is the improvement of midwifery. In this chapter, we have studied the efforts states made to invest in midwifery from the end of the early modern period onward, concentrating, as in the rest of the book, on the nineteenth and early twentieth centuries. Our main finding is that midwifery is different from all the other services we study in this book, since there was no convergence among countries: by the end of the period

---

[14] Those were not the only differences between the capital and the rest of the country. Already in the early twentieth century, for example, most women in Stockholm gave birth in hospitals, not in their homes, decades earlier than women in the countryside (Öberg 1996, 338).

we are studying, midwifery was a strong, publicly trained and funded profession in some countries, but it had become banned in others. In countries where midwifery did develop into a strong profession, *training* for midwives was often one of the very earliest public health interventions by the modern state, but the actual provision of midwifery services varied greatly even among those countries: there were countries in which midwives became public employees already in the late eighteenth and early nineteenth centuries, but there were also countries where midwifery remained a private profession.

The only instances we find of centralization to the national level are on the one hand Fascist Italy and Nazi Germany, on the other hand liberal New Zealand. In other words, there were two paths to centralization when it came to midwifery, as in other policy areas. Regional initiatives in liberal Australia, Progressive Era United States, liberal Norway, and liberal Sweden in the interwar period lend further support to this idea. The desire of the fascist governments in Italy and Germany to control the midwifery profession is an especially noteworthy example of the authoritarian path to centralization. For Italian Fascists and German National Socialists, empowering but also controlling the midwifery profession was a means for the state to reach into families and to implement racial,nativist, and eugenic policies.

When it comes to the role of the church and the provision of public support for midwives in private practice, we note that secularization happened early, and the fusion of church and state was rare even in the nineteenth century (although it had been common in the early modern period). Subsidization, on the other hand, typically happened late; it was most common in religiously mixed societies – which is a pattern that we find in most policy areas where subsidization existed – but we find little evidence that subsidization was treated as a solution to religious conflict. Our interpretation of these patterns is that the mix of public, church, and private authority was largely a matter of convenience and capacity and not a result of conflicts over principles.

The main conflict, instead, was the professional conflict between midwives and doctors over how to best care for mothers and children. This conflict was different from the political conflicts over centralization and the role of religious organizations and private providers that we have concentrated on in this book, but it was certainly not unrelated to politics, for midwives and doctors mobilized their organizations and their political connections to defend their legitimacy and status and, if possible, gain a monopoly on birth attendance and maternal and infant care.

It is no coincidence, in our view, that the countries in which midwifery developed into a strong profession already in the early modern period and the early nineteenth century are also the countries in which midwives continue to play an important role in national public health systems. In this area, too, the way in which public services are provided today is largely a result of professional and political struggles that were fought in the nineteenth and early twentieth centuries.

PART V

THE ORIGINS OF PUBLIC SERVICES

10

Conclusions

I see what you are driving at. I knew it from the first. Centralisation.
No. Never with my consent. Not English.

Charles Dickens, *Our Mutual Friend* (1864–1865)

It is sometimes said that were born alone, live alone, and die alone.[1] For more than 200 years, the state has begged to differ. The modern state trains and employs midwives and obstetricians, who assist our mothers when we are born; teachers, who mold our minds; police officers, who protect us or keep us in check; and doctors and public health officers, who try, with some success, to preserve us from an early death. For better or worse, the state just won't leave us alone.

Over the preceding seven chapters, we have seen how the nineteenth- and early twentieth-century state made its presence felt across the domain of human life, involving itself deeply in the behavior, the minds, and the physical well-being of its citizens. We often think of the interwar period as the political nadir of the modern world, and in many ways it was, but when it comes to the public provision of order, knowledge, and health, it was a new zenith. In most countries, crime was controlled by largely law-abiding, uniform-wearing police.[2] Primary education was more or less universal. Smallpox was on its way to eradication. The mentally ill and the criminal were not banished and punished arbitrarily, but housed, albeit coercively, in modern, purpose-built institutions. Governments had

---

[1] The source of the quote is Orson Welles's film *Someone to Love* from 1985.
[2] For an overview of policing in interwar Europe, see Blaney (2007).

rationalized and universalized the communal treatment of every stage of life, from birth to the inevitabilities of mental and physical decline.

Indeed, one of the causes of the political crisis in the inter-war period was arguably that prewar institutions and political organizations had failed to keep up with the ongoing transformation of state power. Conservatives and liberals – the nineteenth century's dominant political forces – struggled with the demands of mass politics. The expansion of the market system, both in its reach globally and in its purview domestically, had exposed ever more citizens to the vagaries of capitalism, which led, as Polanyi (1944) famously argued, to endemic social disorder. Teeming cities, festering crime, surging populations: these byproducts of industrialization and urbanization could not be managed by decentralized markets. Citizens therefore expected more from their governments.[3] As we discussed in Chapter 2, both conservatives and liberals were reluctant to empower governments to address these problems through a further expansion of public services. In this volatile political climate, as Sheri Berman (2006) has shown, socialism and fascism held out the promise of a new reconciliation of state power and state purpose.[4]

In this concluding chapter, we bring together all the evidence we have considered in our book, drawing conclusions from the main trends over time, the main differences among the seven policy areas we have studied, and the main differences among the nineteen countries in our analysis. Until now, our analysis has been largely qualitative, and the quantitative data we have presented have been univariate and descriptive. After summarizing the results of our qualitative findings, we now adopt a large-*n* approach, examining public-service reforms in all policy areas between the early nineteenth century and the Second World War. We are therefore able to say more about whether the political forces we outlined earlier in the book – the debates between liberals and conservatives, the conflicts between church and state and between majority and minority religions, and the rise of authoritarian regimes – explain the choices states made about how to govern their public services.

The chapter ends by casting forward. In the final two sections, we explore how public services were organized in the period after the Second

---

[3] Ruggie (1982, 50–52) observes that there was also a contradiction between state power and the social purposes of the state in *international* society in the interwar period.

[4] Hong (1998) argues in her study of social policy in Weimar Germany that the shared authority and responsibility of the state, voluntary associations, and churches in the Weimar Republic contributed to a crisis of 'parliamentary government within the welfare sector,' which 'created a situation in which the Nazi critique of republican "welfare" could acquire broad political resonance.'

World War; we discuss whether the 'worlds of welfare' that social scientists have identified in the postwar period correspond with the prewar cross-national differences our book describes, and we bring the narrative up to the present. In the postwar era, with its many conflicts over the levels of taxation and public spending, political debates over 'how much' often dominated debates over 'by whom.' Since the 1980s, however, the prewar conflicts that we discuss in this book have resurged, and the organization of public services has become politically salient once more (see, for example, Gingrich 2011). Meanwhile, moral debates over the merits of institutions such as private prisons, faith schools, and compulsory vaccination are back on the political agenda, and the balance between the central state and local government has tipped once more. The nineteenth century's revolution in government continues to define political conflicts in the twenty-first century.

10.1 THE EXPANSION OF PUBLIC SERVICES

The first objective of our book was to account for the sheer expansion of public services in the nineteenth and early twentieth centuries. Relying on several types of evidence – including data on legislation, government employment, and the proportion of the population that was incarcerated, attended school, or were committed to mental institutions – we have shown when, where, and how the provision of public services increased in Western Europe, North America, Japan, and Oceania between 1800 and 1939. Table 10.1, which summarizes our main findings concerning the expansion of public services, sorts the seven services in our study in the approximate order of their period of greatest expansion.

Let us begin by considering the last column, which summarizes our findings concerning the uniformity of public-service provision once we reach the interwar years of the 1920s and 1930s. Perhaps the most important conclusion to be drawn from our study is that the adoption and expansion of public services was near-universal. The one important exception – midwifery – resulted from the often intense professional conflicts between midwives and doctors in the late nineteenth and early twentieth centuries. By the turn of the twentieth century, almost all countries in our study had established comprehensive systems of policing, imprisonment, schooling, library services, mental health care, and vaccination.

There was not only convergence in the provision of public services, but also in their outward form. Civilian police wore conspicuous uniforms

TABLE 10.1 *Main findings: Expansion*

	First steps	Main expansion	Convergence
Vaccinations	First programs in early nineteenth century, compulsory vaccination in Denmark, Sweden, and many German states before 1820	Early to mid-nineteenth century, many big reforms after Franco-Prussian War	Some program in all countries, but no national program in federal Australia, Canada, and United States; compulsory vaccinations in 75 percent of countries by early twentieth century, in just over 60 percent by 1930s
Police	Civilian: creation of modern police force in London, 1829 National-military: French Revolution, Napoleonic invasions	Diffusion of modern civilian policing in middle third of nineteenth century	All countries in our study introduced modern civilian policing before the late 1880s; by then, 70 percent had national-military police; by 1930s, only 40 percent did
Asylums	Early initiatives in late eighteenth century, First national lunacy law in France, 1838	Most countries adopted lunacy laws in middle third of the nineteenth century	All countries constructed large mental institutions and increased institutionalization rates; Japan was the last country in our study to adopt modern lunacy law in early twentieth century.
Prisons	Mass imprisonment emerged according to the Auburn (1817) and Pennsylvania (1829) models	Mass expansion of imprisonment in middle of nineteenth century in England and France, late nineteenth century in Scandinavia, North America, Japan	All countries replaced exile and corporal punishments with imprisonment, reduction of capital punishment, prisons conformed to the same cellular model

	First steps	Main expansion	Convergence
Schools	First compulsory public schools in Prussia, late eighteenth century	Second half of nineteenth century	Most countries had enrollment rates close to 100 percent by the early twentieth century.
Libraries	England, 1850 (early initiatives in Southern Europe not implemented)	Second third of nineteenth century and beginning of twentieth century, inspired by expansion in England and the United States	Public libraries in all countries, but they remained fee paying in Australia and New Zealand
Midwifery	National midwifery training paid by parishes in Sweden from 1757	Large differences among countries; the Scandinavian countries introduced national midwifery programs at the turn of the nineteenth century; English-speaking settler countries only took steps in that direction in early twentieth century	No convergence: some countries even banned the practice of midwifery altogether

and took control over public order, crime detection, apprehension, and traffic control. Prisons were often constructed along similar architectural lines, with individual cells for prisoners and a radial design that reached outward from a central observation tower (Johnston 2000, 55). Schools expanded in size and were staffed by state-trained, registered teachers, who typically taught to a national curriculum in large, multi-classroom buildings. Like prisons, mental institutions were architecturally similar, as were the methods used, until the so-called deinstitutionalization of the world's great asylums and mental hospitals in the second half of the twentieth century.

An early modern visitor to the early twentieth century's industrialized countries would thus have been struck by the uniformity in the provision and outward form of public services across countries. This uniformity was in sharp contrast to the piecemeal and locally contingent precursors of modern public services that were provided by monarchs, parishes, and religious orders in the eighteenth century and earlier.

Meanwhile, the seven public services we have studied became increasingly distinct from one another.[5] We have found many fascinating *connections* among different public services in the nineteenth and twentieth centuries. Prison libraries are one example. Vaccination as a condition of school enrollment is another. But public services were much more *differentiated* in the nineteenth century than they had been in the eighteenth. If prisons and libraries had not emerged as separate services in the nineteenth century, no one would have thought of combining them in the twentieth.[6]

Next, consider the first column in Table 10.1, which describes the beginnings of modern services. One notes immediately that public services were only introduced prior to the nineteenth century in a few exceptional cases (such as the public provision of midwifery in Age of Liberty Sweden and the beginnings of compulsory schooling in eighteenth-century Prussia). In almost all cases, recognizably modern public services emerged in the first half of the nineteenth century. Not

---

[5] There are a few interesting exceptions. For example, as a result of Australia's history as a penal colony, the police played a significant role in decisions about confinement to asylums and mental hospitals in Australia during a longer period than elsewhere (Coleborne 2003).

[6] The first 'recorded designation of a librarian for correctional library service' occurred in Iowa in the early twentieth century (see the entry on prison libraries in Kent 1968–2003): Iowa's State Board of Control decided to set up a library in each prison in 1903, and a woman named Miriam E. Carey was appointed supervising librarian in 1907.

coincidentally, the timing of these innovations corresponds with the early stages of industrialization and with the growth of cities. The emergence of public services is also synchronous with the early political success of liberalism in many countries, and with the decline in monarchical absolutism and the rise of constitutional government.

The middle column in Table 10.1 identifies the period in which each service expanded and spread among countries once it had been introduced in a few pioneering states. This expansion and diffusion typically occurred in the middle third of the nineteenth century, sometimes accelerating at the turn of the twentieth century. Those were also periods of increasing industrialization in most of the countries in our sample, as well as being periods of rising nationalism, intensifying colonial empire-building, and geopolitical rivalry. These economic, social, and geopolitical changes provided further motivation for policies that could secure a compliant, educated, and healthy population.

Table 10.1 also notes a few instances in which our main categories of local, regional, and central and public, church, and private fail to capture important differences in how public services were provided. The important distinction between national-civilian and national-military police forces is one example. The great nineteenth-century debates on compulsory vaccination is another. We discuss these policy differences and political debates in detail in the empirical chapters. In general, however, the categories of local, regional, and central on the one hand and public, church, and private on the other hand do capture the most important differences among countries, when it comes how public services were provided, and by whom. We turn to those differences in the next section.

10.2 GOVERNING PUBLIC SERVICES

Despite the convergence in public-service provision per se – and despite the convergence in outer form – public services were governed very differently among the advanced states by the 1930s, just as they were in the nineteenth century. As we discussed in Chapter 2, public services were on average becoming more centralized over time. The 'fusion' of state and church was gradually coming to an end. The subsidization of private providers became more common. But the cross-country differences remained significant. In some countries, police forces, prisons, schools, libraries, asylums, vaccinations, and midwives were regulated, governed, and controlled by ministries and bureaucracies in the national capital.

Elsewhere, localities remained in control. In some countries, the church maintained significant control over at least some public services by the interwar period; in most places, secular authorities had stripped religious institutions and orders of their ancient prerogatives and responsibilities. In some countries, public-service-providing organizations remained in private hands, but benefited from government funding; elsewhere, public and private provision remained entirely distinct. Even today, the organization of many public services reflect political choices that were made in the nineteenth and early twentieth centuries.

To understand this variation in how public services were provided – and, importantly, by whom – was the second main objective of our study. We have emphasized two conflicts of interest: a conflict of the vertical distribution of power among localities, regions, and central authorities, which pitted conservatives against liberals and socialists, and a conflict over the horizontal distribution of power among secular authorities, churches, and voluntary associations, which pitted secular modernizers against religious conservatives, and religious communities against one another.

In Table 10.2, we summarize our main findings concerning the organization of each of the seven public services in our study.

The first thing to note is that there is considerable support for the idea that there were two main paths to centralization. We have found prominent examples of the authoritarian path to centralization in every policy area in our study. In some authoritarian political regimes – such as in the fascist regimes of the 1920s and 1930s – nearly every policy area was centralized, even midwifery (although vaccinations, interestingly, were not). But those are not the only examples of the authoritarian path. We also find important examples of centralization among the early nineteenth century's absolutist monarchies and in an autocratic, modernizing regime such as Meiji and early Showa Japan. Centralization was also common in dominions where colonial authorities faced indigenous rebellion, especially when it comes to policing, as in nineteenth-century Ireland and New Zealand. Britain was not authoritarian in itself, but its colonial interventions were. Indeed, it seems to be a general pattern that states have set up more centralized institutions for services that were provided to, or directed at, indigenous populations than when they have organized services for the settler population – note the federal insane asylum for Native Americans in the United States (Chapter 7) and the early centralization of vaccination policy for the Maori population in New Zealand (Chapter 8).

TABLE 16.2 *Main findings: Organization*

	Centralization		Public–church–private	
	Authoritarian path	Liberal–democratic path	Liberalism → secularization	Heterogeneity → subsidies
Police	Yes. Most national-military forces and some national-civilian forces were created in authoritarian regimes.	Yes. Several national-civilian forces were created in liberal-democratic regimes.	No. Secular, public monopoly by nineteenth century.	
Prisons	Yes. Examples: Meiji Japan, Nazi Germany, and colonial government in Ireland.	Yes. Examples: New Zealand and Norway in the twentieth century.	No. Secular monopoly by nineteenth century.	Public funding for private prisons most common in religiously mixed societies but rarely as a solution to religious conflict. Prison labor was sometimes sold to private employers (reverse subsidies).
Schools	Yes. Examples: Meiji Japan and twentieth-century authoritarian regimes.	Yes. Examples: Belgium, France (nineteenth century), Norway and Sweden (twentieth century).	Yes. State–church confrontation in Southern Europe; gradual secularization under liberal and socialist governments in Northern Europe.	Yes. Either public funding for private schools or parallel public school boards in most mixed societies.

	Centralization		Public–church–private	
	Authoritarian path	Liberal–democratic path	Liberalism → secularization	Heterogeneity → subsidies
Libraries	Yes. Examples: Fascist Italy and Nazi Germany.	No. But some liberal and socialist governments created *regional* library authorities.	Yes. Early library initiatives in Southern Europe were results of state–church conflict. Parish libraries lost relevance in Northern Europe.	No. Almost all countries funded private libraries at some point. Private funding for public libraries was common (reverse subsidies).
Asylums	Yes. Early centralizers were typically absolute monarchies; late centralizers were typically fascist regimes.	Yes, in New Zealand.	Mixed support – liberals secularized asylums in Spain, Conservatives did so in England.	A mixed economy was rare in Lutheran countries but common everywhere else.
Vaccinations	Yes. In nineteenth-century monarchies, but not in twentieth-century fascist regimes.	Yes, in New Zealand.	Transfer of authority from clergy to doctors often promoted by nineteenth-century liberals, but conservative examples also exist.	Public funding for private vaccinators was most common in religiously mixed societies, but rarely as a solution to religious conflict.
Midwifery	Yes. Examples: Fascist Italy and Nazi Germany.	Yes, in New Zealand. Regional midwifery programs in other twentieth-century liberal and socialist regimes.	No. Uncontroversial nineteenth-century shift to medical authorities.	Public funding for midwives in private practice was most common in religiously mixed societies, but rarely as a solution to religious conflict.

We also find considerable support for the idea of a liberal-democratic path to centralization led by liberal and socialist parties in democratic states. The evidence is strongest in the domains of public order and education, which are areas in which liberals and socialists in democracies were especially keen for the nation-state to provide services more uniformly. There is least support for the idea of a liberal-democratic path to centralization in the case of public libraries, which have remained local institutions in all democracies. The evidence in the public-health domains is more mixed: there are examples of the liberal-democratic path, but only one or two per policy domain.

Meanwhile, the baseline level of centralization has historically been much higher in some domains than others. There is a strong correlation between how coercive public services were and how centralized they were: prisons and insane asylums were most centralized; then comes the police; then vaccinations and schools, which were often compulsory; and only then come midwives and libraries, which were typically not compulsory, and therefore least coercive. Two possible explanations for this pattern are connected with our argument about two paths to centralization – more coercive public services may have been centralized because state leaders wanted to control those policies and use them for their own ends (the authoritarian path), but they may also have been centralized in order for legislatures to put in place legal checks and put them out of the reach of capricious and idiosyncratic local elites (the liberal-democratic path).

Another idea we discussed in Chapter 2 concerns the fusion of church and state – or, rather, the end of it: secularization. We find some support for our main idea that secularization was the result of liberal or socialist groups getting the upper hand in national politics, but as expected, only clearly so in the case of education. When it comes to public order – policing and prisons – secular institutions had already become predominant before the period we have studied, often long before. When it comes to health care and public health – mental institutions, vaccinations, and midwifery – there is also some evidence for a liberal path to secularization, but it is weaker than in education, since public health reforms were on the whole less contested. We do find that the clergy were often relieved of their duties in national vaccination programs under more liberal governments in the nineteenth century, and out of the few reforms we find in mental health care – which was typically secularized early on – two were adopted by liberals. Nevertheless, Lipset and Rokkan (1967) were right – as was Kalyvas (1998) – to identify schooling as the main area of contention in state–church conflicts in the nineteenth and early twentieth centuries; in other domains, secularization occurred sooner and was less controversial.

Finally, the subsidization of private providers of services has always been more common in religiously mixed societies than in either predominantly Catholic countries or, especially, predominantly Protestant countries. This finding is consistent with the idea that subsidization was as a means of resolving conflicts among denominations, and in the domain of schooling, that has quite clearly been an important mechanism. But we have also found that the subsidization of private providers has been more common in religiously mixed countries than in either Catholic or Protestant countries ever since the first half of the nineteenth century. In other words, the introduction of subsidies was not always a response to rising popular demand for special amenities for religious minorities in democratizing societies. It seems, rather, that governments have long opted to provide public services through subsidization in mixed societies – perhaps because private and religious organizations were better equipped to take on such tasks where Catholics and Protestants lived side by side. Relying on private providers was often a practical choice for governments that lacked the administrative capacity required for setting up new bureaucracies to meet the rising demand for public services in the nineteenth and early twentieth centuries.

In deed, in many of the cases of subsidization that we have discussed in the empirical chapters, other motives than a desire to resolve religious conflict explain why governments opted for a mixed economy. In the area of mental health, for instance, we noted in Chapter 7 that countries often turned to private hospitals and asylums when they could not house all public patients in public institutions. These findings serve as a reminder that governments were often constrained by a lack of infrastructure when the overall demand for public services increased in the nineteenth and early twentieth centuries; state capacity, or rather the lack thereof, is often the best explanation of what governments did, not ideology or party.

10.3 CENTRAL, LOCAL, PUBLIC, CHURCH, PRIVATE

In the chapters on each of the public services in our study, we relied on descriptive evidence and case-by-case discussions of important reforms. In this section, we test our main claims in a different way – by bringing

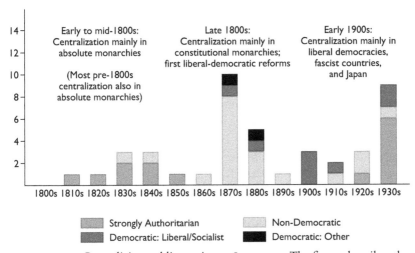

FIGURE 10.1 Centralizing public services, 1800–1939. The figure describes the number of country-years in each decade in which a reform occurred that centralized a public service to the national level. 'Highly authoritarian' corresponds to a Polity score of −6 or lower. 'Not democratic' corresponds to a Polity score that exceeds −6 but is lower than 6. 'Democratic' corresponds to a Polity score of at least 6.

the evidence from all seven different public services together and by conducting a simple statistical analysis of the quantitative data.

Our main hypotheses about centralization are, first, that there was an authoritarian path to centralization (nondemocracies – both nineteenth-century monarchies and twentieth-century authoritarian governments – were more likely to centralize public services than democracies), and second, that there was a liberal-democratic path to centralization (in democracies, liberals and socialists were more likely than conservatives or religious parties to centralize services).

In Figure 10.1, we describe each centralizing reform in each of the policy domains in our study (for the police, we consider the creation of state–civilian and state–military police forces separately). The figure shows when these reforms occurred, as well as the nature of the regimes that adopted them. We distinguish among four types of political systems: strongly authoritarian, nondemocratic but not strongly authoritarian, democratic with a liberal or socialist government, and democratic with any other type of government (mainly conservative or Christian parties). Our data on democracy are from the Polity project (Marshall and Jaggers 2012). Our data on the ideology of heads of governments come from Ansell and Lindvall (2013) and Brambor, Lindvall, and Stjernquist (2017), to which we have added new data on the ideological orientation of heads of government in countries that were democratic before 1870.[7]

Figure 10.1 reveals several important patterns in the history of the centralization of public services. When it comes to the idea of two paths to centralization, one notes immediately that there have been very few instances of centralizing reforms in democratic countries with governments that were not either liberal or social democratic. The only two exceptions we have found are the creation of national services for policing and prisons in New Zealand in the late 1870s and early 1880s, but as we discussed in Chapters 3 and 4, those reforms are in fact quite ambiguous, since – like the centralization of mental institutions and education – they resulted from the wholesale abolition of New Zealand's provincial layer of government in 1876. That larger administrative transformation was not conservative in tendency, for it was pushed through by a prime minister – Julius Vogel – who was in important respects a liberal (although such labels should be used with caution, as New Zealand's political parties had not yet formed at the time). For instance, Vogel was a leading advocate of votes for women (Sinclair 1961, 147; Sinclair suggests that 'adventurer' would be a more fitting label for Vogel's ideological tendency).

Turning to the governments that *did* pursue a policy of centralization, Figure 10.1 shows, as Table 10.2 did, that there is a great deal of support for the idea of two paths to centralization, one authoritarian and one liberal-democratic. We base this conclusion on two observations: among democracies, there are many more reforms under liberal and social democratic governments than under conservative governments,

---

[7] Ansell and Lindvall (2013) and Brambor, Lindvall, and Stjernquist (2017) disagree on the categorization of some heads of government. This is because the Brambor, Lindvall, and Stjernquist heads-of-government data set is mainly concerned with economic ideology, whereas Ansell and Lindvall (2013) distinguishes between conservative and liberal parties even if both were right-wing in the economic dimension. Since we are not only interested in economic issues narrowly defined but also in the conflict between church and state, and other issues, the Brambor, Lindvall, and Stjernquist data are not always right for us. We have recategorized the heads of government in Denmark in 1870–1874, 1902–1909, 1911–1912, 1920–1923, and 1927–1928; in the Netherlands in 1870–1871, 1878–1879, 1883–1887, 1892–1901, 1906–1907, and 1914–1918; in Norway in 1910–1911 and 1923–1924; and in the United States in 1885–1888 and 1893–1896 as 'liberal.' We have recategorized the heads of government in Canada in 1918–1919, France in 1927–1929, Germany in 1923, and Ireland in 1932–1939 as 'not liberal.' We have coded Switzerland as liberal during the period of liberal hegemony until 1891; after that year, we have coded it as not liberal, since liberal parties no longer held power alone.

and among nondemocracies, the most authoritarian governments in each period described in Figure 10.1 were the most likely to pursue a policy of centralization.

Between the eighteenth century (starting before Figure 10.1 begins) and the early 1850s, almost all of the centralizing reforms we have identified in this book were adopted by governments in absolute monarchies. It is noteworthy that most of these reforms concerned the more coercive services among those we study in this book: they involved the introduction of state-civilian and especially state-military state policing, national prison services, state-run insane asylums, and, in one case, compulsory vaccinations. The only two reforms that were *not* introduced in countries with strongly authoritarian institutions before the middle of the nineteenth century were the French law on insane asylums in 1838 and the creation of the Spanish national-military police force, the Guardia Civil, in 1844.

In the second half of the nineteenth century, there were few strongly authoritarian regimes among the countries in our sample, since most of the absolute monarchical regimes had been replaced by more constitutional forms of government. In this period – specifically between 1868 and 1899 (there were no centralizing reforms at all between 1853 and 1868), most centralizing reforms, outside the unusual case of New Zealand, which we discussed earlier, occurred in constitutional monarchies or other nondemocratic but not strongly authoritarian regimes. This is the period in which several constitutional monarchies created more centralized vaccination programs (Chapter 8), and there were important reforms of policing and prisons in Canada, Italy, Japan, New Zealand, the Netherlands, and the United Kingdom (Chapters 3 and 4). But the second half of the nineteenth century also witnessed the first centralized education systems (Chapter 5), two of which were introduced by liberal parties or factions in democracies – Belgium and France – and one of which was introduced in a modernizing authoritarian regime, Meiji Japan.

In the first four decades of the twentieth century, finally, most centralizing reforms were adopted by liberal and social-democratic governments in democracies on the one hand and by authoritarian governments on the other. Schooling was now centralized in a growing number of countries, both in liberal democracies and in authoritarian states. Meanwhile, among the authoritarian states, libraries and midwifery – services that have almost never been centralized anywhere else – were sometimes placed under the control of national bureaucracies (or, in some cases, under the control of parallel organizations that were loyal to the ruling party). Authoritarian governments in countries that had not yet centralized their mental hospitals typically increased the central government's control over those institutions. Finally, liberal and social democratic governments in democracies centralized policing in a few countries in the beginning of the twentieth century.

The patterns we see in this sequence of reforms broadly reflect our main expectations about social services along the vertical and horizontal dimensions we have discussed throughout this book. But it is possible to make more use of the data by also taking control variables and period-specific effects into account. Is it the case that centralizing reforms occurred *because* liberal, socialist, or authoritarian governments come to power? Can we be sure that these reforms were politically motivated and not simply a result of changes in overall economic development or the passing of time?

In Ansell and Lindvall (2013), we examine a cross-time, cross-country data set on the centralization, secularization, and subsidization of education in the period 1870–1939. Education is the policy domain in which we have found the most variation in governance – both across countries and over time. In other policy areas, there is typically less variation in the data, especially over time. Replicating the same sort of statistical analysis for every policy area in this book therefore makes little sense; the policy-specific data are simply not appropriate for quantitative analysis. Instead, our approach is to examine episodes of reform across *all* of our policy areas. For example, if a centralizing reform in any one of our policies is introduced in a particular country in a given year, what are the correlates of that change? We are able to extend our analysis fifty years further back than Ansell and Lindvall (2013), so that the data set covers 1820 to 1939.

We begin by analyzing centralization. Our dependent variable is a binary indicator of whether a centralizing reform in any policy area occurred in a particular country-year. We include all the seven main policy areas, as well as the data we have compiled on national gendarmeries. We have forty-seven instances of centralization in our data. To analyze this outcome statistically, we follow a conventional technique used for discrete-time event analysis by employing a logit specification with controls for our variables of interest along with a cubic polynomial of time since the last reform, to capture temporal dependence, and a variable that counts the number of previous reforms in each country (Beck, Katz, and

Tucker 1998; Carter and Signorino 2010); we cluster our standard errors by country to capture group dependence.

Our core political variables are our measures of regime type. As before, we split regimes into four groups: highly authoritarian regimes (those with a Polity score of under minus five), including both fascist countries in the twentieth century and a number of absolute monarchies in the nineteenth century; non-democracies (with a Polity score between minus five and positive five), sometimes referred to as 'anocracies'; liberal and socialist democracies (those with a Polity score above five and a liberal or socialist government in power); and other democracies (those with a Polity score above five but run by conservative, confessional, or other parties or leaders). Doing so allows us to test our core idea that centralization is most likely through an authoritarian path or through a liberal or socialist democratic path.

We include a number of important controls. We include a measure of GDP per capita from Maddison (2011), to control for economic development, and binary indicators for the presence of an established church and of federalism (both are based on our own coding, which builds, in turn, on Ansell and Lindvall 2013).

Rather than presenting regression tables from the logit models, which are hard to interpret in substantive terms, we display changes in the predicted probability of a centralizing reform in Figure 10.2 which examines the period 1820–1939 (totaling 1,492 observations).[8] The figure shows the estimated marginal effects of a unit shift in each independent variable on the probability of centralization, and the 95 percent confidence interval around that estimate. The omitted political regime category is 'other democracies.'

Figure 10.2 demonstrates that all the three other regime types were more likely to centralize public services than democracies governed by conservative, confessional, or regional parties. Our idea of two paths to centralization appears to hold up: there is one path in authoritarian countries, especially strongly authoritarian ones, and another path where liberal and social-democratic governments are in power in democracies. It is important to note that these two paths emerge even as we control for economic development, church status, federalism, temporal patterns in the data, and each country's history of prior reforms. In terms of magnitude, liberal, socialist and authoritarian governments were between 4

---

[8] The regression tables are presented in the appendix.

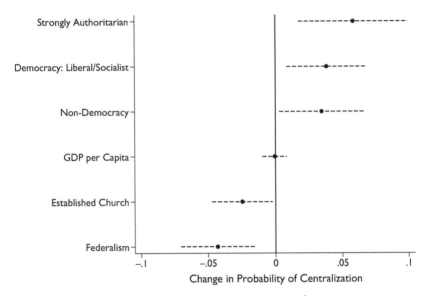

FIGURE 10.2 Likelihood of centralization after 1820.

and 6 percentage points more likely to adopt a centralizing reform in a given year than were conservative or confessional governments in democracies, all else equal. The size of this effect is similar to, or larger than, the countervailing effect of federalism (four percent age points).

There are some other interesting patterns in the data. Economic development does not appear to be positively related to centralization. In other words, centralization did not simply occur because states became rich enough to manage a national system effectively. There is also some evidence that having an established church is associated with a lower likelihood of centralization. This may be a consequence of the networks of church-controlled public services that were prevalent in countries with established churches, which meant that a ready-made – but typically decentralized – basis of provision was available to political leaders. Finally, and unsurprisingly, we find that federal countries were much less likely to centralize public services than unitary states.

Next, we consider our main hypotheses about the relationship between church and state, and in particular about the 'fusion' of secular and religious authority (spiritual and temporal institutions), which are, quite simply, that the role of the church varied greatly among policy domains and that liberal and socialist governments were especially likely to push for secularization.

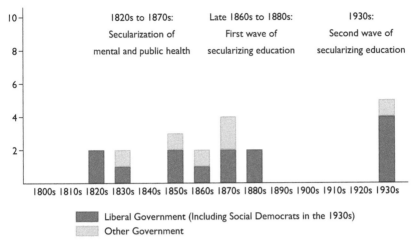

FIGURE 10.3 Ending the fusion of church and state, 1800–1939. The figure describes the number of country-years in each decade in which a reform occurred that ended the 'fusion' of church and state concerning a public service.

In Figure 10.3, we describe reforms that put an end to the 'fusion' of church and state in each of the policy domains in our study. Like Figure 10.1 – which illustrated the history of centralization – Figure 10.3 reveals important patterns in the history of the secularization of public services.

First, Figure 10.3 illustrates the point we made about the differences among policy areas already in Chapter 2, which is that the relationship between church and state varied greatly among the domains of public order, education, and public health: there are no secularizing reforms of public order, for the simple reason that public order had been secularized already in the early-modern period; the secularization of mental and public health, where those domains were not already secularized, occurred in the middle of the nineteenth century; the secularization of education, however, occurred in two major waves, in the 1860s to 1880s and again in the 1930s.

Second, Figure 10.3 shows that the fusion of church and state, to the extent that it persisted into the nineteenth century, typically ended during liberal and social-democratic governments, beginning with the secularization of health in the Spanish *Trienio Liberal* in the 1820s and ending with the secularization of Denmark's and Sweden's Lutheran school systems in the 1930s. There are examples of secularizing reforms under conservative governments, but they are relatively few, especially when

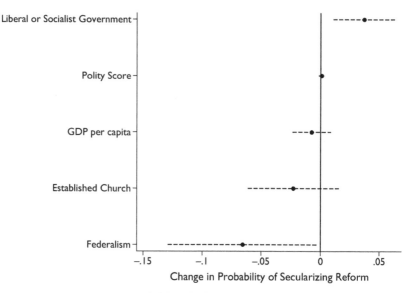

FIGURE 10.4 Likelihood of secularization after 1870.

one considers the fact that conservative governments were more frequent among the countries in our study.

We turn next to our statistical analysis of secularization. Here we have fewer instances of reforms. We are also constrained to a time period for which we have consistent data on the ideological orientation of governments (1870 onward), which means that our analysis relies heavily on the secularization of education. We limit our analysis to those countries where further secularization was actually possible (in a number of country-years, *all* public services were fully secular and no further reform was logically possible). Rather than examining several different political regimes *per se*, our interest now is in whether liberals and socialists were able to achieve their goal of removing public services from the purview of the church, no matter which political regime they were in. This goal was as important to liberals in democratic regimes as it was to their counterparts in democracies. We thus estimate the effect of a liberal or socialist government, with the regime type included as a simple control variable.

The results show that liberals and socialists sought to secularize public services when they were in power. Having a liberal or socialist government is associated with an increase in the likelihood of secularization in a given country-year by approximately 3 percentage points; meanwhile, there does not appear to be any relationship between political regime type and secularization.

The control variables also tell an interesting story. In particular, we do not find that economic development – as measured by GDP per capita – is positively associated with secularization, in sharp contrast to the classic secularization thesis dating back to Durkheim and Weber (which suggests that secularization is driven by rising incomes). Perhaps surprisingly, we see only a weak relationship between having an established church and secularization. One might have assumed that an established church would be more effective at preventing secularization, but this does not appear to be the case. But one must keep in mind that the likelihood of *having* a fusion of church and state in the first place was much higher in countries with established churches. Finally, there is some evidence that federalism was negatively associated with secularization. It was harder to override the privileges of strong interest groups where the government itself was not unitary, as modern theories of veto points and veto players suggest (Immergut 1992; Tsebelis 2002).

Finally, we turn to the last hypothesis, which concerns the subsidization of private service providers and its relationship with the religious composition of the country's population. Since the cross-sectional variation is much greater than the over-time variation in this dimension of the governance of public services, we concentrate on cross-sectional differences in levels (Figure 10.5).

Our argument is that subsidization is most likely in religiously mixed societies, in part as a solution to conflict over the control of public services driven by the fear among adherents of minority religions that the majority religion would dominate provision. Broadly speaking, we find that the expected cross-sectional pattern holds across the various public services where subsidization occurred at all (we have no instance of subsidized policing in our study). Religiously mixed countries typically had the highest rates of subsidization: in prisons, schools, libraries, vaccines, and (at the margin) midwifery. Only in the case of mental asylums do we find that mixed societies had less subsidization on average than Catholic countries. Moreover, there is no area in which Protestant countries had higher rates of subsidization. This is in part a result of the fusion of the Lutheran church with the state in the religiously homogeneous Nordic countries – , an institutional mechanism that long contained state–church conflicts.

What we cannot be sure of is the degree to which this correlation reflects the mechanism of subsidization as a solution to religious conflict

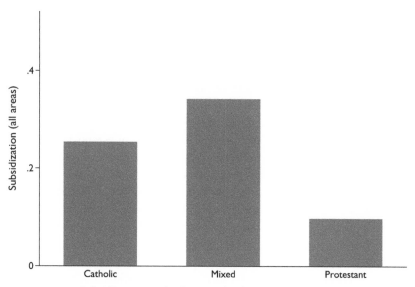

FIGURE 10.5 Subsidization and religion. The figure describes the proportion of country-years in which private service providers received public funding (on average across public services).

per se. It is also the case, for example, that settler colonies such as Canada and Australia were religiously heterogeneous because of immigration from different (mostly European) countries. They were also low-density countries where developing state capacity was inherently challenging, thereby creating a reliance on private provision that might ultimately become subsidized. Thus, issues of state capacity may have been as important as the need to resolve religious conflict in some cases.

10.4 SERVICES AND THE POSTWAR WELFARE STATE

We end our story in 1939 since our main goal in this book is to describe, explain, and analyze the expansion of public services before the large increases in the generosity of social insurance and other types of government benefits after the Second World War. We wanted to show that recognizably modern public services emerged early on, long before the tax-and-transfer state – notwithstanding the fact that the tax-and-transfer state is precisely what the vast majority of all studies of the welfare state are concerned with.

But political conflicts over public services before the Second World War mattered indirectly for the development of the welfare state after the war had ended. Modern party systems, and therefore also the political parties that built and grew the post-war welfare state, were themselves products of the nineteenth and early twentieth centuries' divisive conflicts over schooling, health care, and other services. This is especially true for Christian democratic parties, which are the successors of pre-war Christian parties that were created to defend the prerogatives of the church (Kalyvas 1996). As is well known, Christian democratic parties went on to play a crucial role in the development of the postwar welfare state (Huber and Stephens 2001; van Kersbergen 1995; van Kersbergen and Manow 2009). Meanwhile, the survival of liberal parties into the twenty-first century, even as socialist parties grew in prominence, reflects in part their success at earning the votes of the often secular teachers, doctors, and lawyers whom their public service reforms before 1939 had empowered.

With a few important exceptions, however, the manner in which the public services *themselves* were governed changed only gradually in the postwar period. Indeed, the institutional arrangements that countries put in place in the period before the Second World War typically remained intact long thereafter – sometimes even until today. The explanation is political. Since the nineteenth and early twentieth centuries' conflicts over public services shaped modern party systems, the 'freezing' of those party systems in the interwar period (Lipset and Rokkan 1967) contributed to a consolidation of the institutions that countries had created before then.

In some cases, the stability of those institutional arrangements is remarkable. Consider, for instance, Canadian prisons. As we noted in Chapter 1, the Canadian prison system is based on a division of labor between provincial and federal prisons: those who serve prison sentences longer than two years are housed in federal prisons, whereas those who serve shorter prison sentences are housed in provincial prisons. This particular arrangement, two-year cut-off and all, has existed at least since the 1870s (Wetherell 1979, 146–147) – that is, since the very beginnings of the Canadian federation.

The governance of policing has also been stable in most countries. In the United States, policing remains divided between local, state, and federal jurisdictions, for instance, and in France, it remains divided between the local and national level and between the civilian police and the *Gendarmerie nationale*. England also retains its prewar, decentralized police structure, with thirty-nine separate police forces that in some cases match counties and in others match collections of counties (for example West Mercia Police and Thames Valley Police) or the metropolitan areas.

The compromises that political parties and other political decision makers reached over schooling in the nineteenth and early twentieth centuries also continue to shape modern school systems. Public schools in the United States remain local, secular institutions funded by local property taxes. Private, typically religious schools in the Netherlands continue to receive public funding, no matter which religious community they are associated with. The vast majority of all children in New Zealand still attend state schools (although the small private Catholic school sector was incorporated in the state system in the 1970s, in a manner that is reminiscent of pre–World War II compromises on public and Catholic schools elsewhere). In most countries, public libraries also continue to be governed in much the same way today as in the interwar period. So does midwifery, although it has typically become more fully integrated in the health care system, which means that governance structures have changed in some cases (as in the United Kingdom with the introduction of the National Health Service immediately after the Second World War).

The areas that have changed the most are vaccinations and mental institutions. In the case of vaccinations, the explanation is simple: since smallpox has been eradicated, smallpox vaccination programs have been abolished. But other immunization programs remain, often modelled on the old vaccination programs. In the case of mental institutions, the explanation is that most of the great mental hospitals have been shut down because of the so-called deinstitutionalization of mental health care in the second half of the twentieth century (for a comparative study, see Goodwin 1997). As we noted in Chapter 7, mental institutions are unique among the public services we study in this book: there are few other examples of services that emerge, then disappear. One phase in the deinstitutionalization process was typically the decentralization of mental health care from the national to the regional or local level, or from the regional to the local.

In other policy areas, major changes in the governance of public services were typically associated with great regime changes. For example, most of the centralizing policies that were introduced in Germany under the Nazis were abolished after the Second World War. For example, there is no national-military police in Germany any more, nor is there one in Japan (in Austria, the gendarmerie disappeared even earlier, in

TABLE 10.3 *The roots of modern welfare regimes*

	Liberal	Cons.	Nordic	Southern	Japanese
Overall centralization	0.38	0.30	0.50	0.44	0.66
Overall secularization	0.93	0.94	0.81	0.95	1.00
Overall subsidization	0.27	0.41	0.15	0.36	0.11
Observations	338	344	203	210	70

Notes: The table describes the mean levels of centralization, secularization, and subsidization across all public services between 1870 and 1939 in four groups of countries that have had similar welfare-state institutions in the twentieth century, and in Japan.

connection with another regime change: the creation of the First Republic after the First World War).

France is another interesting example of the importance of regime changes. In the Third Republic, as we saw in Chapter 5, private (typically Catholic) schools did not receive public funding. But after the war, in the Fourth Republic, support for private schools was introduced through the Barangé Law, adopted in 1951 (Williams 1964, 39). In the new party system that emerged in the Fourth Republic, the *Mouvement Républicain Populaire*, a Christian democratic party – notably absent in the Third Republic (Kalyvas 1996) – had become pivotal in the French parliament. The right-wing parties used the divisive issue of religious schooling to split clerical and anticlerical parties on the center-left. In the Fifth Republic, after another regime change, the socialists sought to abolish funding for Catholic schools once they won power in the early 1980s, but they had to back down following widespread protests (see, for instance, Keeler and Hall 2001).

We end this section by considering the relationship between the governance of public services before the Second World War and the structure of postwar welfare states. In Table 10.3, we describe the mean level of centralization, secularization, and subsidization across all public services between 1870 and 1939 in four groups of countries: those that scholars of the welfare state, following Esping-Andersen (1990), categorize as 'liberal' (the English speaking countries in Europe, North America, and Oceania), 'conservative' (continental Western Europe north of the Alps), 'social democratic' or 'Nordic' (Scandinavia and Finland), and 'Southern' (continental Western Europe south of the Alps). For comparison, we place Japan in a separate column. We are interested in whether the patterns that we have found in this book are predictive of how the modern welfare state developed after the Second World War.

There are several interesting patterns to note here. First of all, the level of centralization in the period we have studied was lowest in the 'conservative' welfare states in Continental Western Europe north of the Alps. This is not only consistent with what we know about the subsequent development of the welfare states in these countries, but also with our argument that as countries democratized, more liberal parties – not conservative or religious ones – sought to centralize public services.

Centralization, highest in Japan, is also high in Northern and Southern Europe. The high levels in Southern Europe are unsurprising, since the Southern European welfare states are often described as 'statist' in the scholarly literature. The high level of centralization in the Nordic countries is perhaps more surprising, since local government is traditionally regarded as strong in that region. Clearly, many public services were nevertheless centralized historically. The fact that centralization is as high as it is in the 'liberal' welfare states is mainly due to the fact that New Zealand is in this group (0.7 on a scale from 0 to 1); the other liberal states have lower levels of centralization (ranging from 0.2 for the United States to 0.5 for Ireland).

Turning to secularization, two things stand out in the table: the low level of secularization, historically, in the Nordic countries, three of which had Lutheran state churches, and the high level of secularization in Meiji and post-Meiji Japan.

Finally, turning to subsidization, the main things that stand out in the table are the low levels of subsidization in the Nordic countries and in Meiji Japan and the high levels of subsidization in Continental Western Europe – both north and south of the Alps. In the more northerly countries, this reflects high levels of religious (and sometimes linguistic) heterogeneity, as in Belgium, Germany, and the Netherlands. In the more southerly countries, which are fully Catholic, this reflects weaker state capacity and long-standing reliance on the church to provide services. Most of the countries that had high levels of subsidization historically continue to have a more mixed welfare-state economy today – not only when it comes to public services, but also when it comes to social insurance, with pension systems and other insurance programs being fragmented along occupational lines.

10.5 THE PAST IS NOT EVEN PAST

The political struggles and reforms that we have studied in this book do not only matter because they shaped the modern welfare state. They also matter because political conflicts over public services are back on the political agenda in most modern democracies. The issues that divide us today are in many ways similar to the issues that divided interest groups and political parties in the nineteenth and early twentieth centuries.

For a long time after the Second World War, conflicts over public services were not as politically salient as they had been in the period before World War I, or in the interwar period. With a few important exceptions – some of which we discussed in the previous section – postwar conflicts concerned things such as taxes, social insurance, and the role of the government in the economy, not public services. In other words, political parties in the postwar era disagreed mainly on what we have called 'How much?' questions; most of the 'By whom?' questions appeared, at the time, to have been resolved.

But since the 1980s, as Goerres and Kumlin (2019, Chapter 4) note, public services such as schooling, child care and elderly care have become more salient in European politics than they were in the first postwar decades. So has crime, with important implications for conflicts over policing and prisons: mass incarceration has become a major political issue in the United States, but also in other countries. Meanwhile, as Goerres and Kumlin show, conflicts over social insurance have, if anything, become *less* salient in the last few decades. Conflicts over public services often encompass conflicts over 'How much?' questions, of course, but today, as in the nineteenth and early twentieth centuries, the 'By whom?' questions are often even more divisive.

Contemporary conflicts over schooling are a clear example of how the politics of public services has changed in ways that resemble the great conflicts over control in the nineteenth and early twentieth centuries. In the first half of the 1990s, to take one noteworthy example, Sweden both decentralized its state-run primary school system and introduced a nation-wide voucher system, allowing parents to take their children out of the public system and enroll them in private schools (although the private schools are not allowed to charge fees if they accept public funding) (Gingrich 2011, 152–162). The introduction of vouchers was welcomed by politically influential middle-class and high-income voters – who were much more likely than low-income earners to favor private education – but also by religious groups, who saw an opportunity to set up their own schools. The political divisions over income and class that we recognize from twentieth-century conflicts over the welfare state have thus combined with old political divisions over group and religion that we recognize from pre–Second World War conflicts over public services, especially schooling.

Another example of how today's political conflicts resemble political conflicts more than century ago is the salience of antivaccinationism in contemporary politics. For much of the twentieth century, the issue of vaccination appeared to have been settled, but in the last two or three decades, vaccine refusal has been on the increase. Vocal interest groups now lead the opposition to government vaccination programs.

On January 20, 2017, the former British doctor Andrew Wakefield appeared at one of President Donald Trump's inauguration balls. This was not a coincidence. Some twenty years earlier, Wakefield had been the lead author of an article in *The Lancet* that claimed to have found a link between autism and the vaccine against measles, mumps, and rubella. That article was later retracted since the claims were found fraudulent, and Wakefield, who had several undeclared conflicts of interest, was discredited (after an investigation by the General Medical Council, he was prohibited from practicing medicine in the United Kingdom). By the late 2010s, however, Wakefield had become a leading figure in the antivaccinationist movement and was popular in right-wing populist circles and among supporters of Donald Trump (Boseley 2018).

Scholars of public health have noted many similarities between today's antivaccinationists and those of the nineteenth century (Wolfe and Sharp 2002). Today, as in the past, antivaccinationists exaggerate the risks of vaccination and minimize its benefits (Omer et al. 2009, 1985). Today, as in the past, antivaccinationist propaganda contains false and misleading claims about the purposes, benefits, and risks of vaccination – and in today's internet fora, as in the nineteenth century's own changing media landscape, such propaganda is widely available. Finally, today, as in the past, vaccine refusal is concentrated in ethnic and religious minority groups that are suspicious of the majority culture. In the contemporary United States, for instance, measles have spread in the Amish community, which is concentrated in Ohio; in the Somali community in Minneapolis, Minnesota; and in the Orthodox Jewish community in New York City.

Finally, in a strange return to early nineteenth-century practice, prison services have been partially privatized in a number of countries, and receive public subsidies. The United States is the most well-known example, with the growing private prison sector often described as a 'big business' (Alexander 2010, 230) that is reliant for profit on a continuous stream of prisoners, arrested by public police forces and paid for from public funds. This is a relatively recent phenomenon, for the end of the convict-leasing system in the 1920s led to a long period of exclusively public imprisonment in the United States. But in 1984, the state of

Tennessee contracted out the running of the Shelby prison to the Corrections Corporation of America, and by 2013, over 8 percent of American prisoners were housed in privately run jails, with some states such as New Mexico and Montana holding at least 40 percent of their prisoners in private facilities (Carson 2014, 13). The United Kingdom also returned to the use of private prisons, after over a century's abeyance, in 1992; Australia opened a private prison in 1990, and New Zealand did the same in 2000 (Canada also briefly operated private prisons between 2001 and 2006). Notably, the new world of subsidized private prisons is largely an English-speaking one, and it is driven by profit-making motivations rather than the religious impulses of the first penitentiary movement.

Thus, although we have come to the end of our story, we have not come to the end of political conflicts over public services. The history of those conflicts is an integral part of the history of the modern state.

For the great historian of ideas Michel Foucault, prisons, schools, and mental hospitals were disciplinary institutions, representing a new form of social power. But without the public services we have discussed in this book, much of the social progress that we have witnessed over the past two centuries would have been impossible. And once new public services had been created, citizens held political leaders to account: as democratic elections spread across the advanced countries in the late nineteenth and early twentieth centuries, citizens had the opportunity to vote for the parties that provided order, education, and health most effectively, and to their liking. Today's mass politics is the child of yesterday's political struggles over the control of behavior, minds, and bodies.

Appendix

TABLE A1 *Correlates of centralizing reforms, 1820–1939*

Strongly authoritarian	2.337^*
	(0.941)
Liberal/socialist democracy	1.530^*
	(0.719)
Nondemocracy	1.385^*
	(0.705)
GDP per capita	-0.020
	(0.187)
Established church	-0.985^*
	(0.403)
Federalism	-1.718^{***}
	(0.486)
Observations	$1,492$

Note. Standard errors are in parentheses.
$^*p < 0.05.\ ^{**}p < 0.01.\ ^{***}p < 0.001.$

TABLE A2 *Correlates of secularizing reforms, 1870–1939*

Liberal or socialist government	1.931^{**}
	(0.695)
Polity score	0.050
	(0.073)
GDP per capita	-0.351
	(0.498)
Established church	-1.538
	(1.484)
Federalism	-3.604
	(1.992)
Observations	479

Note. Standard errors are in parentheses.
$^*p < 0.05.\ ^{**}p < 0.01.\ ^{***}p < 0.001.$

References

Ahlskog, Rafael. 2017. *Essays on the Collective Action Dilemma of Vaccination.* PhD thesis, Uppsala University.

Akenson, Donald H. 1970. *The Irish Education Experiment.* London: Routledge and Kegan Paul.

Alexander, Michelle. 2010. *The New Jim Crow: Mass Incarceration in the Age of Colorblindness.* New York: The New Press.

Andersen, Otto. 1973. 'Dødelighedsforholdene i Danmark 1735–1839.' *Nationaløkonomisk Tidsskrift* 111 (2):277–305.

Anderson, Benedict. 1983. *Imagined Communities.* London: Verso Books.

Anisef, Paul, and Priscilla Basson. 1979. 'The Institutionalization of a Profession: A Comparison of British and American Midwifery.' *Sociology of Work and Occupations* 6 (3):353–372.

Ansell, Ben, and Johannes Lindvall. 2013. 'The Political Origins of Primary Education Systems.' *American Political Science Review* 107 (3):505–522.

Aparicio Basauri, Victor. 1997. *Origenes y fundamentos de la psiquiatria en España.* Madrid: Libro del ano.

Appleton, V. E. 1967. 'Psychiatry in Canada a Century Ago.' *Canadian Psychiatric Association Journal* 12 (4):345–361.

Archambault, Joseph. 1938. *Report of the Royal Commission to Investigate the Penal System of Canada.* JO Patenaude, ISO, printer to the King.

Arnold, Mavis, and Heather Laskey. 2012. *Children of the Poor Clares: The Collusion between Church and State That Betrayed Thousands of Children in Ireland's Industrial Schools.* Bloomington, IN: Trafford Publishing.

Arthur, James. 1995. *The Ebbing Tide: Policy and Principles of Catholic Education.* Leominster, MA: Gracewing.

Atherton, William Henry. 1914. *Montreal 1535–1914: Under British Rule 1760–1914.* Montreal: S. J. Clarke.

Atlestam, Ingrid, Madeleine Bergmark, and Eva Halász. 1997. *Fullbokat: Göteborgs folkbibliotek 1862–1997.* Gothenburg, Sweden: Göteborgs stadsbibliotek.

Axelsson, Runo. 2000. 'The Organizational Pendulum: Healthcare Management in Sweden 1865–1998.' *Scandinavian Journal of Public Health* 28 (1):47–53.

Baker, Ernest A. 1922. *The Public Library.* London: Daniel O'Connor.

Baldwin, Peter. 1990. *The Politics of Social Solidarity*. Cambridge: Cambridge University Press.

———. 1999. *Contagion and the State in Europe*. Cambridge: Cambridge University Press.

Balmer-Engel, Catherine. 1994. *Festschrift zum 100-Jahr-Jubiläum: 100 Jahre Schweizerischer Hebammenverband 1894–1994*. Schweizerischer hebammenverband.

Banks, Arthur S. 2009. 'Cross-National Time-Series Data Archive.' Distributed by Databanks International, Jerusalem, Israel.

Barker, Ernest. 1943. *The Development of Public Services in Western Europe 1660–1930*. London: Oxford University Press.

Barnett, Graham Keith. 1987. *Histoire des bibliothèques publiques en France*. Paris: Promodis.

Barreto, Luis, and Christopher J. Rutty. 2002. 'The Speckled Monster: Canada, Smallpox and Its Eradication.' *Canadian Journal of Public Health* 93 (July–August):special insert.

Barrett Litoff, Judy. 1978. *American Midwives, 1860 to the Present*. Westport, CT: Greenwood Press.

———. 1982. 'The Midwife throughout History.' *Journal of Midwifery & Women's Health* 27 (6):3–11.

Barrington, Ruth. 1987. *Health, Medicine & Politics in Ireland, 1900–1970*. Dublin: Institute of Public Administration.

Bartlett, Peter. 1999. *The Poor Law of Lunacy*. London: Leicester University Press.

Bartolini, Stefano. 2000. *The Political Mobilization of the European Left, 1860–1980*. Cambridge: Cambridge University Press.

Bartolomé Martínez, Bernabé. 1989. 'Las bibliotecas publicas provinciales (1835–1885).' *Revista de educación* 288:271–304.

Bassett, Michael. 1998. *The State in New Zealand, 1840–1984*. Auckland: Auckland University Press.

Basso, Rosanna. 2015. *Levatrici: l'assistenza ostetrica nell'Italia liberale*. Rome: Viella.

Bayley, David. 1975. *The Police and Political Development in Europe*. Princeton, NJ: Princeton University Press.

———. 1990. *Patterns of Policing*. New Brunswick, NJ: Rutgers University Press.

———. 1992. 'Comparative Organization of the Police in English-Speaking Countries.' *Crime and Justice* 15:509–545.

———. 1996. *Police for the Future*. Oxford: Oxford University Press.

Bazin, Hervé. 2000. *The Eradication of Smallpox*. San Diego, CA: Academic Press.

———. 2011. *Vaccination: A History*. Montrouge, France: J. Libbey Eurotext.

Beck, Nathaniel, Jonathan Katz, and Richard Tucker. 1998. 'Taking Time Seriously: Time-Series Cross-Section Data with a Binary Dependent Variable.' *American Journal of Political Science* 42 (4):1260–1288.

Benedict, Susan, Mary Lagerwey, and Linda Shields. 2014. 'The Medicalization of Murder.' In *Nurses and Midwives in Nazi Germany*, edited by Susan Benedict and Linda Shields. New York: Routledge, 48–80.

Benoit, Cecilia, Sirpa Wrede, and Jane Sandall. 2001. 'The State and Birth/The State of Birth.' In *Birth by Design*, edited by Raymond De Vries, Cecilia Benoit, Edwing R. van Teijlingen, and Sirpa Wrede. London: Routledge, 28–51.

Beramendi, Pablo. 2012. *The Political Geography of Inequality*. New York: Cambridge University Press.

Bercé, Yves-Marie. 1983. 'Le clergé et la diffusion de la vaccination.' *Revue d'histoire de l'eglise de France* 69 (182):87–106.

Berlière, Jean-Marc, and René Lévy. 2011. *Histoire des polices en France de l'ancien régime à nos jours*. Paris: Nouveau Monde éditions.

Berman, Sheri. 2006. *The Primacy of Politics*. Cambridge: Cambridge University Press.

Besley, Timothy, and Torsten Persson. 2011. *Pillars of Prosperity*. Princeton, NJ: Princeton University Press.

Bieri, Matthias. 2015. 'Beständiger Aufstieg: Private Sicherheitsunternehmen in der Schweiz.' *Bulletin zur schweizerischen Sicherheitspolitik* 2015:63–86.

Biskup, Peter, and Doreen Goodman. 1982. *Australian Libraries*. 3rd ed. London: Clive Bingley.

Bjerrum, Merete. 2005. *Dansk hospitalspsykiatri 1930–1990 med særlig henblik på organisatoriske og administrative forhold*. PhD thesis, Aarhus University.

Blaney, Gerald, Jr., ed. 2007. *Policing Interwar Europe*. Basingstoke, UK: Palgrave.

Bliss, Michael. 1991. *Plague: A Story of Smallpox in Montreal*. Toronto: HarperCollins.

Blom, Ida. 1988. *Den haarde dyst*. Bergen: J. W. Cappelens.

Bobinski, George S. 1969. *Carnegie Libraries*. Chicago: American Library Association.

Bonderup, Gerda. 2001. *En kovending. Koppevaccinationen og dens udfordring til det danske samfund omkring 1800*. Aarhus: Aarhus Universitetsforlag.

Bonger, W. A. 1933. 'Development of the Penal Law in the Netherlands.' *Journal of the American Institute of Criminal Law and Criminology* 24 (1): 260–270.

Borst, Charlotte G. 1995. *Catching Babies*. Cambridge, MA: Harvard University Press.

Borthwick, John Douglas. 1886. *History of the Montreal Prison, from A. D. 1784 to A. D. 1886*. Montreal: A. Periard.

Boschma, Geertje. 2003. *The Rise of Mental Health Nursing: A History of Psychiatric Care in Dutch Asylums, 1890–1920*. Amsterdam: Amsterdam University Press.

Boseley, Sarah. 2018. 'How Disgraced Anti-Vaxxer Andrew Wakefield Was Embraced by Trump's America.' *The Guardian*, July 18.

Bossé, Sébastien, and Chantal Bouchard. 2013. *Bordeaux: l'histoire d'une prison*. Boisbriand, France: Éditions au Carré.

Botsman, Daniel V. 2013. *Punishment and Power in the Making of Modern Japan*. Princeton, NJ: Princeton University Press.

Bowles, Samuel, and Herbert Gintis. 1976. *Schooling in Capitalist America*. New York: Basic Books.

Brambor, Thomas, Agustín Goenaga, Johannes Lindvall, and Jan Teorell. 2019. 'The Lay of the Land: Information Capacity and the Modern State.' *Comparative Political Studies* 53 (2):175–213.

Brambor, Thomas, Johannes Lindvall, and Annika Stjernquist. 2017. 'The Ideology of Heads of Government, 1870–2012.' Version 1.5. Department of Political Science, Lund University.

Breathnach, Ciara. 2016. 'Handywomen and Birthing in Rural Ireland, 1851–1955.' *Gender & History* 28 (1):34–56.

Brennan, Damien. 2014. *Irish Insanity 1800–2000*. London: Routledge.

Briggs, Asa. 1959. *The Age of Improvement*. London: Longmans.

——— 1961. 'The Welfare State in Historical Perspective.' *Archives européennes de sociologie* 2 (2):221–258.

British Medical Journal. 1898. 'The Vaccination Act, 1898.' 2 (1966):637–639.

Brockman, Ann-Marie. 1994. *Göteborgs hospital S:t Jörgen*. Uddevalla: Bohusläns museum.

Brogden, Mike. 1987. 'The Emergence of the Police—The Colonial Dimension.' *The British Journal of Criminology* 27 (1):4–14.

Brouwere, De. 2007. 'The Comparative Study of Maternal Mortality over Time.' *Social History of Medicine* 20 (3):541–562.

Brundage, James A. 2009. *Law, Sex, and Christian Society in Medieval Europe*. Chicago: University of Chicago Press.

Brunton, Deborah. 2008. *The Politics of Vaccination: Practice and Policy in England, Wales, Ireland, and Scotland, 1800–1874*. Rochester, NY: University of Rochester Press.

Brunton, Warwick. 2001. '*A Choice of Difficulties*': National Mental Health Policy in New Zealand, 1840–1947. PhD thesis, University of Otago.

Bugge, Knud Eyvin. 1982. 'Kirke og skole i Danmark 1930–1945.' In *Kirken, Krisen og Krigen*, edited by Ingun Montgomery and Stein Ugelvik Larsen. Oslo: Universitetsforlaget, 69–74.

Burdett, Henry C. 1891. *Hospitals and Asylums of the World*. London: J. & A. Churchill.

Bureau of Statistics, US Treasury Department. Various years. *Statistical Abstract of the United States*. Washington, DC: Government Printing Office.

Busse, Reinhard, Miriam Blümel, Franz Knieps, and Till Bärnighausen. 2017. 'Statutory Health Insurance in Germany.' *The Lancet* 390 (10097):882–897.

Campbell, Janet M. 1917. *Report on the Physical Welfare of Mothers and Children*. Vol. 2. Liverpool, UK: C. Tinling.

Cantor, Nathaniel. 1934. 'Prison Reform in Germany—1933.' *Journal of the American Institute of Criminal Law and Criminology* 25:84.

Caramani, Daniele. 2004. *The Nationalization of Politics*. Cambridge: Cambridge University Press.

Cardona, Álvaro. 2005. *La salud pública en España durante el trienio liberal, 1820–1923*. Vol. 39. Madrid: Editorial CSIC-CSIC Press.

Carlsson, Sten. 1966. 'Den sociala omgrupperingen i Sverige efter 1866.' In *Samhälle och riksdag*. Stockholm: Almqvist & Wiksell, 3–374.

Carson, E. Ann. 2014. 'Prisoners in 2013.' *Bureau of Justice Statistics: Bulletin*.

Carter, David B., and Curtis S. Signorino. 2010. 'Back to the Future: Modeling Time Dependence in Binary Data.' *Political Analysis* 18 (3):271–292.

Castel, Robert. 1988. *The Regulation of Madness*. Berkeley: University of California Press.

Cellard, André, and Dominique Nadon. 1986. 'Ordre et désordre: le Montreal Lunatic Asylum et la naissance de l'asile au Québec.' *Revue d'histoire de l'Amérique française* 39 (3):345–367.

Census and Statistics Office of the Dominion of New Zealand. Various years. *New Zealand Official Yearbook*. Wellington: Government Printer.

Centeno, Miguel A. 2002. *Blood and Debt: War and the Nation-State in Latin America*. University Park: Pennsylvania State University Press.

Centraal Bureau voor de Statistiek. Various years. *Jaarcijfers voor het Koninkrijk der Nederlanden*. The Hague: Gebr. Belinfante.

Christensen, Cecil. 1987. 'Frie skoler i Danmark, historisk og aktuelt.' In *Skolefrihed i Norden*, edited by Henning Lysholm Christensen and Helmut Wolffhechel. Slagelse: Nordisk Privatskole Union, 45–55.

Christie, Nils. 1968. 'Changes in Penal Values.' *Scandinavian Studies in Criminology* 2:161–172.

Cliff, Helen. 1992. *Jordemoderliv*. Copenhagen: Borgens.

Coleborne, Catharine. 2003. 'Passage to the Asylum: The Role of the Police in Committals of the Insane in Victoria, Australia, 1848–1900.' In *The Confinement of the Insane*, edited by Roy Porter and David Wright. Cambridge: Cambridge University Press, 129–148.

Commonwealth Bureau of Census and Statistics. Various years. *Official Year Book of the Commonwealth of Australia*. Melbourne: McCarron, Bird.

Conseil National des Accoucheuses. 2006. 'Profil Professionnel de la Sage-femme en Belgique.' Réunion plénière du 18/12/2006.

Conway, Vicky. 2013. *Policing Twentieth Century Ireland: A History of An Garda Síochána*. New York: Routledge.

Corcos, Arlette. 1997. *Montréal, les Juifs et l'école*. Sillery: Septentrion.

Crawford, Alice. 2015. 'Introduction.' In *The Meaning of the Library*, edited by Alice Crawford. Princeton, NJ: Princeton University Press, xiii–xxix.

Crichton, Anne. 1990. *Slowly Taking Control? Australian Governments and Health Care Provision, 1788–1988*. Sydney: Allen & Unwin.

Cruickshank, Marjorie. 1963. *Church and State in English Education*. London: St. Martin's Press.

Cumpston, John Howard Lidgett. 1914. *The History of Small-Pox in Australia, 1788–1908*. Melbourne: Albert J. Mullett.

———. 1925. 'History of Smallpox in Australia, 1909–1925.' *Public Health Reports* 40 (33):1686–1692.

Cusack, Thomas R., Torben Iversen, and David Soskice. 2007. 'Economic Interests and the Origins of Electoral Systems.' *American Political Science Review* 101 (3):373–391.

Dagenais, Michèle. 2006. *Faire et fuir la ville: espaces publics de culture et de loisirs à Montréal et Toronto aux XIXe et XXe siècles*. Montreal: Les presses de l'Université Laval.

Dain, Phyllis. 1996. 'American Public Libraries and the Third Sector.' *Libraries & Culture* 31 (1):56–84.

Dal Passo, Fabrizio, and Alessandra Laurenti. 2017. *La scuola italiana*. Anzio-Lavinio, Italy: Novalogos.

Darmon, Pierre. 1986. *La longue traque de la variole*. Paris: Librairie Académique Perrin.

Davis, Donald G., and John M. Tucker. 1989. *American Library History: A Comprehensive Guide to the Literature*. Santa Barbara, CA: ABC-CLIO.

De Swaan, Abram. 1988. *In Care of the State*. Oxford: Oxford University Press.

de Tocqueville, Alexis. 2012 [1835–1840]. *Democracy in America*. Chicago: University of Chicago Press.

Dean, Elizabeth A. 1983. 'The Organization of Italian Libraries from the Unification until 1940.' *The Library Quarterly* 53 (4):399–419.

deGruyter, Lisa. 1980. 'The History and Development of Rural Public Libraries.' *Library Trends* 28 (4):513–524.

Dekker, Jeroen J. H., Hilda T. A. Amsing, and Inge J. M. Wichgers. 2019. 'Education in a Nation Divided.' In *School Acts and the Rise of Mass Schooling*, edited by Johannes Westerberg, Lukas Boser, and Ingrid Brühwiler. London: Palgrave, 93–118.

Depaepe, Marc, Maurice De Vroede, Luc Minten, and Frank Simon. 1998. 'L'enseignement primaire.' In *Histoire de l'enseignement en Belgique*, edited by D. Grootaers. Brussels: CRISP, 111–191.

Devries, Raymond, and Rebeca Barroso. 1997. 'Midwives among the Machines.' In *Midwives, Society and Childbirth*, edited by Hilary Marland and Anne Marie Rafferty. London: Routledge, 248–273.

Dixon, C. W. 1962. *Smallpox*. London: J. & A. Churchill.

Dondici, Danilo. 2017. *Italy's Prison System and the Reforms of 1889–1891*. PhD thesis, University of East Anglia.

Donley, Joan. 1986. *Save the Midwife*. Auckland: New Women's Press.

Donnelly, Michael. 1992. *The Politics of Mental Health in Italy*. London: Routledge.

Donnison, Jean. 1977. *Midwives and Medical Men*. London: Heinemann.

Dow, Derek A. 1995. *Safeguarding the Public Health: A History of the New Zealand Department of Health*. Wellington: Victoria University Press.

Dowbiggin, Ian. 2011. *The Quest for Mental Health*. Cambridge: Cambridge University Press.

Dowdall, George W. 1996. *The Eclipse of the State Mental Hospital*. Albany: State University of New York Press.

Drenth, Petra. 1998. *Honderd jaar vroedvrouwen verenigd: 1898/1998*. Nederlandse Organisatie van Verloskundigen (NOV).

Du Mont, Rosemary Ruhig. 1977. *Reform and Reaction: The Big City Public Library in American Life*. Westport, CT: Greenwood Press.

Ducpetiaux, Édouard. 1835. *Statistique comparée de la Criminalité en France, en Belgique, en Angleterre et en Allemagne*. Brussels: Hauman.

Dufour, Andrée. 1997. *Histoire de l'éducation au Québec*. Montreal: Boréal.

Dyrbye, Martin, Ilkka Mäkinen, Tiiu Reimo, and Magnus Torstensson, eds. 2009. *Library Spirit in the Nordic and Baltic Countries*. Tampere, Finland: Hibolire.

Earle, Pliny. 1841. *A visit to Thirteen Asylums for the Insane in Europe.* Philadelphia: Dobson.

1854. *Institutions for the Insane in Prussia, Austria and Germany.* Utica: New York State Asylum.

Edwardes, Edward J. 1902. *A Concise History of Smallpox and Vaccination in Europe.* London: H. K. Lewis.

Ehrenreich, Barbara, and Deirdre English. 1973. *Witches, Midwives and Nurses: A History of Women Healers.* London: Writers and Readers Publishing Cooperative.

Eisner, Manuel, and M. Killias. 2004. 'Country Survey: Switzerland.' *European Journal of Criminology* 1:257–293.

Ellefsen, Birgitte. 2015. 'The Making of a New Police: An Analysis of the Norwegian Police Discourse 1814–1866.' In *The Past, the Present and the Future of Police Research*, 103. Växjö, Sweden: Linnaeus University Press.

Emsley, Clive. 1983. *Policing and Its Context, 1750–1870.* London: Macmillan.

1999a. *Gendarmes and the State in Nineteenth-Century Europe.* Oxford: Oxford University Press.

1999b. 'A Typology of Nineteenth-Century Police.' *Crime, History & Societies* 3 (1):29–44.

2013. *Crime and Society in England: 1750–1900.* London: Routledge.

Engelbrecht, Helmut. 1982–1988. *Geschichte des österreichischen Bildungswesens.* 5 vols. Vienna: Österreichischer Bundesverlag.

Engstrom, Eric J. 2003. *Clinical Psychiatry in Imperial Germany.* Ithaca, NY: Cornell University Press.

Eriksson, Bengt Erik. 1989. *Vägen till centralhospitalet.* Gothenburg, Sweden: Daidalos.

Eskola, Eija. 2001. 'Finnish Public Libraries between the World Wars.' In *Finnish Libraries in the 20th Century*, edited by Ilkka Mäkinen. Tampere, Finland: Tampere University Press, 73–87.

Esping-Andersen, Gøsta. 1985. *Politics against Markets.* Princeton, NJ: Princeton University Press.

1990. *The Three Worlds of Welfare Capitalism.* Princeton, NJ: Princeton University Press.

Esquirol, Étienne. 1838. *Des maladies mentales considérées sous les rapports médical, hygiénique et médico-légal.* Vol. 1. Jean-Baptiste Baillière.

Evans, Richard J. 2005. *The Third Reich in Power.* London: Allan Lane.

Fallwell, Lynne Anne. 2013. *Modern German Midwifery, 1885–1960.* London: Pickering & Chatto.

Fawcett, Edmund. 2015. *Liberalism.* Princeton, NJ: Princeton University Press.

Feeley, Malcolm M. 2002. 'Entrepreneurs of Punishment: The Legacy of Privatization.' *Punishment & Society* 4 (3):321–344.

Fenner, Frank, Donald A. Henderson, Isao Arita, Zdeněk Ježek, and Ivan D. Ladnyi. 1988. *Smallpox and Its Eradication.* Geneva: World Health Organization.

Finer, Samuel E. 1997. *The History of Government.* 3 vols. Oxford: Oxford University Press.

Finnane, Mark. 1981. *Insanity and the Insane in Post-famine Ireland.* London: Croon Helm.

2005. 'A "New Police" in Australia.' In *Policing: Key Readings*, edited by Tim Newburn. Cullompton, UK: Willan, 48–68.

Flamm, Heinz, and Christian Vutuc. 2010. 'Geschichte der Pocken-Bekämpfung in Österreich.' *Wiener klinische Wochenschrift* 122 (9–10):265–275.

Fleming, Valerie E. M. 1996. 'Midwifery in New Zealand: Responding to Changing Times.' *Health Care for Women International* 17 (4):343–359.

Flora, Peter, and Jens Alber. 1981. 'Modernization, Democratization, and the Development of Welfare States in Western Europe.' In *The Development of Welfare States in Europe and America*, edited by Peter Flora and Arnold J. Heidenheimer. New Brunswick, NJ: Transaction Books, 37–80.

Flora, Peter, Jens Alber, Richard Eichenberg, Jürgen Kohl, Franz Kraus, Winfried Pfenning, and Kurt Seebohm. 1983. *State, Economy, and Society in Western Europe 1815–1975*. London: Macmillan.

Floud, Jean, and Albert H. Halsey. 1958. 'The Sociology of Education.' *Current Sociology* 7 (3):165–193.

Fonseca Ruiz, Isabel. 1977. 'La lectura pública en España. Pasado, presente y deseable futuro.' *Boletín de la ANABAD* 27 (2):3–27.

Forsythe, Bill, Joseph Melling, and Richard Adair. 1999. 'Politics of Lunacy: Central State Regulation and the Devon Pauper Lunatic Asylum, 1845–1914.' In *Insanity, Institutions and Society, 1800–1914*, edited by Joseph Melling and Bill Forsythe. London: Routledge, 68–92.

Foth, Thomas. 2013. *Caring and Killing: Nursing and Psychiatric Practice in Germany, 1931–1943*. Göttingen, Germany: V&R Unipress.

Foucault, Michel. 1961. *Folie et déraison*. Paris: Librairie Plon.

1975. *Surveiller et punir*. Paris: Gallimard.

1976. *Histoire de la sexualité I: La volonté de savoir*. Paris: Gallimard.

2004a. *Naissance de la biopolitique*. Paris: Gallimard.

2004b. *Sécurité, territoire, population*. Paris: Gallimard.

Fox, Lionel W. 1952. *The English Prison and Borstal Systems*. London: Routledge.

Fraser, Derek. 1973. *The Evolution of the British Welfare State*. London: Palgrave Macmillan.

Fraser, Gertrude Jacinda. 1998. *African American Midwifery in the South*. Cambridge, MA: Harvard University Press.

Fuchs, Rachel G., and Paul E. Knepper. 1989. 'Women in the Paris Maternity Hospital.' *Social Science History* 13 (2):187–209.

Furuhagen, Björn. 2009. *Från fjärdingsman till närpolis*. Växjö, Sweden: Växjö universitet.

2017. 'The Police as a Municipal or State Agency.' *Nordisk politiforskning* 4 (2).

Fyfe, Nicholas R. 1991. 'The Police, Space and Society.' *Progress in Human Geography* 15 (3):249–267.

Fyson, Donald. 2012. 'La police au Québec, 1760–1878.' In *Polices d'Empires*. Rennes, France: Presses universitaires de Rennes, 95–112.

Gasser, Jacques. 2003. 'The Confinement of the Insane in Switzerland, 1900–1970.' In *The Confinement of the Insane*, edited by Roy Porter and David Wright. Cambridge: Cambridge University Press, 54–78.

Gellner, Ernest. 1983. *Nations and Nationalism*. Ithaca, NY: Cornell University Press.

General Board of Health. 1857. *Papers Relating to the History and Practice of Vaccination*. London: General Board of Health.

Gerring, John, Daniel Ziblatt, Johan Van Gorp, and Julián Arévalo. 2011. 'An Institutional Theory of Direct and Indirect Rule.' *World Politics* 63 (3):377–433.

Gerstle, Gary. 2015. *Liberty and Coercion: The Paradox of American Government from the Founding to the Present*. Princeton, NJ: Princeton University Press.

Gezelius, Karl Johan. 1923. 'Göteborgs stads hälso- och sjukvård.' In *Göteborg*, edited by Nils Wimarson. Gothenburg, Sweden: Elanders boktryckeri, 338–376.

Gibson, Mary. 2019. *Italian Prisons in the Age of Positivism, 1861–1914*. London: Bloomsbury.

Gijbels, Jolien, and Kaat Wils. Forthcoming. 'Medicine, Health and Gender.' In *Medical Histories of Belgium*. Manchester, UK: Manchester University Press.

Gijswijt-Hofstra, Marijke. 2005. 'Within and Outside the Walls of the Asylum: Caring for the Dutch Mentally Ill, 1884–2000.' In *Psychiatric Cultures Compared*, edited by Marijke Gijswijt-Hofstra, Harry Oosterhuis, Joost Vijselaar, and Hugh Freeman. Amsterdam: Amsterdam University Press, 35–72.

Gingrich, Jane R. 2011. *Making Markets in the Welfare State*. Cambridge: Cambridge University Press.

2015. 'Varying Costs to Change?' *Governance* 28 (1):41–60.

Gloyne, S. Roodhouse. 1944. *Social Aspects of Tubercolosis*. London: Faber and Faber.

Gómez Hernández, J. A. 1993. 'La preocupación por la lectura pública en España.' *Revista General de Información y Documentación* 3 (2):55–94.

Goerres, Achim, and Staffan Kumlin. 2019. 'Election Campaigns and Welfare State Change.' Unpublished manuscript.

Goffman, Erving. 1961. *Asylums*. Garden City, NY: Anchor Books.

Goldstein, Jan E. 1987. *Console and Classify: The French Psychiatric Profession in the Nineteenth Century*. Cambridge: Cambridge University Press.

Goodwin, Simon. 1997. *Comparative Mental Health Policy*. London: Sage.

Gorski, Philip S. 2003. *The Disciplinary Revolution*. Chicago: University of Chicago Press.

Gralén, Josef S. 1955. *Folkskoleinspektionen i Gävleborgs län II: Åren 1877–1914*. Stockholm: Föreningen för svensk undervisningshistoria.

Green, Andy. 1990. *Education and State Formation*. London: Macmillan.

Green, Rebecca Fields. 2014. '"Simple, Easy, and Intelligible": Republican Political Ideology and the Implementation of Vaccination in the Early Republic'. *Early American Studies* 12 (2):301–337.

Greenwood, Thomas. 1902. *Edward Edwards: The Chief Pioneer of Municipal Public Libraries*. London: Scott, Greenwood.

Greer, Allan. 1992. 'The Birth of the Police in Canada.' In *Colonial Leviathan*, edited by Allan Greer and Ian Radforth. Toronto: University of Toronto Press, 17–49.

Grew, Raymond, and Partick J. Harrigan. 1991. *School, State, and Society: The Growth of Elementary Schooling in Nineteenth-Century France.* Ann Arbor: University of Michigan Press.

Grob, Gerald N. 1994. *The Mad among Us.* New York: Free Press.

Gryzmala-Busse, Anna. 2015. *Nations under God.* Princeton, NJ: Princeton University Press.

Guarnieri, Patrizia. 2005. 'Madness in the Home: Family Care and Welfare Policies before Fascism.' In *Psychiatric Cultures Compared,* edited by Marijke Gijswijt-Hofstra, Harry Oosterhuis, Joost Vijselaar, and Hugh Freeman. Amsterdam: Amsterdam University Press, 312–328.

Guyer, Walter, ed. 1936. *Erziehungsgedanke und Bildungswesen in der Schweiz.* Leipzig, Germany: Huber.

Habermas, Jürgen. 1989 [1962]. *The Structural Transformation of the Public Sphere.* Cambridge, MA: MIT Press.

Hackett, Ursula. 2020. *America's Voucher Politics.* New York: Cambridge University Press.

Halliday, Jane, and Stephen Halliday. 2007. 'Zepherina Veitch (1836–94), Childbed Fever and the Registration of Midwives.' *Journal of Medical Biography* 15 (4):241–245.

Halls, Wilfred D. 1976. *Education, Culture and Politics in Modern France.* Oxford: Pergamon Press.

Harvey, Ross. 2015. 'Australia.' In *A History of Modern Librarianship,* edited by Wayne A. Wiegand, Pamela Spence Richards, and Marija Dalbello. Santa Barbara, CA: Libraries Unlimited, 179–204.

Hasenfeld, Yeheskel. 1983. *Human Service Organizations.* Upper Saddle River, NJ: Prentice Hall.

Hassenforder, Jean. 1967. *Développement comparé des bibliothèques publiques en France, en Grande-Bretagne et aux États-Unis dans la seconde moitié du XIXe siècle.* Paris: Cercle de la librairie.

He, Wenkai. 2018. 'Legitimating Early Modern States: England, Japan, and China.' Unpublished manuscript.

Heidenheimer, Arnold J. 1986. 'Politics, Policy and Policey as Concepts in English and Continental Languages.' *The Review of Politics* 48 (1): 3–30.

Heijder, Alfred. 1973. 'Some Aspects of the Dutch Probation System.' *International Journal of Offender Therapy and Comparative Criminology* 17 (1):106–110.

Heitz, Ernst. 1872. *Die öffentlichen Bibliotheken der Schweiz im Jahre 1868.* Basel, Switzerland: Schweighauserische Verlagsbuchhandlung.

Hennock, E. P. 1973. *Fit and Proper Persons.* London: Edward Arnold.

——— 1998. 'Vaccination Policy against Smallpox, 1835–1914: A Comparison of England with Prussia and Imperial Germany.' *Social History of Medicine* 11 (1):49–71.

——— 2000. 'The Urban Sanitary Movement in England and Germany.' *Continuity and Change* 15 (2):269–296.

Hietaniemi, Tuija. 1992. *Lain vartiossa: poliisi Suomen politiikassa 1917–1948.* Helsinki: Suomen historiallinen seura.

Hill, Richard S. 1991. 'The Policing of Colonial New Zealand.' In *Policing the Empire*, edited by David M. Anderson and David Killingray. Manchester, UK: Manchester University Press, 52–70.

Hiramatsu, Yoshiro. 1973. 'History of Penal Institutions: Japan.' *Law in Japan* 6:1–48.

Hirst, John. 1995. 'The Australian Experience: The Convict Colony.' In *The Oxford History of the Prison–The Practice of Punishment in Western Society.* Oxford: Oxford University Press, 235–265.

Hoare, Peter, and Alistair Black. 2006. *The Cambridge History of Libraries in Britain and Ireland.* Cambridge: Cambridge University Press.

Högberg, Ulf. 2004. 'The Decline in Maternal Mortality in Sweden.' *American Journal of Public Health* 94 (8):1312–1320.

Hollingsworth, J. Rogers. 1990. *State Intervention in Medical Care.* Ithaca, NY: Cornell University Press.

Hong, Young-Sun. 1998. *Welfare, Modernity, and the Weimar State, 1919–1933.* Princeton, NJ: Princeton University Press.

Hood, Christopher. 1983. *The Tools of Government.* London: Macmillan.

Hopkins, Donald R. 2002. *The Greatest Killer.* Chicago: University of Chicago Press.

Horrock, Norman. 1968–2003. 'Australia.' In *Encyclopedia of Library and Information Sciences*, vol. 2, edited by Allen Kent. New York: Dekker, 98–100.

Horwitz, Morton J. 1982. 'History of the Public/Private Distinction.' *University of Pennsylvania Law Review* 130 (6):1423–1428.

House of Commons. 1885. 'Reports from Her Majesty's Representatives at European Courts and in the United States on the Working of the Lunacy Laws in the Countries in Which They Reside.' Miscellaneous. No. 1.

Howard, John. 1777. *The State of the Prisons in England and Wales.* London: William Eyres.

Howells, John G., and M. Livia Osborn. 1975. 'Great Britain.' In *World History of Psychiatry*, edited by John G. Howells. New York: Brunner/Mazel, 168–206.

Hubber, Brian. 1994. 'A Slight Encouragement: The Colonial Book Grant and the Victorian Parliament, 1857–1860.' In *Pioneering Culture: Mechanics Institutes and Schools of Art in Australia*, edited by Phillip C. Candy and John Laurent. Adelaide: Auslib Press, 92–101.

Huber, Evelyne, and John D. Stephens. 2001. *Development and Crisis of the Welfare State.* Chicago: University of Chicago Press.

Hubert, Ollivier. 2013. 'Sulpician Cultural Strategies: Books.' In *The Sulpicians of Montreal*, edited by Dominique Deslandres, John A. Dickinson, and Ollivier Hubert. Montreal: Bibliothèque et Archives nationales du Québec, 499–514.

Huerkamp, Claudia. 1985. 'The History of Smallpox Vaccination in Germany.' *Journal of Contemporary History* 20 (4):617–635.

Hughes, Robert. 1987. *The Fatal Shore.* New York: Knopf.

Hughes, Steven. 2017. 'Fear and Loathing in Bologna and Rome: The Papal Police in Perspective.' In *Theories and Origins of the Modern Police*, edited by Clive Emsley. London: Routledge, 155–174.

Hume, L. J. 1967. 'Jeremy Bentham and the Nineteenth-Century Revolution in Government.' *The Historical Journal* 10 (3):361–375.

Humphreys, Kenneth W. 1994. 'Church and Cathedral Libraries in Western Europe.' In *Encyclopedia of Library History*, edited by Wayne A. Wiegand and Donald G. Davis Jr. Abingdon, UK: Routledge, 139–142.

Hurd, Henry M., William F. Drewry, Richard Dewey, Charles W. Pilgrim, G. Adler Blumer, and T. J. W. Burgess. 1916. *The Institutional Care of the Insane in the United States and Canada*. Baltimore: Johns Hopkins University Press.

Hvenegaard Lassen, Harald. 1962. *De danske folkebibliotekers historie, 1876–1940*. Copenhagen: Dansk Bibliografisk Kontor.

Immergut, Ellen M. 1992. *Health Politics*. Cambridge: Cambridge University Press.

Irwin, Fairfax. 1910. 'Smallpox in Japan.' *Public Health Reports* 25 (35): 1205–1208.

Jackson, Charles L. 1969. 'State Laws on Compulsory Immunization in the United States.' *Public Health Reports* 84 (9):787. www.ncbi.nlm.nih.gov/pmc/articles/PMC2031602/.

Jacobson v. Massachusetts, 197 US 11. (1905).

Jägerskiöld, Stig. 1959. *Från prästskola till enhetsskola*. Stockholm: Almqvist & Wiksell.

Jannetta, Ann. 2007. *The Vaccinators: Smallpox, Medical Knowledge, and the 'Opening' of Japan*. Stanford, CA: Stanford University Press.

——— 2009. 'Jennerian Vaccination and the Creation of a National Public Health Agenda in Japan, 1850–1900.' *Bulletin of the History of Medicine* 83 (1):125–140.

Japan International Cooperation Agency. 2005. 'Japan's Experiences in Public Health and Medical Systems.' Research Group, Institute for International Cooperation, Japan International Cooperation Agency (JICA).

Jenner, Edward. 1798. 'An Inquiry into the Causes and Effects of the Variolæ Vaccinæ, or Cow-Pox.' Reprinted in *The Three Original Publications on Vaccination against Smallpox*, vol. XXXVIII, part 4, *The Harvard Classics*. New York: P. F. Collier, 1909–14.

Johnson, F. Henry. 1968. *A Brief History of Canadian Education*. Toronto: McGraw-Hill.

Johnston, Les. 1992. *The Rebirth of Private Policing*. London: Routledge.

Johnston, Norman. 2000. *Forms of Constraint*. Urbana-Champaign: University of Illinois Press.

Johnston, Norman, Kenneth Finkel, and Jeffrey A. Cohen. 1994. *Eastern State Penitentiary*. Philadelphia: Philadelphia Museum of Art.

Jones, David J. 2001. 'Public Libraries.' In *A History of the Book in Australia, 1891–1945*. St Lucia: University of Queensland Press, 157–175.

Jones, Kathleen. 1955. *Lunacy, Law and Conscience, 1744–1845*. London: Routledge.

——— 1972. *A History of the Mental Health Services*. London: Routledge.

Kahan, Alan. 2003. *Liberalism in Nineteenth Century Europe*. Basingstoke, UK: Palgrave.

Kalyvas, Stathis N. 1996. *The Rise of Christian Democracy in Europe.* Ithaca, NY: Cornell University Press.

1998. 'Democracy and Religious Politics.' *Comparative Political Studies* 31 (3):292–320.

Kaspersen, Lars Bo, and Johannes Lindvall. 2008. 'Why No Religious Politics?' *Archives européennes de sociologie* 49 (1):119–143.

Katznelson, Ira, and Margaret Weir. 1985. *Schooling for All.* New York: Basic Books.

Keeler, John T. S., and Peter A. Hall. 2001. 'Interest Representation and the Politics of Protest.' In *Developments in French Politics 2.* Basingstoke, UK: Palgrave, 50–67.

Kelly, Brendan D. 2016. *Hearing Voices: The History of Psychiatry in Ireland.* Newbridge: Irish Academic Press.

Kelly, Thomas. 1973. *A History of Public Libraries in Great Britain, 1845–1965.* London: Library Association.

Kenneally, Rhona Richman. 1983. *The Montreal Maternity, 1843–1926.* Master's thesis, McGill University.

Kent, Allen, ed. 1968–2003. *Encyclopedia of Library and Information Science.* New York: Dekker.

Ketelaar, Eric, Frank Huysmans, Peter van Mensch, M. J. Bates, and M. N. Maack. 2010. 'Netherlands: Archives, Libraries and Museums.' In *Encyclopedia of Library and Information Sciences.* Boca Raton, FL: CRC Press/Taylor & Francis, 3874–3900.

Kjærheim, Kristina. 1987. *Mellom kloke koner og kvitkledde menn.* Oslo: Det Norske samlaget.

Kleppner, Paul. 1979. *The Third Electoral System 1853–1892.* Chapel Hill: University of North Carolina Press.

Knemeyer, Franz-Ludwig. 1980. 'Polizei.' *Economy and Society* 9 (2):172–196.

Knippenberg, Hans, and Herman van der Wusten. 1984. 'The Primary School System in the Netherlands 1900–1980.' *Tijdschrift voor Economische en Sociale Geografie* 73 (3):177–185.

Koch, Christine. 2003. *Das Bibliothekswesen im Nationalsozialismus.* Marburg, Germany: Tectum.

Kohn, George C. 2007. *Encyclopedia of Plague and Pestilence.* New York: Infobase.

Korpi, Walter. 1983. *The Democratic Class Struggle.* London: Routledge and Kegan Paul.

Korsgaard, Ove. 2004. *Kampen om folket.* Copenhagen: Nordisk Forlag.

Kringlen, Einar. 2004. 'A History of Norwegian Psychiatry.' *History of Psychiatry* 15 (3):259–283.

2007. *Norsk psykiatri gjennom tidene.* Oslo: N. W. Damm.

Kuhnle, Stein, and Anne Sander. 2010. 'The Emergence of the Western Welfare State.' In *The Oxford Handbook of the Welfare State*, edited by Francis G. Castles, Stephan Leibfried, Jane Lewis, Herbert Obinger, and Christopher Pierson. Oxford: Oxford University Press, 61–80.

Kunkel, Wolfgang. 1973. *An Introduction to Roman Legal and Constitutional History.* Oxford: Clarendon Press.

Kurian, George Thomas. 1989. *World Encyclopedia of Police Forces and Penal Systems.* New York: Facts on File.

Kusters, Walter, and Marc Depaepe. 2011. 'The French Third Republic: Popular Education, Conceptions of Citizenship and the Flemish Immigrants.' *Historical Studies in Education* 23 (1):22–39.

LaBrum, B. 1992. 'Looking beyond the Asylum: Gender and the Process of Committal in Auckland, 1870–1910.' *New Zealand Journal of History* 26 (1):553–574.

Ladd-Taylor, Molly. 1992. 'Why Does Congress Wish Women and Children to Die?' In *Women and Children First*, edited by Valerie Fildes, Lara Marks, and Hilary Marland. London: Routledge, 121–132.

Laing, Ronald D. 1967. *The Politics of Experience.* Harmondsworth, UK: Penguin Books.

Lambert, R. J. 1962. 'A Victorian National Health Service: State Vaccination 1855–71.' *The Historical Journal* 5 (1):1–18.

Lamberti, Marjorie. 1989. *State, Society and the Elementary School in Imperial Germany.* Oxford: Oxford University Press.

2002. *The Politics of Education: Teachers and School Reform in Weimar Germany.* Monographs in German History 8. New York: Berghahn Books.

Langan, Patrick A., John V. Fundis, Lawrence A. Greenfeld, and Victoria W. Schneider. 1988. *Historical Statistics on Prisoners in State and Federal Institutions 1925–86.* Washington, DC: US Department of Justice, Bureau of Justice Statistics.

Larsen, Kristian. 2012. 'Opbrud i medicinen fra 1750–1850.' *Praktiske Grunde* 6 (1):25–67.

Laugesen, Amanda. 2014. 'UNESCO and the Globalization of the Public Library Idea, 1948 to 1965.' *Library & Information History* 30 (1):1–19.

Laurent, Helene. 2012. 'War and the Emerging Social State: Social Policy, Public Health and Citizenship in Wartime Finland.' In *Finland in World War II*, edited by Tiina Kinnunen and Ville Kivimäki. Leiden, Netherlands: Brill, 313–354.

Leavitt, Judith W. 1976. 'Politics and Public Health: Smallpox in Milwaukee, 1894–1895.' *Bulletin of the History of Medicine* 50 (4):553–568.

1986. *Brought to Bed: Childbearing in America 1750 to 1950.* Oxford: Oxford University Press.

Lederer, David. 2006. *Madness, Religion and the State in Early Modern Europe.* Cambridge: Cambridge University Press.

Lee, Jong-Wha, and Hanol Lee. 2016. 'Human Capital in the Long Run.' *Journal of Development Economics* 122 (C):147–169.

Levi, Margaret. 1977. *Bureaucratic Insurgency.* New York: Lexington Books.

1988. *Of Rule and Revenue.* Berkeley: University of California Press.

Lewis, Jane. 1980. *The Politics of Motherhood: Child and Maternal Welfare in England, 1900–1939.* London: Croom Helm.

Lewis, Milton. 1988. *Managing Madness: Psychiatry and Society in Australia 1788–1980.* Canberra: Australian Institute of Health.

Liesen, Bruno. 2014. 'Des bibliothèques populaires aux bibliothèques publiques en Belgique.' In *Des bibliothèques populaires à la lecture publique*, edited by Agnes Sandras. Lyon, France: Presses de l'enssib, 327–372.

Lijphart, Arend. 1968. *The Politics of Accommodation.* Berkeley: University of California Press.
1979. 'Religious vs. Linguistic vs. Class Voting: The Crucial Experiment of Comparing Belgium, Canada, South Africa and Switzerland.' *American Political Science Review* 73 (2):442–458.
Lindegren, Alina M. 1941. 'Education and Service Conditions of Teachers in Scandinavia, the Netherlands and Finland.' *US Office of Education Bulletin* 1940 (9).
Lindert, Peter. 2004. *Growing Public.* Cambridge: Cambridge University Press.
Lipset, Seymour Martin, and Stein Rokkan. 1967. *Party Systems and Voter Alignments.* New York: Free Press.
Lisner, Wiebke. 2006. *Hüterinnen der Nation: Hebammen in Nationalsozialismus.* Frankfurt, Germany: Campus.
Lisner, Wiebke, and Anja K. Peters. 2014. 'German Midwifery in the "Third Reich."' In *Nurses and Midwives in Nazi Germany,* edited by Susan Benedict and Linda Shields. New York: Routledge, 164–197.
Løkke, Anne. 1997. 'The "Antiseptic" Transformation of Danish Midwives, 1860–1920.' In *Midwives, Society and Childbirth,* edited by Hilary Marland and Anne Marie Rafferty. London: Routledge, 102–133.
1998. *Døden i barndommen.* Copenhagen: Gyldendal.
Lopez Ibor, Juan José. 1975. 'Spain and Portugal.' In *World History of Psychiatry,* edited by John G. Howells. New York: Brunner/Mazel, 90–118.
Loss, Daniel. 2013. *The Afterlife of Christian England, 1944–1994.* PhD thesis, Brown University.
Loudon, Irvine. 1986. 'Deaths in Childbirth from the Eighteenth Century to 1935.' *Medical History* 30 (1):1–41.
1992. *Death in Childbirth.* Oxford: Clarendon Press.
Lowell, A. Lawrence. 1896. *Governments and Parties in Continental Europe.* London: Longmans, Green.
Lundberg, Sven. 1997. *Härlanda fängelse – en tidsspegel.* Gothenburg, Sweden: Tre böcker.
Lundh, Atle. 1957. *Frimurare Barnhuset i Göteborg 1757–1957.* Gothenburg, Sweden: Frimuraresamhället.
Lundqvist, Birger. 1940. *Det svenska barnmorskeväsendets historia.* Stockholm: Svenska barnmorskor.
MacDonagh, Oliver. 1958. 'The Nineteenth-Century Revolution in Government: A Reappraisal.' *The Historical Journal* 1 (1):52–67.
Machin, Howard. 1977. *The Prefect in French Public Administration.* London: Croom Helm.
Maclean, Francis S. 1964. *Challenge for Health: A History of Public Health in New Zealand.* Wellington: Government Printer.
MacLeod, Roderick, and Mary Anne Poutanen. 2004. *Meeting of the People: School Boards and Protestant Communities in Quebec.* Montreal: McGill-Queen's Press.
Maddison, Angus. 2011. 'Statistics on World Population, GDP and Per Capita GDP, 1–2008 AD.' University of Groningen.
Mallinson, Vernon. 1963. *Power and Politics in Belgian Education: 1815 to 1961.* London: Heinemann.

Mann, Michael. 1984. 'The Autonomous Power of the State.' *Archives européennes de sociologie* 25:185–213.

    1993. *The Sources of Social Power: Vol. 2. The Rise of Classes and Nation States 1760–1914*. Cambridge: Cambridge University Press.

    2004. *Fascists*. Cambridge: Cambridge University Press.

Marks, Lara. 1992. 'Mothers, Babies and Hospitals: "The London" and the Provision of Maternity Care in East London, 1870–1939.' In *Women and Children First*, edited by Valerie Fildes, Lara Marks, and Hilary Marland. London: Routledge, 48–73.

Marland, Hilary. 1992. 'The Medicalization of Motherhood: Doctors and Infant Welfare in the Netherlands, 1901–1930.' In *Women and Children First*, edited by Valerie Fildes, Lara Marks, and Hilary Marland. London: Routledge, 74–96.

Marland, Hilary, ed. 1993. *The Art of Midwifery*. London: Routledge.

Marshall, Monty G., and Keith Jaggers. 2012. 'Polity IV Project: Political Regime Characteristics and Transitions, 1800–2010.' University of Maryland.

Martin, Cathie Jo, and Duane Swank. 2012. *The Political Construction of Business Interests*. Cambridge: Cambridge University Press.

Marx, Karl. 1977 [1867]. *Capital*. New York: Vintage Books.

Marx, Otto M. 2008. 'German Romantic Psychiatry.' In *History of Psychiatry and Medical Psychology*, edited by Edwin R. Wallace and John Gach. New York: Springer, 313–351.

McAdam, Doug, Sidney Tarrow, and Charles Tilly. 2001. *Dynamics of Contention*. Cambridge: Cambridge University Press.

McCarthy, Rebecca Lea. 2010. *Origins of the Magdalene Laundries*. New York: McFarland.

McConville, Seàn. 1981. *A History of Prison Administration, 1750–1877*. London: Routledge.

McEldowney, W. J. 1994. 'New Zealand.' In *Encyclopedia of Library History*, edited by Wayne A. Wiegand and Donald G. Davis Jr. Abingdon, UK: Routledge, 469–470.

McGowen, Randall. 1995. 'The Well-Ordered Prison: England, 1780–1865.' In *The Oxford History of the Prison*, edited by Norval Morris and David J. Rothman. Oxford: Oxford University Press, 79–109.

McKeown, Thomas. 1979. *The Role of Medicine*. Oxford: Basil Blackwell.

McLeod, Hugh. 1997. *Religion and the People of Western Europe 1789–1990*. Oxford: Oxford University Press.

McNair, John M. 1984. *Education for a Changing Spain*. Manchester, UK: Manchester University Press.

Mein Smith, Philippa. 1986. *Maternity in Dispute: New Zealand, 1920–1939*. Wellington: Historical Publications Branch, Department of Internal Affairs, Government Printer.

    1993. 'Mothers, Babies, and the Mother and Babies Movement: Australia through Depression and War.' *The Society for the Social History of Medicine* 6 (1):51–83.

Melosi, Martin V. 1981. *Garbage in the Cities*. College Station: Texas A&M University Press.

Melossi, Dario. 2001. 'The Cultural Embeddedness of Social Control.' *Theoretical Criminology* 5 (4):403–424.

Melossi, Dario, and Massimo Pavarini. 1981. *The Prison and the Factory.* London: Macmillan.

Meyer, John W., Francisco O. Ramirez, and Yasemin N. Soysal. 1992. 'World Expansion of Mass Education, 1870–1980.' *Sociology of Education* 65:128–149.

Meyer, John W., and George M. Thomas. 1984. 'The Expansion of the State.' *Annual Review of Sociology* 10:461–482.

Miliband, Ralph. 1969. *The State in Capitalist Society.* New York: Basic Books.

Millen, Julia. 2014. 'Public Libraries.' In *Te Ara – the Encyclopedia of New Zealand.* https://teara.govt.nz/en.

Miller, Wilbur R. 1999. *Cops and Bobbies.* Columbus: Ohio State University Press.

Milner, Henry. 1986. *The Long Road to Reform: Restructuring Public Education in Quebec.* Kingston: McGill-Queen's University Press.

Milton, Lena. 2001. 'Folkhemmets barnmorskor.' Department of History, Uppsala University.

Ministère de l'Agriculture et du Commerce. Various years. *Annuaire Statistique de la France.* Paris: Ministère de l'Agriculture et du Commerce.

Minto, John, and James Hutt. 1932. *A History of the Public Library Movement in Great Britain and Ireland.* London: G. Allen & Unwin.

Møllerhøj, Jette. 2008. 'On Unsafe Ground: The Practices and Institutionalization of Danish Psychiatry, 1850–1920.' *History of Psychiatry* 19 (3):321–337.

Monk, Lee-Ann. 2008. *Attending Madness: At Work in the Australian Colonial Asylum.* Amsterdam: Rodopi.

Moran, Catherine, and Pearl Quinn. 2006. 'The Irish Library Scene.' In *The Cambridge History of Libraries in Britain and Ireland*, vol. 3. Cambridge: Cambridge University Press, 253–265.

Moran, James. 2001. *Committed to State Asylum: Insanity and Society in 19th Century Québec and Ontario.* Montreal: McGill-Queen's University Press.

Moreno, P., and A. Calixto, eds. 2013. 'Ética y modelos de atención a las personas con trastorno mental grave.' Universidad Pontificia Comillas.

Morgan, Kimberly J. 2002. 'Forging the Frontiers between State, Church, and Family.' *Politics & Society* 30 (1):113–148.

2006. *Working Mothers and the Welfare State.* Palo Alto, CA: Stanford University Press.

Mulhall, Michael G. 1884. *Mulhall's Dictionary of Statistics.* London: Routledge.

Munthe, Wilhelm. 1964. *American Librarianship from a European Angle.* Hamden, UK: Shoe string Press.

Murison, William J. 1950. 'Social Significance of the Public Library Service.' *Library Review* 12 (7):424–432.

1988. *The Public Library.* London: Clive Bingley.

Murphy, Elaine. 2003. 'The Administration of Insanity in England 1800 to 1870.' In *The Confinement of the Insane*, edited by Roy Porter and David Wright. Cambridge: Cambridge, 334–349.

Needell, Jeffrey D. 1987. 'The Revolta Contra Vacina of 1904.' *The Hispanic American Historical Review* 67 (2):233–269.

Neumann, Franz L. 1957. *The Democratic and the Authoritarian State.* Glencoe, IL: Free Press.

Newbold, Greg. 2007. *The Problem of Prisons: Corrections Reform in New Zealand since 1840.* Wellington: Dunmore.

Nilsson, Roddy. 1999. *En välbyggd maskin, en mardröm för själen.* PhD thesis, Lund University.

Nitschke, Peter. 1996. *Die Deutsche Polizei und ihre Geschichte.* Vol. 2. Hilden, Germany: Verlag Deutsche Polizeiliteratur.

North, Douglass C. 1990. *Institutions, Institutional Change, and Economic Performance.* Cambridge: Cambridge University Press.

Ó hÓgartaigh, Margaret. 2012. 'Irish Nurses, Emerging States and Trade Unions, 1918–39.' *Saothar* 37:57–70.

Öberg, Lisa. 1994. 'Privatpraktiserande barnmorska – ett yrke som försvann.' In *Det evigt kvinnliga*, edited by Ulla Wikander. Stockholm: Tiden, 188–213. 1996. *Barnmorskan och läkaren.* Stockholm: Ordfront.

O'Brien, Patricia. 2014. *The Promise of Punishment: Prisons in Nineteenth-Century France.* Princeton, NJ: Princeton University Press.

Ohlander, Joh. 1923. 'Folkskolorna.' In *Göteborg*, edited by Nils Wimarson. Gothenburg, Sweden: Elanders boktryckeri, 812–838.

Olagüe de Ros, Guillermo, and Mikel Astrain Gallart. 2004. '¡Salvad a los niños! Los primeros pasos de la vacunación antivariólica en España (1799–1805).' *Asclepio* 56 (1):7–32.

Olson, Mancur. 1993. 'Dictatorship, Democracy, and Development.' *American Political Science Review* 87 (3):567–576.

Omer, Saad B., Daniel A. Salmon, Walter A. Orenstein, M. Patricia deHart, and Neal Halsey. 2009. 'Vaccine Refusal, Mandatory Immunization, and the Risks of Vaccine-Preventable Diseases.' *New England Journal of Medicine* 360 (19):1981–1988.

Onorato, Massimiliano Gaetano, Kenneth Scheve, and David Stasavage. 2014. 'Technology and the Era of the Mass Army.' *The Journal of Economic History* 74 (2):449–481.

Ortiz, Teresa, and Clara Martínez Padilla. 2002. 'How to Be a Midwife in Late Nineteenth-Century Spain.' In *Midwives, Society and Childbirth.* New York: Routledge, 75–94.

Osler, Mogens. 2002. *Fødselshjælpens historie.* Copenhagen: FADL's Forlag.

O'Sullivan, Eoin, and Ian O'Donnell. 2007. 'Coercive Confinement in the Republic of Ireland: The Waning of a Culture of Control.' *Punishment & Society* 9 (1):27–48.

O'Toole, George. 1978. *The Private Sector: Rent a Cop, Private Spies and the Police Industrial Complex.* New York: Norton.

O'Toole, Sean. 2006. *The History of Australian Corrections.* New South Wales: UNSW Press.

Oyler, Patricia. 1968–2003. 'Scandinavia.' In *Encyclopedia of Library and Information Sciences*, edited by Allen Kent. New York: Dekker, 339–358.

Palmgren, Uno. 1923. 'Göteborgs polisväsen.' In *Göteborg*, edited by Nils Wimarson. Gothenburg, Sweden: Elanders boktryckeri, 219–243.

Palmgren, Valfrid. 1911. *Förslag angående de åtgärder, som från statens sida böra vidtagas för främjande af det allmänna biblioteksväsendet i Sverige.* Stockholm: Ivar Hæggströms boktryckeri.

Parris, Henry. 1960. 'The Nineteenth-Century Revolution in Government: A Reappraisal Reappraised.' *The Historical Journal* 3 (1):17–37.

Parry-Jones, William L. 1972. *The Trade in Lunacy.* London: Routledge and Kegan Paul.

Parsons, Talcott. 1959. 'The School Class as a Social System.' *Harvard Educational Review* 29 (4):297–318.

Partridge, Percy H. 1973. *Society, Schools and Progress in Australia.* Rushcutters Bay, UK: Pergamon Press.

Passin, Herbert. 1982 [1965]. *Society and Education in Japan.* Tokyo: Kodansha International.

Patel, Vikram, Harry Minas, Alex Cohen, and Martin J. Prince. 2013. *Global Mental Health.* Oxford: Oxford University Press.

Peel, Brue. 1982. 'Librarianship in Canada before 1952.' *Archivaria* 1982/1983 (15):78–85.

Peters, Edward M. 1995. 'Prison before the Prison: The Ancient and Medieval Worlds.' In *The Oxford History of the Prison*, edited by Norval Morris and David J. Rothman. Oxford: Oxford University Press, 3–43.

Peters, Rudolph. 2005. *Crime and Punishment in Islamic Law.* Cambridge: Cambridge University Press.

Peterson, Anna M. 2013. *The Birth of a Welfare State: Feminists, Midwives, Working Women and the Fight for Norwegian Maternity Leave, 1880–1940.* PhD thesis, Ohio State University.

———. 2018. *Maternity Policy and the Making of the Norwegian Welfare State, 1880–1940.* Cham, Switzerland: Palgrave Macmillan.

Pettersson-Lidbom, Per. 2014. 'Midwifes and Maternal Deaths: Evidence from a Midwifery Policy Experiment in Sweden in the 19th Century.' Unpublished manuscript.

Philips, David. 1989. 'Good Men to Associate and Bad Men to Conspire: Associations for the Prosecution of Felons in England, 1760–1860.' In *Policing and Prosecution in Britain, 1750–1850*, edited by Douglas Hay and Francis Snyder. Oxford: Clarendon Press, 113–170.

Phillips, Sean P. 2016. *Pox and the Pulpit.* PhD thesis, University of Notre Dame.

Pine, Lisa. 2010. *Education in Nazi Germany.* Oxford: Berg.

Pitkänen, Kari J., James H. Mielke, and Lynn B. Jorde. 1989. 'Smallpox and Its Eradication in Finland.' *Population Studies* 43 (1):95–110.

Plato. 1892 [369 BC]. 'Theaetetus.' In *The Dialogues of Plato*, edited by Benjamin Jowett. London: Oxford University Press, 107–280.

Platt, Brian. 2004. *Burning and Building: Schooling and State Formation in Japan, 1750–1890.* Cambridge, MA: Harvard University Asia Center and Harvard University Press.

Plummer, Kate. 2000. 'From Nursing Outposts to Contemporary Midwifery in 20th Century Canada.' *Journal of Midwifery & Women's Health* 45 (2):169–175.

Polanyi, Karl. 1944. *The Great Transformation.* New York: Farrar & Rinehart.

Porras Gallo, María Isabel. 2004. 'Luchando contra una de las causas de invalidez: Antecedentes, contexto sanitario, gestación y aplicación del decreto de vacunación obligatoria contra la viruela de 1903.' *Asclepio* 56 (1):145–168.

Porter, Dorothy. 1999. *Health, Civilization, and the State.* London: Routledge.

Porter, Roy. 1987a. *Madmen.* Stroud, UK: Tempus.

———. 1987b. *Mind-Forg'd Manacles.* Cambridge, MA: Harvard University Press.

Poslethwaite, T. Neville, ed. 1995. *International Encyclopedia of National Systems of Education.* Oxford: Pergamon.

Poulantzas, Nicos. 1969. 'The Problem of the Capitalist State.' *New Left Review* I (58):67–78.

Punell, Georg. 1995. *Farväl Lillhagen.* Partille, Sweden: Warne.

Pylkkänen, Kari. 2012. 'Finnish Psychiatry—Past and Present.' *Nordic Journal of Psychiatry* 66 (1):14–24.

Quétel, Claude. 2012. 'La vote de la loi de 1838.' In *Nouvelle histoire de la psychiatrie,* new ed., edited by Jacques Postel and Claude Quétel. Paris: Dunod, 180–186.

Qvarsell, Roger. 1982. *Ordning och behandling. Psykiatri och sinnessjukvård i Sverige under 1800-talets första hälft.* Stockholm: Almqvist & Wiksell International.

Raeff, Marc. 1975. 'The Well-Ordered Police State and the Development of Modernity in Seventeenth-and Eighteenth-Century Europe.' *The American Historical Review* 80 (5):1221–1243.

Raftery, Deirdre, and Catherine Nowlan-Roebuck. 2007. 'Convent Schools and National Education in Nineteenth-Century Ireland.' *History of Education* 36 (3):353–365.

Rawlings, Philip. 2002. *Policing: A Short History.* Cullompton, UK: Willan.

Reardon, Sara. 2014. '"Forgotten" NIH Smallpox Virus Languishes on Death Row'. *Nature* 514 (7524):544.

Rehn, Margareta, and Donald Boström, eds. 2011. *300 år i livets tjänst.* Stockholm: Svenska barnmorskeförbundet.

Reiger, Kerreen. 2014. 'The Politics of Midwifery in Australia.' *Annual Review of Health Social Science* 10 (1):53–64.

Reith, Charles. 1943. *British Police and the Democratic Ideal.* Oxford: Oxford University Press.

———. 1956. *A New Study of Police History.* Edinburgh: Oliver and Boyd.

Relyea, Joyce M. 1992. 'The Rebirth of Midwifery in Canada.' *Midwifery* 8:159–169.

Retterstöl, Nils. 1975. 'Scandinavia and Finland.' In *World History of Psychiatry,* edited by John G. Howells. New York: Brunner/Mazel, 207–237.

Richter, Noë. 1977. 'Histoire de la lecture publique en France.' *Bulletin des bibliothèques* 1977 (1).

Ringdal, Nils Johan. 1985. *By, bok og borger: Deichmanske bibliotek gjennom 200 år.* Oslo: Aschehoug.

Ritzmann, Iris. 2015. 'Vaccination.' *Dictionaire historique de la Suisse.* https://hls-dhs-dss.ch/.

Riving, Cecilia. 2008. *Icke som en annan människa: psykisk sjukdom i mötet mellan psykiatrin och lokalsamhället under 1800-talets andra hälft*. PhD thesis, Lund University.

Robbins, Kevin C. 1995. 'Municipal Justice, Urban Police and the Tactics of Counter-Reformation in La Rochelle, 1618–1650.' *French History* 9 (3):273–293.

Roekens, Anne, and Benoît Majerus. 2017. 'Deadly Vulnerabilities: The Provisioning of Psychiatric Asylums in Occupied Belgium (1914–1918).' *Revue Belge de Histoire Contemporaine* 4 (47):18–48.

Rokkan, Stein. 1973. 'Cities, States, and Nations.' In *Building States and Nations*, vol. I, edited by Shmuel N. Eisenstadt and Stein Rokkan. Beverly Hills, CA: Sage, 73–97.

Rolleston, John D. 1933. 'The Smallpox Pandemic of 1870–1874.' *Proceedings of the Royal Society of Medicine* 27 (2):177–192.

Romlid, Christina. 1998. *Makt, motstånd och förändring*. Stockholm: Vårdförbundet.

Rosen, George. 1958. *A History of Public Health*. New York: MD Publications.

———. 1963. 'The Hospital: Historical Sociology of a Community Institution.' In *The Hospital in Modern Society*, edited by Eliot Freidson. London: The Free Press, 1–36.

Rosenberg, Charles E. 1995 [1987]. *The Care of Strangers*. Baltimore: The Johns Hopkins University Press.

Rosenberg, Karen, and Wenda Trevathan. 2002. 'Birth, Obstetrics and Human Evolution.' *BJOG: An International Journal of Obstetrics & Gynaecology* 109 (11):1199–1206.

Rothman, David R. 1990 [1971]. *The Discovery of the Asylum*. London: Little, Brown.

Rousseau, Jean-Jacques. 1762. *Émile, ou De l'éducation*. Amsterdam: Jean Néaulme.

Ruggie, John G. 1982. 'International Regimes, Transactions, and Change: Embedded Liberalism in the Postwar Economic Order.' *International Organization* 36 (2):379–415.

Rusche, Georg, and Otto Kirchheimer. 1939. *Punishment and Social Structure*. New York: Columbia University Press.

Rutten, Willibrord. 1997. *'De vreselijkste aller harpijen': Pokkenepidemieën en pokkenbestrijding in Nederland in de achttiende en negentiende eeuw*. PhD thesis, Afd. Agrarische Geschiedenis, Landbouwuniversitet, Wageningen.

Sacks, Oliver. 2009. 'The Lost Virtues of the Asylum.' *New York Review of Books* 56 (14):50–52.

Sage-Pranchère, Nathalie. 2014. 'L'appel à la sage-femme.' *Annales de Démographie Historique* 2014 (1):181–208.

———. 2018. *L'école des sages-femmes: Naissance d'un corps professionnel, 1786–1917*. Tours, France: Presses universitaires François-Rabelais.

Sandiford, Peter, ed. 1918. *Comparative Education*. London: J. M. Dent.

Saraceno, Chiara. 1991. 'Redefining Maternity and Paternity: Gender, Pronatalism and Social Policies in Fascist Italy.' In *Maternity and Gender Policies*, edited by Gisela Bock and Pat Thane. London: Routledge, 196–212.

Saville Muzzey, David. 1911. 'State, Church, and School in France II: The Campaign for Lay Education.' *The School Review* 19 (4):248–265.

Schadewitz, Leo. 1903. *Folkbiblioteken i Finland*. Helsinki: Folkupplysningssällskapet i Finland.

Scheipl, Josef, and Helmut Seel. 1985. *Die Entwicklung des Österreichischen Schulwesens von 1750–1938*. Graz, Germany: Leykam.

Scheuermann, Karen. 1995. 'Midwifery in Germany.' *Journal of Nurse-Midwifery* 40 (5):438–447.

Schlaug, Rudolf. 1989. *Psykiatri, lag och samhälle*. Stockholm: Askelin & Hägglund.

Schneider, Gabi. 2012. 'Libraries in Switzerland.' In *Libraries in the Early 21st Century*, vol. 2, edited by Ravindra N. Sharma. Berlin: De Gruyter Saur, 473–490.

Schneiders, Paul. 1998. 'Libraries in the Netherlands.' *IFLA Journal* 24 (3):145–156.

Schumpeter, Joseph A. 1942. *Capitalism, Socialism, and Democracy*. New York: Harper.

Schwartz, Richard D., and James C. Miller. 1964. 'Legal Evolution and Societal Complexity.' *American Journal of Sociology* 70 (2):159–169.

Scott, James. 1998. *Seeing Like a State*. New Haven, CT: Yale University Press.

Scull, Andrew T. 1979. *Museums of Madness*. New York: St. Martin's Press.

Seavey, Charles. 1994. 'Public Libraries.' In *Encyclopedia of Library History*, edited by Wayne A. Wiegand and Donald G. Davis Jr. Abingdon, UK: Routledge, 518–528.

2003. 'The American Public Library during the Great Depression.' *Library Review* 52 (8):373–378.

Sellin, Thorsten. 1944. *Pioneering in Penology: The Amsterdam Houses of Correction in the Sixteenth and Seventeenth Centuries*. Philadelphia: University of Pennsylvania Press.

Senser, Christine. 1991. *Die Bibliotheken der Schweiz*. Wiesbaden, Germany: Reichert.

Sessa, Frank B. 1968–2003. 'Public Libraries, History.' In *Encyclopedia of Library and Information Sciences*, vol. 24, edited by Allen Kent. New York: Dekker.

Sharp, Rachel. 1980. *Knowledge, Ideology and the Politics of Schooling*. London: Routledge.

Sheikh, Sukhera, Inithan Ganesaratnam, and Haider Jan. 2013. 'The Birth of Forceps.' *Journal of the Royal Society of Medicine Short Reports* 4 (7):1–4.

Shichor, David. 1995. *Punishment for Profit: Private Prisons/Public Concerns*. Thousand Oaks, CA: Sage.

Shorter, Edward. 1990. 'Private Clinics in Central Europe 1850–1933.' *The Society for the Social History of Medicine* 3 (2):159–195.

1991 [1982]. *Women's Bodies*. New Brunswick, NJ: Transaction.

1998. *A History of Psychiatry*. New York: John Wiley.

Silver, Allan. 2017. 'The Demand for Order in Civil Society.' In *Theories and Origins of the Modern Police*, edited by Clive Elmsley. New York: Routledge, 23–46.

Simon, J. 1857. *Papers Relating to the History and Practice of Vaccination.* London: General Board of Health.

Sinclair, Keith. 1961. *A History of New Zealand.* London: Oxford University Press.

Sköld, Peter. 1996a. 'From Inoculation to Vaccination: Smallpox in Sweden in the Eighteenth and Nineteenth Centuries.' *Population Studies* 50 (2):247–262.

1996b. *The Two Faces of Smallpox: A Disease and Its Prevention in Eighteenth- and Nineteenth-Century Sweden.* Umeå: Umeå University.

Skocpol, Theda. 1979. *States and Social Revolutions.* Cambridge: Cambridge University Press.

Slack, Paul. 1985. *The Impact of Plague in Tudor and Stuart England.* London: Routledge.

Smith, Leonard. 1999a. 'The County Asylum in the Mixed Economy of Care.' In *Insanity, Institutions and Society, 1800–1914*, edited by J. Melling and B. Forsythe. London: Routledge, 33–47.

1999b. *Cure, Comfort and Safe Custody: Public Lunatic Asylums in Early Nineteenth Century England.* London: Leicester University Press.

Smith, Michael M. 1974. 'The "Real Expedición Marítima de la Vacuna" in New Spain and Guatemala.' *Transactions of the American Philosophical Society* 64 (1):1–74.

Smith, Peter Scharff. 2004. 'A Religious Technology of the SelfReligion in the Rise of the Modern Penitentiary.' *Punishment & Society* 6 (2):195–220.

Socialstyrelsen. 2011. 'Statistik om hälso- och sjukvårdspersonal.' Stockholm: National Board of Health and Welfare.

Söderberg, Verner. 1901. *Sveriges sockenbibliotek och öfriga anstalter för folkläsning.* Stockholm: P. A. Norstedt.

Soifer, Hillel. 2015. *State Building in Latin America.* Cambridge: Cambridge University Press.

SOU 1937:28. *Betänkande med förslag till Lag om Skyddskoppympning.* Stockholm: Beckmans Boktryckeri.

Spierenburg, Pieter. 1995. 'The Body and the State: Early Modern Europe.' In *The Oxford History of the Prison*, edited by Norval Morris and David J. Rothman. Oxford: Oxford University Press, 49–77.

Statistiska centralbyrån. Various years. *Sveriges officiella statistik i sammandrag.* Stockholm: P. A. Norstedt.

Stephens, John D. 1979. *The Transition from Capitalism to Socialism.* London: Macmillan.

Stevenson, Christine. 1988. 'Madness and the Picturesque in the Kingdom of Denmark.' In *The Asylum and Its Psychiatry.* New York: Routledge, 13–47.

Stojanovic, Jane. 2008. 'Midwifery in New Zealand 1904–1971.' *Contemporary Nurse* 30 (2):156–167.

Stone, Lawrence. 1969. 'Literacy and Education in England 1640–1900.' *Past & Present* 42:69–139.

Sussman, Sam. 1998. 'The First Asylums in Canada.' *Canadian Journal of Psychiatry* 43 (3):260–264.

Suzuki, Akihito. 2003a. 'A Brain Hospital in Tokyo and its Private and Public Patients, 1926–45.' *History of Psychiatry* 14 (3):337–360.

2003b. 'State, Family, and the Insane in Japan, 1900–1945.' In *The Confinement of the Insane*, edited by Roy Porter and David Wright. Cambridge: Cambridge, 193–225.

Svenska barnmorskeförbundet. *1986. Jubileumsskrift Svenska Barnmorskeförbundet 1886–1986.* Solna: Alliance.

Symphorien-Louis, F. E. C., frère. 1921. *Les Frères des Écoles chrétiennes au Canada.* Montreal: Les Frères des Écoles chrétiennes.

Szasz, Thomas. 1961. *The Myth of Mental Illness.* New York: Harper & Row.

Tannenbaum, Edward R. 1974. 'Education.' In *Modern Italy*, edited by Edward R. Tannenbaum and Amiliana P. Noether. New York: New York University Press, 231–253.

Taylor, David. 1997. *The New Police in Nineteenth-Century England.* Manchester, UK: Manchester University Press.

Teese, Richard. 1986. 'Private Schools in France.' *Comparative Education Review* 30 (2):247–259.

Teeters, Negley King. 1944. *World Penal Systems: A Survey.* Philadelphia: Pennsylvania Prison Society.

Tegborg, Lennart. 1969. *Folkskolans sekularisering 1895–1909.* Stockholm: Föreningen för svensk undervisningshistoria.

Tegnér, Esaias. 1922 [1832]. 'Om fattigvården i Vexiö stift.' In *Samlade skrifter*, vol. 7, edited by Ewert Wrangel and Fredrik Böök. Stockholm: P. A. Norstedt, 132–143.

Telhaug, Alfred Oftedal, and Odd Asbjørn Mediås. 2003. *Grunnskolen som nasjonsbygger.* Oslo: Abstrakt.

Terazawa, Yuki. 2018. *Knowledge, Power, and Women's Reproductive Health in Japan, 1690–1945.* Cham, Switzerland: Palgrave Macmillan.

Thane, Pat. 1991. 'Visions of Gender in the Making of the British Welfare State.' In *Maternity and Gender Policies*, edited by Gisela Bock and Pat Thane. London: Routledge, 93–118.

Thauer, Wolfgang, and Peter Vodosek. 1978. *Geschichte der öffentlichen Bücherei in Deutschland.* Wiesbaden, Germany: Otto Harrassowitz.

Thelen, Kathleen. 2004. *How Institutions Evolve.* Cambridge: Cambridge University Press.

Thießen, Malte. 2013. 'Vom immunisierten Volkskörper zum "präventiven Selbst": Impfen als Biopolitik und soziale Praxis vom Kaiserreich zur Bundesrepublik.' *Vierteljahrshefte für Zeitgeschichte* 61 (1):35–64.

Thorsen, Leif. 1972. *Public Libraries in Denmark.* Copenhagen: Det Danske Selskab.

Tilly, Charles. 1992. Coercion, Capital, and European States. Oxford: Blackwell.

Timasheff, N. S. 1957. 'The Dutch Prison System.' *Journal of Criminal Law, Criminology & Police Science* 48:608–612.

Tipton, Elise K. 1990. *The Japanese Police State: Tokko in Interwar Japan.* Honolulu: University of Hawaii Press.

Tobias, John J. 1972. 'Police and Public in the United Kingdom.' *Journal of Contemporary History* 7 (1):201–219.

Tortella, Gabriel. 2000. *The Development of Modern Spain.* Cambridge, MA: Harvard University Press.

Traniello, Paolo. 1997. *La biblioteca pubblica*. Bologna, Italy: il Mulino.

2002. *Storia delle biblioteche in Italia dall'Unità a oggi*. Bologna, Italy: Il Mulino.

Traue, J. E. 1998. 'Legislating for Un-Free Public Libraries: The Paradox of New Zealand Public Library Legislation, 1869–1877.' *Libraries & Culture* 33 (2):162–174.

2007. 'The Public Library Explosion in Colonial New Zealand.' *Libraries & Cultural Record* 42 (2):151–164.

Tribe, Keith. 1984. 'Cameralism and the Science of Government.' *The Journal of Modern History* 56 (2):263–284.

Triolo, Nancy. 1994. 'Fascist Unionization and the Professionalization of Mid-wives in Italy.' *Medical Anthropology Quarterly, New Series* 8 (3):259–281.

Tsebelis, George. 2002. *Veto Players*. Princeton, NJ: Princeton University Press.

Tung, Louise Watanabe. 1956. 'Library Development in Japan. II.' *The Library Quarterly* 26 (3):196–223.

Tynell, Knut. 1931. *De svenska folkbiblioteken*. Stockholm: P. A. Norstedt.

United Nations Educational, Scientific and Cultural Organisation. 1949. 'The Public Library.' UNESCO/LBA/1 (Rev.), Paris, May 16.

Unterkircher, Franz, Rudolf Fiedler, and Michael Stickler. 1981. *Die Bibliotheken Österreichs in Vergangenheit und Gegenwart*. Wiesbaden, Germany: Reichert.

Vallgårda, Signild. 2004. *Folkesundhed som politik*. Aarhus: Aarhus Universitetsforlag.

Van Den Abeele, Manuel. 2006. *De pokken in Oost-Vlaanderen in de periode 1815–1840*. MA thesis, Ghent University.

van Kersbergen, Kees. 1995. *Social Capitalism*. London: Routledge.

van Kersbergen, Kees, and Philip Manow, eds. 2009. *Religion, Class Coalitions, and Welfare States*. Cambridge: Cambridge University Press.

Van Lieburg, M. J., and Hilary Marland. 1989. 'Midwife Regulation, Education, and Practice in the Netherlands during the Nineteenth Century.' *Medical History* 33 (3):296–317.

Van Slyck, Abigail A. 1995. *Free to All: Carnegie Libraries and American Culture, 1890–1920*. Chicago: University of Chicago Press.

Vanhulle, Bert. 2010. 'Dreaming about the Prison: Edouard Ducpétiaux and Prison Reform in Belgium (1830–1848).' *Crime, History & Societies* 14 (2):107–130.

Varese, Federico. 2001. *The Russian Mafia*. Oxford: Oxford University Press.

Varney, Helen. 1997. *Varney's Midwifery*. 3rd ed. London: Jones and Bartlett.

Vaughan, Michalina, and Margaret S. Archer. 2010. *Social Conflict and Educational Change in England and France 1789–1848*. Cambridge: Cambridge University Press.

Veith, Ilza. 1975. 'The Far East.' In *World History of Psychiatry*, edited by John G. Howells. New York: Brunner/Mazel, 662–703.

Vervliet, Hendrik D. L. 1977. 'Libraries and Librarianship in Belgium.' *IFLA Journal* 3 (1):9–11.

Villasante, Olga. 2003. 'The Unfulfilled Project of the Model Mental Hospital in Spain.' *History of Psychiatry* 14 (3):3–23.

Vodosek, Peter. 2001. 'The Usual Delay: Public Libraries in Nineteenth Century Germany.' *Library History* 17 (3):197–202.

Voisine, Nive. 1987. *Les Frères des écoles chrétiennes au Canada.* Sainte-Foy, France: Éditions Anne Sigier.

Wachsmann, Nikolaus. 2015. *Hitler's Prisons.* New Haven, CT: Yale University Press.

Walsh, Dermot, and Antoinette Daly. 2004. *Mental Illness in Ireland 1750–2002.* Dublin: Health Research Board.

Weber, Eugen. 1976. *Peasants into Frenchmen.* Palo Alto, CA: Stanford University Press.

Weindling, Paul. 1989. *Health, Race, and German Politics between National Unification and Nazism, 1870–1945.* Cambridge: Cambridge University Press.

Welch, Theodore F. 1976. *Toshokan: Libraries in Japanese Society.* Chicago: American Library Association.

——— 1997. *Libraries and Librarianship in Japan.* Westport, CT: Greenwood Press.

Wetherell, Donald G. 1979. 'To Discipline and Train: Adult Rehabilitation Programmes in Ontario Prisons, 1874–1900.' *Histoire sociale* 12 (23):145–165.

Wetterberg, Lennart. 2012. 'History of Psychiatry in Sweden during a Millennium.' *Nordic Journal of Psychiatry* 66 (1):42–53.

Whitaker, Elizabeth D. 2000. *Measuring Mamma's Milk: Fascism and the Medicalization of Maternity in Italy.* Ann Arbor: University of Michigan Press.

Whitehill, Walter M. 1956. *Boston Public Library.* Cambridge, MA: Harvard University Press.

Wiegand, Wayne A. 1989. *An Active Instrument for Propaganda: The American Public Library during World War I.* New York: Greenwood Press.

——— 2015. *Part of Our Lives: A People's History of the American Public Library.* Oxford: Oxford University Press.

Wiegand, Wayne A., and Donald G. Davis Jr., eds. 1994. *Encyclopedia of Library History.* Abingdon, UK: Routledge.

Wilkinson, Ian R., Brian J. Caldwell, R. J. W. Selleck, Jessica Harris, and Pam Dettman. 2007. *A History of State Aid to Non-government Schools in Australia.* Canberra: Department of Education, Science, and Training.

Williams, Gareth. 2010. *The Angel of Death: The Story of Smallpox.* Basingstoke, UK: Palgrave.

Williams, Philip M. 1964. *Crisis and Compromise.* 3rd ed. London: Longman.

Williamson, Stanley. 2007. *The Vaccination Controversy.* Liverpool, UK: Liverpool University Press.

Willrich, Michael. 2011. *Pox: An American History.* New York: Penguin.

Wines, Enoch Cobb. 1873. *Report on the International Penitentiary Congress of London, July 3–13, 1872.* Washington, DC: US Government Printing Office.

Wirz, Hans Georg. 1933. 'Die öffentlichen Bibliotheken in der Schweiz.' *Der Schweizer Sammler* 7 (31).

Wolfe, Robert M., and Lisa K. Sharp. 2002. 'Anti-vaccinationists Past and Present.' *British Medical Journal* 325 (7361):430–432.

Wrede, Sirpa. 2001. *Decentering Care for Mothers: The Politics of Midwifery and the Design of Finnish Maternity Services.* Åbo: Åbo Akademis.

Wright, David. 1997. 'Getting Out of the Asylum.' *Social History of Medicine* 10 (1):137–155.

Wåhlin, L., and A. L. Romdahl. 1923. 'Bibliotek och muséer.' In *Göteborg*, edited by Nils Wimarson. Gothenburg, Sweden: Elanders boktryckeri, 219–243.

Yanagisawa, Satoko. 2009. 'Childbirth in Japan.' In *Childbirth across Cultures*, edited by Helaine Selin. Dordrecht, Netherlands: Springer, 85–94.

Zalewski, Barbara. 2008. 'St. Hans Hospital i København 1612–1808.' In *Psykiatriens historie i Danmark*, edited by Jesper Vaczy Kragh. Copenhagen: Reitzels, 19–58.

Zedner, Lucia. 2005. 'Policing before and after the Police.' *British Journal of Criminology* 46 (1):78–96.

Ziblatt, Daniel. 2008. *Structuring the State*. Princeton, NJ: Princeton University Press.

Zocchi, P. 2006. *Il Comune e la salute: Amministrazione municipale e igiene pubblica a Milano*. Milan, Italy: Franco Angeli.

Index